WESTERN HATCHES

Hafele/Hughes

Dedication

Janel and Graham Hafele

Pam Jaasko

ISBN 0-936608-12-9
© Copyright, 1981, by Rick Hafele and Dave Hughes
Printed in U.S.A.

Fourth Printing 1988

THE COMPLETE BOOK OF WESTERN HATCHES

An Angler's Entomology and Fly Pattern Field Guide

by
Rick Hafele and Dave Hughes

Illustrations by Richard Bunse and Paul Mooney
Flies Tied by Dave McNeese
Photos of Flies by Russ Davies
Cover Photo by Russ Davies

Frank Amato Publications
P.O. Box 02112 Portland, Oregon 97202

About the Authors

Rick Hafele works as a professional aquatic entomologist for an environmental consulting firm. He has studied the insects of streams, rivers and lakes from Alaska to California, and from the Pacific Coast to Montana. He received his B.S. degree in biology in 1973 from Western Washington University at Bellingham, Washington. In 1979 he earned an M.S. in aquatic entomology from Oregon State University at Corvallis, Oregon.

Rick started fly fishing for bluegills and bass as a young man in Illinois. His interest in fly fishing and entomology fully developed after he moved to the Northwest in 1969. Since then he has traveled throughout the West, fishing for his favorite wild native trout and collecting and studying the insects on which they feed. He has fished waters from tiny coastal cutthroat streams to large western brown trout rivers. He has visited, fished and collected insects on the chalk streams of southern England, the birthplace of angling entomology.

Rick has written articles that have appeared in several fly fishing magazines. His work has also appeared in scientific technical journals. He is a member of the American Entomological Society, the Federation of Fly Fishermen, the Flyfisher's Club of Oregon and the Santiam Flycasters. He lives in Portland, Oregon with his wife Janel and son Graham.

Dave Hughes is a professional writer and amateur aquatic entomologist. He was born and raised in Astoria, Oregon and has lived in the West all of his life. He has fly fished throughout the West for more than twenty years. His hobbies include collecting, identifying and photographing aquatic insects.

Dave is outdoor columnist for the *Daily Astorian* newspaper. His articles and photographs have appeared in most of the major fishing magazines. He teaches fly fishing and fly tying classes at Clatsop Community College. He is a member of the Federation of Fly Fishermen, the Flyfishers Club of Oregon and the Sunset Empire Fly Fishing Club. Dave lives and works in Astoria, Oregon.

Rick and Dave teach a workshop for western fly fishermen. Entitled "Entomology and the Artificial Fly", it is a one-day slide and lecture presentation on collecting and identifying the insects on which trout feed, and on selecting and presenting flies that match them. It is given to fly fishing clubs and other groups throughout the western states.

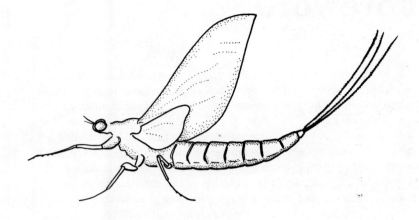

Contents

FOREWORD ———————————————————— 8

ACKNOWLEDGEMENTS ———————————————— 9

INTRODUCTION ——————————————————— 11

ONE: KNOWING THE ORDERS OF INSECTS ———— 13

TWO: MAYFLIES
         (ORDER: EPHEMEROPTERA) —————— 31

THREE: STONEFLIES
         (ORDER: PLECOPTERA) ——————————— 101

FOUR: DRAGONFLIES AND DAMSELFLIES
         (ORDER: ODONATA) —————— 127

FIVE: WATERBOATMEN AND BACKSWIMMERS
         (ORDER: HEMIPTERA) —————— 142

SIX: CADDISFLIES
         (ORDER: TRICHOPTERA) —————— 148

SEVEN: ALDERFLIES AND DOBSONFLIES
         (ORDER: MEGALOPTERA) —————— 178

EIGHT: WATER BEETLES
         (ORDER: COLEOPTERA) —————— 184

NINE: TRUE FLIES
         (ORDER: DIPTERA) —————— 190

GLOSSARY ——————————————————— 204

BIBLIOGRAPHY ——————————————— 206

BIOLOGICAL SUPPLY HOUSES ——————— 208

INDEX ——————————————————— 210

Foreword

I t is with some trepidation that this writer is composing the fore-word for an outstanding new book on aquatic entomology. I have written several books, it is true, and also numerous magazine articles, but never a foreword.

The Complete Book of Western Hatches is a fine and long needed book. I have begged and cajoled other aquatic entomologists for years to give us something of this scope, to no avail. They all feel they have done their thing, but one and all, with the exception of the late Paul Needham in his *Trout Streams,* have practically ignored those of us west of the Rockies. Don't they think we have our own families of "bugs" out here? In this book now before you all that will be changed, inasmuch as the authors are pretty much ignoring everything east of the Rockies, and that is as it should be because here in the West we not only have many families of insects unknown in the East, but be it known we also have a goodly complement still unclassified. I feel certain that oversight will be rapidly and thoroughly researched by Rick and Dave in the near future.

As new findings and proofs are made I am sure they will pass same on to their readers. On at least two or three mayflies in my area I have taken it as my responsibility to collect the male spinners and to see that Rick and Dave get them for identifying and classifying.

This is not what could be called a "reader's book" and it is not in-tended as such. It is a fine presentation of needed information in its field, and a first class reference work. What is especially valuable is the presentation of the variations in nomenclature that have been used by many western fly tiers for western insect hatches, the development of their favorite flies to match them, and the contributions these men have made to the lore of angling.

The Complete Book of Western Hatches should be on every angler's bookshelf.

Polly Rosborough
Chiloquin, Oregon

Acknowledgements

Writers dealing with angling entomology owe their thanks first to the men of science who helped them understand the insects. Our special acknowledgment is to Dr. Norman Anderson, professor of aquatic entomology at Oregon State University. It was he who brought us together, Dave as an observer auditing his class to learn more about aquatic insects, Rick as a graduate student assisting Professor Anderson in teaching the class. It was Professor Anderson who patiently directed Rick through the rigors of a Master's program and helped teach him the ways of aquatic insects. He has encouraged us in our writing and has given us much useful advice and criticism.

Our thanks go next to Hal Turner, Shelton, Washington, and Dr. Burt Covert, LaGrande, Oregon. They attended one of our early "Entomology and the Artificial Fly" workshops and were the first to say: "You guys should do a book from this class." The seed they planted grew into the present work.

We would like to thank the many angling writers who have helped us understand the relationship between the fly and the fish: Ernest Schwiebert with his unmatched prose and scholarly work in *Matching the Hatch, Nymphs,* and *Trout;* Charles Brooks, with his stream studies and codification of nymph fishing methods in *The Trout and the Stream* and *Nymph Fishing for Larger Trout;* Al Caucci and Bob Nastasi for their detailed and accurate book on mayflies, *Hatches;* Larry Solomon and Eric Leiser for the first useful treatment of all stages of the caddisflies in *The Caddis and the Angler;* Doug Swisher and Carl Richards for their work on new pattern developments in *Selective Trout* and *Fly Fishing Strategy.*

No list of contributors to angling literature can be complete. But no list on western fishing can begin without thanks to the famous angling entomologist of the West: E. H. "Polly" Rosborough. His *Tying and Fishing the Fuzzy Nymphs* was first published in 1969; it sold out quickly. It was released in a new edition in 1978 and is again available to western fly fishers. In *Nymphs,* Schwiebert said of Polly's book: "Rosborough and his original research are perhaps the first major contribution to the theory and techniques of American nymph fishing since (James) Leisenring." Many of Polly's patterns have been described throughout *The Complete Book of Western Hatches.* He has personally helped us with notes on tying and fishing them.

The fine line drawings and illustrations were done by our friend and fishing partner, Richard Bunse, of Falls City, Oregon and by Paul Mooney, of Portland, Oregon. Without their help the accurate depictions of insect characteristics could not have been shown and the book would have lost much of its value.

Dave McNeese of Salem, Oregon tied most of the flies photographed throughout *The Complete Book of Western Hatches.* Dave is one of the West's best artists with fur, feathers, and steel.

Russ Davies, Warrenton, Oregon, photographed and printed the fly patterns. He also printed the insect pictures throughout the book. He has not only improved the book, but has taught the authors how to improve their own photography.

We want to thank all of those who have taken our "Entomology and the Artificial Fly" workshops. They have inspired the book, and many have contributed their knowledge to its pages.

Our thanks go finally to Don Roberts, editor of *Flyfishing the West.* We sent him a copy of the booklet we give students in our workshops, asking him what he thought of it as the outline for a book on western entomology. His answer was enthusiastic: "It should be written," he told us. By a happy turn of fate Don Roberts became book editor for Frank Amato Publications. He told us to get to work on the book. With his encouragement *The Complete Book of Western Hatches* was written.

Introduction

T he goal of *The Complete Book of Western Hatches* is to introduce the aquatic insects important in fly fishing the West, and to help in the selection of patterns to match them.

Any book about western angling entomology must deal with unique western conditions. Chalk stream hatches in England have long been identified, timed, and matched. Knowledge of our eastern hatches is approaching the same point. As they are catalogued, and matching patterns are codified, anglers begin to approach their fishing with a fair knowledge of what insect will hatch and a certain confidence in the pattern that will match it.

Western anglers face a set of circumstances that may never allow such refinement. There are vast geographic differences, from arid reaches in the desert states to lush rain forests on the Olympic Peninsula; from high alpine lakes in the Sierras to the sometimes brutal blue ribbon rivers in Montana. Elevations can differ by thousands of feet on a single river system; insect inhabitants change along its course to meet the changing conditions of the river. Climatic variations are sharp: the knife-edge crest of a mountain chain may be the dividing line between a forest and a desert.

Insects adapt to the conditions surrounding them. Through the millenia the wide variety of western conditions has given rise to an equally wide variety of insect species. Taxonomists, who have catalogued the insects of England and are on their way toward understanding the aquatic life of our eastern waters, are only beginning to fit together the insect puzzle of the West.

This lack of codification of western hatches leads the western angler to a new approach to hatch matching. He must be prepared to do his own insect collecting. He must have the basic knowledge necessary to classify an insect to a useful level. Finally, he must be imaginative enough to select a matching pattern or to create his own.

What is a useful level to which an angler must identify a hatch? It is that level at which all of the members of an order, family, or genus live in the same type of habitat and have the same behavior. For example, if a hatch of mayflies occurs on a slow, marshy river the ability to identify the hatch as the genus *Siphlonurus* will enable the angler to fish it just as effectively as if it were identified to species. Different *Siphlonurus* species vary in size and color; they do not vary in shape, behavior, or habitat. A pattern can be selected or created based on observation of the natural, and presented with the action that is consistent throughout the genus.

Identification to species is intriguing. It is a quest that spurs your authors into pouring over textbooks and peering through microscopes when they should be fishing. It gives us great satisfaction to identify an insect to species; only occasionally does it increase our ability to match the hatch.

Some western hatches are so famous they have long been identified to species. An example is the Giant Salmon Fly, *Pteronarcys californica*, famous on Oregon's Deschutes, Idaho's Henry's Fork of the Snake, and Montana's Madison. Where such identifications have been made, and specific patterns have evolved to match them, they will be discussed in detail.

The array of western insects, however, is largely uncatalogued even by professional taxonomists. The western angler must not yet look for books filled with species and pattern lists, and emergence charts for specific stretches of specific waters. He must learn to collect his own hatches and select or create matching patterns for them. This is a greater challenge. The angler who accepts it will be able to fish any water, from his backyard stream to the famous rivers in Montana. He will understand and match any hatch he encounters. He will write his own streamside guide.

There are four steps in matching a hatch: *Identify* it, *understand* it, select a pattern to *match* it, and *present* the pattern in the manner of the living insect.

Identification is not always necessary in order to match a hatch. Generations who fished successfully without knowing a Latin name prove this. However, there are useful levels of identification that are almost always helpful. *The Complete Book of Western Hatches* was written to help you identify aquatic insects of fishing importance to those levels, usually family or genus, sometimes species.

Understanding the insects means knowing their habits and habitat. Aquatic insects have adapted in unique ways to specific conditions. Where and how each performs its role tells us where and how to fish patterns selected to match them.

Selection of *matching* patterns should be based on the size, form, color, and action of the natural. Dressings presented in *The Complete Book of Western Hatches* are suggestive, impressionistic, or imitative. Simple suggestive patterns often capture the action of the insect best, and are always easier to tie. Each imitation is given as an idea to help in the selection or creation of a dressing which matches the hatch over which the angler is fishing.

Presentation of the selected imitation is based on the behavior of the insect. If you understand its habits and habitat you will know where fish find it, and how your imitation should be fished.

In his 1955 classic, *Matching the Hatch,* Ernest Schwiebert said: "Stream tactics can be learned by experience, but stream entomology can be learned only by serious study." More than twenty years after he wrote those words, the scientific study of western entomology is still in its infancy. But the groundwork has been laid. It is now possible for the angler, casual or serious, to *identify* western hatches to a useful level, *understand* their habits and habitat, select patterns to *match* them, and *present* those patterns in a life-like manner.

The Complete Book of Western Hatches was written to make your study of insects more enjoyable and your fishing more productive. We hope it will prompt you to practice "stream tactics" more often. We also hope you will develop an appreciation for the environment of the trout, and know that fishermen are only a small part of it.

The best way to use this book is to take it along when you go fishing. We do not recommend carrying it in your vest; if your vest is like ours, it is overloaded already. If the book is handy in the car or camp, though, a quick reference to it might be enough to put you back on the stream or lake with a killing pattern.

Make good use of the space in the margins. Write notes about where and when you found a hatch and the pattern you used to fish it: write your own streamside guide.

RH
DH

Chapter One
Knowing the Orders of Insects

The day breaks clear. By mid-morning the sun kneads the land with a pleasant warmth. Stream temperatures rise, and soon the insects respond with a flurry of activity. The hatch becomes so heavy that insects land on your arms and hat. Swirls mark the feeding lanes of hungry trout. You drift many different imitations over dimpling rises, but only an occasional fish accepts your offerings.

The activity subsides like the passing of a summer squall. Frustrated, you collect a few adults, net some nymphs from a shallow riffle, and take them home hoping to unwrap some of the morning's mysteries. Your favorite fishing books are consulted as you look for the pieces to the puzzle. Names like *Paraleptophlebia adoptavia, Palpomyia americana,* and *Alloperla fraterna* keep popping up until you are lost between costal angulations and anastomosed stigmas. Finally you ask yourself: "Hell, is this a mayfly or a stonefly?"

From teaching our western workshop, "Entomology and the Artificial Fly," we have come to realize that this question is the rule rather than the exception. The best angling-entomology references lack information explaining basic insect life cycles, anatomy, and descriptions of the *orders* of aquatic insects.

The purpose of this chapter is to unravel the basics. With an understanding of the life cycles of insects and some of their anatomical features, recognizing the orders will become second nature, usually taking no more than a streamside glance. This knowledge will provide the groundwork for identifying the families, genera, and species discussed in the following chapters. It will also help you understand the remarkable adaptations aquatic insects have made to their unique environment.

METAMORPHOSIS

Few animals undergo greater changes during their development than aquatic insects. The transformation of the worm-like caterpillar into the beautiful butterfly is familiar to us all. But the changes that occur among aquatic insects are perhaps more amazing. The immature stages live under water. They are used to slow changes in temperature and get their oxygen directly from the water. The adults are not only dramatically different in form, but also in their adaptations to the conditions around them. They emerge into a terrestrial environment, with rapidly fluctuating temperatures and atmospheric oxygen.

Metamorphosis refers to the changes that occur during an insect's life cycle. Despite the diversity among aquatic insects, their life cycles can be grouped into three types of metamorphosis: none, incomplete, and complete. The first do not change in form during their life cycle. Those with incomplete metamorphosis have three distinct stages of development: egg, nymph, and adult. Insects displaying complete metamorphosis have four distinct stages of development: egg, larva, pupa, and adult. Only a few primitive insects have no metamorphosis; none are important to fishermen. The majority of insects have either incomplete or complete metamorphosis. Understanding these two life cycles will aid the fly fisher in identification, pattern selection, and presentation.

Incomplete metamorphosis evolved first and is considered the more primitive of the two. The following description of a stonefly's life cycle is an example of incomplete metamorphosis.

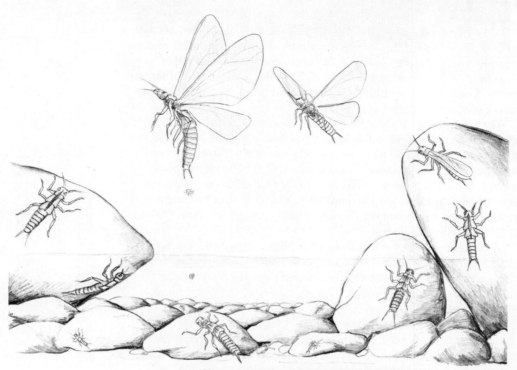

Figure 1. Life cycle of the stonefly (Order: Plecoptera).

The stonefly egg incubates from two days to several months, depending on its species and climatic conditions. The egg hatches and the immature insect, or nymph, immediately begins feeding. The growth of all immatures is limited by their inextensible outer covering, or exoskeleton. A new exoskeleton is formed periodically under the old one, which is then sloughed off, or molted. After each molt growth proceeds to the limit of the new exoskeleton, then another molt occurs. The stages of growth between molts are called instars. The number of instars varies between the different orders. Stonefly nymphs go through twenty to thirty instars.

During each instar there is an increase in nymphal size. Various external changes also occur. Most noticeable of these is the development of wing pads. These develop only on insects with incomplete metamorphosis. You must be careful, however, to look at fairly mature nymphs: wing pads in the early instars will not be developed. Mature nymphs of the orders with incomplete metamorphosis often resemble their forthcoming adult stage.

The nymph requires from one to four years to complete development, depending on its species. After its final instar it is ready to molt to the adult stage. Emergence is usually preceded by an increase in activity as nymphs move to preferred hatching sites. This activity makes them vulnerable to fish and more important to fishermen. With rare exceptions, mature stonefly nymphs crawl out of the water on sticks, plant stems, logs, or stones to emerge. Only a few species emerge in open water.

Emergence may require a few seconds or take more than an hour. Because the nymph crawls from the water to emerge the intial adult stage is seldom available to fish. Stonefly adults mate on streamside foliage several hours to several days after emergence. Laying of eggs follows mating by several minutes to a week or more; a six to twelve hour period is average. Oviposition typically occurs over the water, the female dipping her abdomen to the surface and releasing a cluster of eggs. They are often taken by fish while doing so. Adults die shortly after oviposition, completing the life cycle of the stonefly through the egg, nymph, and adult stages.

An example of an insect with complete metamorphosis is the caddisfly (Order: Trichoptera). The initial stages of complete and incomplete metamorphosis are similar. After the egg incubates for a varying period the immature, called a larva in orders with complete metamorphosis, hatches and begins feeding. Larval growth again proceeds in a series of instars separated by molts. The number of caddis instars is typically five; a few specimens have six. As the larva grows its external features remain nearly the same; there is little or no resemblance to the adult stage, just as there is no similarity between a caterpillar and a butterfly. No development of external wing pads takes place. This lack of wing pads easily distinguishes larvae, with complete metamorphosis, from nymphs, with incomplete metamorphosis. When mature, typically after one year, the larva does not transform directly to the adult stage. Instead it changes into a pupal stage. Pupation occurs under water. The pupa is protected by a gravel, sand, or stick case lined with silk. Adult characteristics take shape during pupal development. External wing pads appear, legs change in shape, antennae increase in size, and the reproductive organs develop. The duration of the pupal stage varies from one week to several months. Some mature caddis pupae remain dormant until the right environmental conditions trigger emergence.

Figure 2. Life cycle of the caddisfly (Order: Trichoptera).

When the pupa is mature and conditions are right it cuts its way out of the pupal cell and swims or floats to the surface. This ascent can cause heavy feeding by fish and provide excellent fishing. Emergence into the adult stage occurs in or just under the surface film. The adult bursts through the surface film and floats on the surface until its wings dry and it can fly away, this taking a few seconds to several minutes.

Adult caddisflies mate on streamside foliage. Following mating, swarms of females return to the water to deposit their eggs. They may oviposit on the water's surface or crawl under the water to lay eggs on the substrate, beginning the life cycle anew.

Variations in the duration of each stage, habitat preferences, and behavior are great between and even within each order. They will be detailed for each taxa in later chapters. But all insects with incomplete metamorphosis go through egg, nymph, and adult stages, while those with complete metamorphosis have an egg, larva, pupa, and adult stage. Following is a table listing the orders of aquatic insects important to fly fishermen, categorized by their type of metamorphosis.

Incomplete Metamorphosis:

Ephemeroptera	(Mayflies)
Plecoptera	(Stoneflies)
Odonata	(Dragonflies and Damselflies)
Hemiptera	(Water Bugs, Including Water-boatmen and Backswimmers)

Complete Metamorphosis:

Trichoptera	(Caddisflies)
Megaloptera	(Alderflies and Dobsonflies)
Coleoptera	(Beetles)
Diptera	(True Flies)

BASIC ANATOMY

The biggest stumbling block for amateur entomologists is the terminology used by professionals. You don't need to learn a new language; you do need to learn a few new words. Insects are different. No other animals have six legs, four wings, and ten-segmented abdomens. Such uniqueness requires special terms to describe them. The difference between two taxa can be small, resting on the number of tails or of segments in each leg. Understanding some of their basic anatomy is essential in order to distinguish between them. With a bit of fireside study and a lot of streamside practice, recognizing the different orders and even families of aquatic insects will become second nature and often take but a glance at the specimen.

Certain anatomical characteristics distinguish insects from other aquatic organisms. A typical insect has:

A. Three major body divisions: head, thorax, and abdomen.
B. Three thoracic segments: prothorax (first), mesothorax (second), and metathorax (third).
C. Normally ten abdominal segments, though this number is reduced in some groups.
D. Six legs, one pair on each thoracic segment. (Some immatures lack legs.)
E. Usually four, but sometimes two or no, wings (adults only).

Checking for these characteristics will quickly separate insects from possible confusing organisms such as crustaceans, spiders, mites, or underwater worms.

The information in the following labelled diagrams provides the groundwork for separating specific taxa described in the rest of the book. The stonefly nymph and adult, and caddisfly larva, pupa, and adult, exemplify the structures of insects with incomplete and complete metamorphosis. Variations in structure do occur among the other groups. These will be explained individually in each chapter.

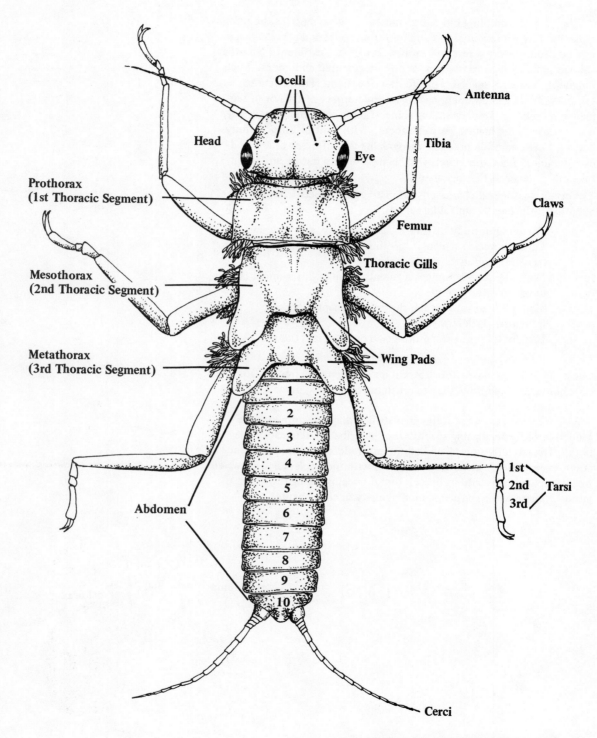

Ocelli

Antenna

Head

Tibia

Eye

Prothorax (1st Thoracic Segment)

Femur

Claws

Thoracic Gills

Mesothorax (2nd Thoracic Segment)

Metathorax (3rd Thoracic Segment)

Wing Pads

1
2
3
4
5
6
7
8
9
10

1st
2nd **Tarsi**
3rd

Abdomen

Cerci

Figure 3. Generalized stonefly nymph.

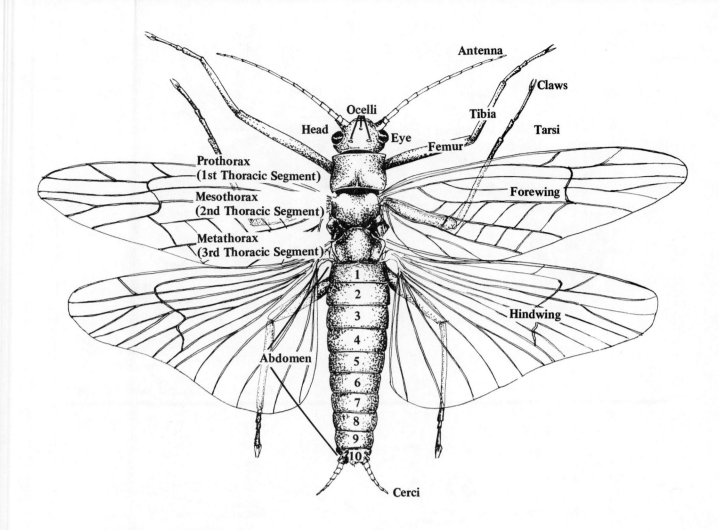

Figure 4. Generalized stonefly adult.

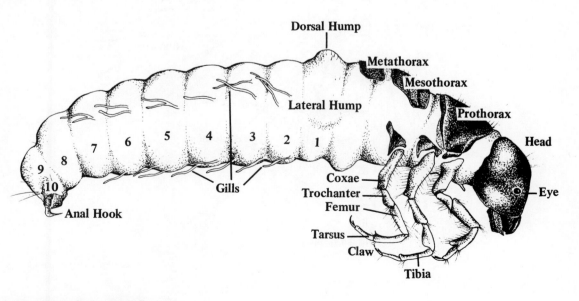

Figure 5. Generalized caddisfly larva.

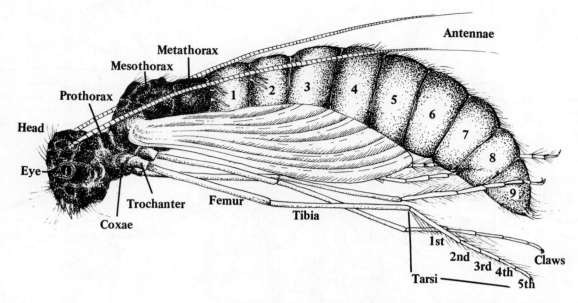

Figure 6. Generalized caddisfly pupa.

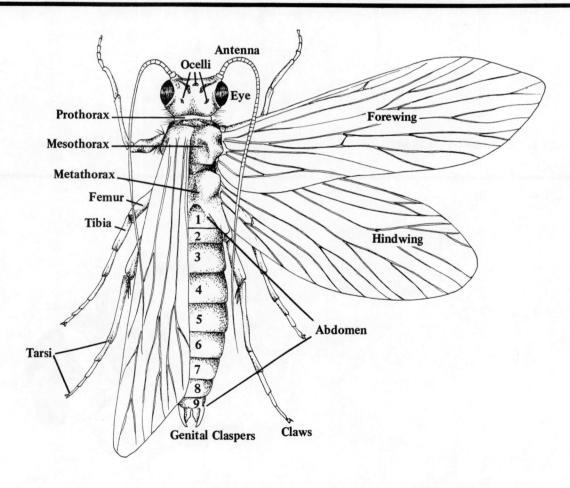

Figure 7. Generalized caddisfly adult.

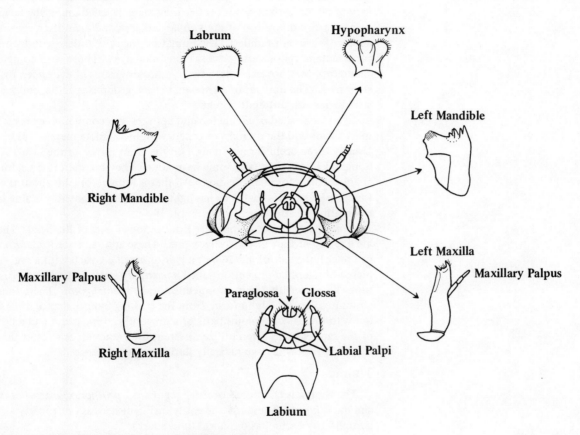

Figure 8. Detail of mouth parts (mayfly nymph).

ANATOMICAL STRUCTURES

Head

The head has many characters that are used to identify insects. The two *antennae* vary widely in size and shape. They are a common identifying characteristic. For example, two mayfly families, Siphlonuridae and Baetidae, are distinguished by the difference in length of their antennae. Antennae are not always obvious. On caddisfly larvae they are very small; on certain water beetles they are concealed under the head.

The size and position of the two large compound *eyes* often separate adults of different families. The immature stages of orders with incomplete metamorphosis also possess compound eyes. Those with complete metamorphosis, however, have two clumps or groups of *eye spots,* or stemmata. The number of stemmata in each group is specific, and may also distinguish different families.

Eye spots called *ocelli* are located between the compound eyes of most adults and the nymphs of orders with incomplete metamorphosis. Usually three ocelli form a triangle on the front or top of the head. Some taxa have only two; some have none. They are therefore useful characteristics for identification. All that is known for sure about the function of ocelli is that they are light sensitive cells, possibly aiding in orientation or affecting night activity.

Mouthparts are located on the front or lower part of the head. They are a group of four major components. These are: an anterior *labrum,* or upper lip; a pair of *mandibles;* a pair of *maxillae,* each with a segmented finger-like projection called a *maxillary palp;* and a *labium* or lower lip, also with a pair of projections called *labial palpi.* These four structures vary widely in form, from the sucking mouthparts of a mosquito to the chewing mouthparts of a dragonfly. Immatures and adults of the same species often utilize different food sources; as a result the mouthparts may change radically during metamorphosis.

Thorax

The thorax is composed of three segments: *prothorax, mesothorax,* and *metathorax.* These may be easily distinguished, as on stonefly nymphs, or obscure, as on most Diptera larvae.

Typically the three thoracic segments each possess a pair of *legs.* Legs vary widely in size and shape; in the larval stages of some groups they may be absent. Legs consist of specific segments. Starting closest to the body they are: *coxae, trochantor, femur, tibia, tarsi* (with one to five segments), and *tarsal claws.*

Wings of adult insects are also attached to the thorax. There are normally two pairs, one on the second thoracic segment and another on the third. Diptera (true flies) have only the pair on the second segment; those on the third segment have evolved into small knobbed stalks called halteres. In the orders Hemiptera (true bugs) and Coleoptera (beetles) the first pair of wings forms a tough covering over the hind wings and abdomen.

The *veins* running through insect wings serve two functions: they supply the wing membranes with blood and they support and stiffen the wings. Veins form specific patterns that are often used to identify different families, genera, and species. Wing venation can be confusing and requires practice to learn. Different systems of naming the veins have been developed. Because of the difficulty in using wing venation, we have avoided its use, and have stressed other characteristics.

Abdomen

The abdomen typically consists of ten segments, but this number may be reduced in certain orders (e.g., Coleoptera and Diptera). The *gills* are prominent structures on the abdomens of many aquatic insects and are excellent distinguishing features. They will be described individually for each taxa.

The *tails,* or cerci, are found on the last abdominal segment. There may be two or three tails of varying length. Some groups, for example, Trichoptera, have no tails at all.

The *reproductive organs* are also found on the last abdominal segments. The shape of the male genitalia is often used to identify specific species.

The pages that follow show pictures and list the distinguishing characteristics of the immature and adult stages for each order. Use the anatomical diagrams in this section to check structures of which you are unsure when trying to identify a specimen. Soon you will be able to distinguish the orders as easily as you can tell horses and cows and pigs from one another. It is just a matter of practice.

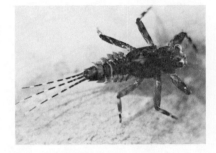

ORDER CHARACTERISTICS

EPHEMEROPTERA (MAYFLIES)

Nymphs

1. Three tails, except the members of the genus *Epeorus* and the species *Baetis bicaudatus,* which have only two.
2. Each leg with only a single claw at the end.
3. Lamellate or platelike gills on abdominal segments only.

Adults (Dun and Spinner Stages)

1. Two or three long tails.
2. Wings held vertically; front pair large and triangular while hind pair is reduced or absent.
3. Body slender and delicate.

PLECOPTERA (STONEFLIES)

Nymphs

1. Two stout tails of varying length.
2. Two claws at the end of each leg.
3. Gills often absent; when present appear on thorax.

Adults

1. Two tails; may be short and 1-segmented or long and multi-segmented.
2. Long antennae.
3. Four wings of equal length; held flat over the abdomen when at rest.

ODONATA (DRAGONFLIES AND DAMSELFLIES)

Nymphs

1. Large compound eyes.
2. Short antennae.
3. Extendible labium (lower lip) for capturing prey.
4. Dragonflies with internal rectal gills; damselflies with three caudal gill lamellae in place of tails.

Adults

1. Large compound eyes.
2. Short antennae.
3. No tails.
4. Two pair of large wings. Dragonflies hold wings horizontally when at rest; damselflies hold wings together above body when at rest.

AQUATIC HEMIPTERA (WATERBOATMEN AND BACKSWIMMERS)

Nymphs and Adults Have Similar Characteristics

1. Antennae short, not more than five segments.
2. Short sucking mouthparts shaped like a slender beak.
3. No tails.
4. First pair of wings thickened and lie flat over abdomen, covering second pair of wings (adults only).
5. Body more or less oval or elliptical in outline.

TRICHOPTERA (CADDISFLIES)

Larvae

1. Antennae minute.
2. No tails; last abdominal segment with small to large anal hooks.
3. Gills, when present, are on abdominal segments.
4. No wing pads on thorax.
5. Many species build tubular cases out of mineral or plant material; other species are free-living (uncased).

Pupae

1. Antennae long, approximately body length.
2. Wing pads well developed and slope under abdomen.
3. No tails or anal hooks.
4. Contained in silk cocoon inside mineral or plant case until just prior to emergence.

Adults

1. Four well developed wings covered with dense fine hairs; wings held in a swept-back, tent-shaped fashion when at rest.
2. No tails.
3. Long antennae, length of body or longer.

MEGALOPTERA (ALDERFLIES AND DOBSONFLIES)
(HELLGRAMMITES)

Larvae

1. Antennae short.
2. No tails; last abdominal segment has either a single long filament, or a pair of anal hooks.
3. Pair of lateral filaments on each abdominal segment for gills.

Pupae

1. Terrestrial; not important to fishermen.

Adults

1. Antennae approximately body length, with beadlike segments.
2. No tails.
3. Wings folded tent-like over abdomen when at rest.
4. Body and wings smooth, without fine hairs.

COLEOPTERA (WATER BEETLES)

Larvae

1. No tails, but may have caudal breathing tubes with stout hairs.
2. Some larvae with filamentous gills on abdomen; others with caudal breathing tube.
3. One or two claws at end of each leg.

Pupae

1. Usually terrestrial; of no importance to fishermen.

Adults

1. Antennae of various lengths; some club-shaped at end.
2. No tails.
3. First pair of wings formed into hard covering, called an elytra, over hind wings and abdomen.

DIPTERA (TRUE FLIES)

Larvae

1. No tails.
2. Antennae minute.
3. No legs; body has the general appearance of a segmented tube.

Pupae

1. Head, thorax, and wing pads closely appressed, or clumped together.
2. No tails.
3. May have filamentous gill fibers on top of thorax.

Adults

1. No tails.
2. Antennae normally well formed but not more than 2-3 times width of head in length.
3. Only first pair of wings developed; second pair of wings reduced to short stalks, called halteres.

COLLECTING INSECTS

The Complete Book of Western Hatches is designed to be most useful at streamside, in camp, or back at home with an insect in hand. When you find an insect that fish take readily, an effective imitation is necessary for consistent success. But you can't match it until you catch it. There is a world of difference between an insect observed with a glance at three feet and the same insect observed carefully at the distance a trout sees it: an inch or two. Colors change; shapes are not what we took them to be; the underside, seen by the fish, is a different shade than the backside, seen by the fisherman.

Just as there are certain tools and techniques for catching fish, so there are certain tools and techniques for catching insects. We will break these into four categories: 1) What will fit conveniently in a fishing vest; 2) what will fit in the trunk of a car; 3) what is best used in your home; and 4) none. Since it is the simplest, the last will be discussed first.

None: This is for the angler whose vest carries an inventory to rival a tackle house catalog. There is no room for additions, so we will tell you a couple of ways to collect with just techniques, no tools. The best way, and the most fun, is to catch a fish. Assuming you are going to kill it anyway, then take the time to examine its stomach contents. This is the surest way to know what the fish has been eating. We do not advocate killing fish for this purpose; we feel it is foolish, however, to kill a fish without doing it. Pay special attention to recently taken insects. These will be near the front of the throat, and stomach acids will not have decomposed them or changed their colors.

Another way of collecting that requires no extra equipment is to carefully lift rocks, gravel, debris, moss, and other substrate from the water with your hands. The advantage of this method is that you can see exactly what habitat the collected specimens prefer. The major disadvantage is that many insects will let go or swim away when they are disturbed and you will never see them. Another disadvantage is that you are limited to collecting areas shallower than the length of your arm. However, the method is always "at hand" and should be standard practice whenever you fish new waters.

Vest Pocket Equipment: There are some small items that fit in one pocket of a fishing vest and greatly aid in collecting. We always carry four items: alcohol-filled vials, tweezers, aquarium net, and a small white jar lid. The net is for capturing specimens. It will be appreciated most by those who have seen a dun emerge and float gracefully down the current to their waiting hand, only to have it slip between their fingers and float on by. This tiny less-than-a-dollar net is handy in a thousand situations and is seldom in the way.

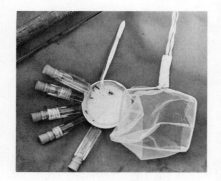

Vials filled with alcohol are used to preserve collected specimens. Be sure to observe the colors of the insect *before* putting it in the vial. Alcohol washes them out quickly, as do all other convenient preservatives. The best alcohol is ethyl diluted to 80% strength with water. Rubbing alcohol (isopropyl) will work but it makes the specimens brittle: when you observe them later their legs, wings, and antennae will break off. We prefer two or three dram vials with rubber stoppers. These are available from the biological supply houses listed in the back of the book.

Tweezers are used to transfer specimens from net to vials. They should have fine points and be soft-sprung. Stiff tweezers are clumsy and damage insects easily. Some fly fishing supply houses list "nymph tweezers." They are perfect for collecting.

The jar lid is for observing insects. If you collect debris with a sample you can put it in the lid and add water. Any insects will be easy to spot as they swim or crawl against the white background. The lid is perfect for examining stomach contents. Put the mess in the lid, add water, and stir it with your tweezers. Any usable specimens will untangle so you can tell what they are.

There are a few other items we carry most of the time. A small magnifying glass makes streamside identification and matching a little more precise. A stak-pak with a small circle of fiberglass screen in the bottom of each compartment is perfect for keeping live specimens. This is especially valuable if you are interested in getting spinners from mayfly duns. Coax the duns into the stak-pak compartment without touching them. In a day or two they will make the final molt. But put no more than three in each space or they will damage each other, and fail to molt.

A stomach pump is handy to get an idea of what a fish has been taking. They must be used gently, however, or the fish will be injured.

Car Trunk Items: We always keep a kick net or screen net in the car, along with an aerial net, a white pan, and a few extra alcohol filled vials.

The best kick net can be made from a broom handle with a twelve to eighteen inch spring wire hoop attached. The bottom of the hoop should be flattened. A twelve inch deep bag made of 24 to 32 meshes-per-inch mosquito netting is sewn to the hoop. It should be reinforced with canvas around the opening. A commercial kick net is available from some supply houses listed in the back of the book.

Easier to make is the hand screen net. Simply cut a three foot square section of fiberglass window screen and sew or staple it at the ends to 3/4 inch dowels four feet long. Leave three inches of dowel exposed at one end to dig into the stream bottom, nine inches at the other to serve as handles.

Either the kick net or the hand screen net can be used by holding it to the bottom in a current, then standing upstream and shuffling your feet in the substrate. Even the most tenacious insects will be dislodged and swept into the net. It is not hit-or-miss like hand collecting: everything will be in the net. When you are finished lift it carefully from the water and take it ashore to examine it. On a rich river there will be an incredible array of critters flipping, crawling, and running across the meshes. The long handled kick net can also be used to sample still waters. Simply swish it through vegetation, over the bottom, or along undercut banks.

Always be sure to sample a wide variety of habitats. In running water collect from riffles, runs, pools, margins, and vegetated areas. There will be different insects in each. In lakes sample the deepest part you can reach and the shallows, too. Sweep clean bottoms and the muck of leaf packs. Be sure to swish the net through vegetation such as watercress and cattail stalks.

Use a freezer pan or enamel tray to accommodate the larger samples taken with these nets. As with the jar lid, the insects can be observed as they swim or crawl against the white background.

The kick net will work for collecting flying adults, but a lighter aerial net is better. You can swing it with more speed, which is often necessary to capture dancing mayflies and erratic caddisflies. A standard butterfly net with a deep bag is perfect for this. Try to make or buy one sturdy enough so you can beat the brush with it. Swishing it through streamside leaves, over conifer boughs, and across ferns will turn up a lot of quiescent bugs in which fish might show an interest.

What Should Be Left At Home: Your collection will be kept at home. It will include the specimens, vialed and labelled, that you have collected over the years. It is amazing how valuable they will become.

The most important part of any collection, next to the insects themselves, is the labels with them. No collection has any merit whatsoever if you cannot look at it and know where and when each insect was taken.

A correct label is made on white note-card paper with a No. 2 lead pencil. Each vial is labelled and each label has the following information: county, state, stream or lake, exact location, date of collection, and the collector's name. On the back should be the order, family, and whatever other level to which you can identify the insect. The label should be placed *in the vial* with the specimens. At the same time be sure the vial is filled to the top with alcohol; an air bubble rolling back and forth is as damaging as a pebble. Each vial should be labelled on the day the collection is made. If you wait you will forget the pertinent data.

Your collection will be more valuable if you start a small card file system. Number each vial and cross reference it to a numbered card. Data that will not fit on the label can go on the card: weather, water and air temperatures, fishing conditions, time of emergence, and patterns which effectively match the specimens. A notebook can be used instead of a file to record the same information.

You should show the same respect for the environment when collecting as when you are fishing. Don't decimate a delicate system. Most healthy western rivers won't be hurt by collecting any more than by wading to fish. But we have fragile systems, too. Show them respect, collect discriminately, and they will stay healthy and productive.

Front

Clatsop Co., Oregon

Pine Cr. 2 miles below Winkles Corner

12 June 1980

Coll. by D. Hughes

Back

Order: Plecoptera

Family: Capniidae

Det. by R. Hafele

Figure 9. Example of correctly written label.

Chapter Two
Mayflies Order: Ephemeroptera

It is difficult to imagine what the earth was like 270 million years ago, when mayflies first appeared. These early mayflies did not contend with hungry trout: there would be none for another 200 million years. The ancestors of trout, however, undoubtedly schooled them on the finer points of survival.

Mayflies were one of the earliest aquatic insect groups to evolve. Some ancestral characteristics are retained in present day members of the order. Their primitive wing venation gives the wings a fluted, accordion-like structure. These wings provide good vertical lift but poor forward flight. This results in the well known, up-and-down, yo-yo like dance of mating mayflies. Their primitive wing-to-body attachment fixes the wings in the vertical position when at rest. Dragonflies and damselflies are the only other group of insects that cannot fold their wings down along the abdomen when not in flight. The most unusual primitive characteristic of mayflies is their two separate winged stages: dun (subimago) and spinner (imago). No other insect has two winged stages.

During their evolution mayflies adapted to almost every freshwater habitat. They are found throughout the world, except for the extreme Arctic, Antarctica, and most small ocean islands. There are over 600 species in North America alone, and more than 200 from the western United States. Great Britain has only forty-eight. The mayflies are a perfect example of the complexity of western hatches.

Mayflies have incomplete metamorphosis. Their eggs are laid at or under the water's surface. They are covered with a sticky substance or with fine coiled filaments which hold them to the substrate. The eggs hatch from a few minutes to several months after oviposition, depending on the species. The newly hatched nymphs are approximately 0.5mm long. They begin feeding immediately on rooted plants, algae, or mosses. They are the primary herbivores of lakes and streams; biologists often refer to them as the cows of the freshwater ecosystem.

Mayfly nymphs can be grouped into four categories, *swimmers, crawlers, clingers, and burrowers,* based on their shape and behavior. Understanding these categories will help you identify them. Behavior unique to each group also gives guidelines for proper fly presentation.

As the nymphs grow they molt twenty or more times. The typical mayfly nymph matures in about one year, although some require two or even three years and others only two or three months. Mature nymphs, ready to emerge, can be recognized by their large, dark wing pads.

Emergence from the nymph to the subimago, or dun, may occur under water, in or just under the surface film, or above water on plant stems, logs, or rocks. It can occur at any time of the day and even during the night. The exact time depends on the species, the time of year, and the weather. Afternoon emergence is typical during the colder months; morning or evening emergence is more common during hot weather.

After emergence the duns fly to streamside vegetation. They have relatively dull body colors and smoky, opaque wings. Mayfly duns are the insect group most imitated by fly fishermen.

Mayflies are not capable of mating until after a final molt to the imago, or spinner stage. This takes place from a few minutes to several days after emergence.

Spinners have brighter, shinier, body colors than duns and have clear, or hyaline, wings. The spinner lives solely for reproduction. Males gather in swarms, generally over or near water, but sometimes miles from the nearest stream or lake. They sometimes mistake asphalt roads for water.

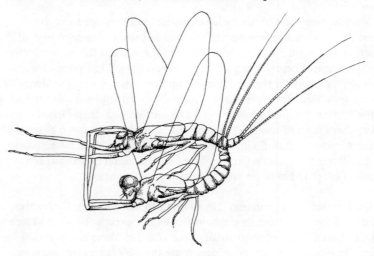

Figure 10. Pair of mating mayflies.

Females fly into the swarm of males and mating occurs in flight. Copulation is rapid, fertilization being completed in the time it takes the male and female to fall a few feet in the air. The females then fly to the water to deposit from several hundred to several thousand eggs. They are laid in small clusters of several hundred eggs each. Spent females usually fall to the water when ovipositing is complete, with their wings flat on the surface, and die. Males generally fly back to the vegetation before dying.

Adult mayflies are specialized for one task: reproduction. They have no mouthparts and cannot feed. Eggs are stored in the abdomen, where once there was a stomach and intestinal tract. The combined winged stages, dun and spinner, may be as short as a few hours, but normally lasts two or three days. From this "ephemeral" existence of the adults the order derives its name: Ephemeroptera.

MAYFLY SWIMMERS

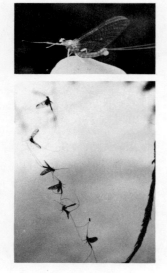

The four mayfly groups—swimmers, crawlers, clingers, and burrowers—are based on the behavior of the nymphs. Swimmers are active in the water, darting from place to place in weedbeds, brush tangles, around aquatic plants and logs, and along the open bottom.

Their shape is molded by their life style. They are slightly tapered from head to tail, streamlined like fish for efficient movement through the water. Their tails are fringed with fine interlocking hairs, forming a paddle-like surface which supplies most of their swimming thrust.

The swimming motion of these nymphs gives us one clue to quick recognition: when seined in a net or held in a hand they flip and flop just like a fish out of water. This also gives us a hint about selection and presentation of imitations: slender patterns should be chosen and fished with a movement that mimics their agility.

Swimmers are found in all fishable habitats: lakes and ponds, and slow pools, rapids, and riffles of rivers. Such wide distribution, combined with active habits and often great numbers, makes them one of the most important groups to both fish and fishermen.

The adults of all swimmers have *only two tails.* This feature is shared with the clingers and burrowers; it does, however, eliminate the crawlers, which have three tails in the adult stages. Such features, which narrow things down, are the kind of hints we look for as we identify hatches.

Throughout the mayfly groups it is always easiest to identify the nymphs. The adults have fewer distinguishing features. One of the best ways to identify a hatching adult is to capture the nymph from which it is emerging. If that is not possible then securing a cast nymphal shuck can be just as valuable: all the key features are on the shuck just as they were on the nymph itself. Shucks can be found floating just under the surface, or attached to underwater vegetation in the area of emergence.

Association of nymph and dun is one of the most important methods of identification. As we introduce the following families and genera of mayflies, keep in mind that the easiest way to key an adult to genus is to associate it with a nymph or cast nymphal skin. If several different species are emerging be careful not to confuse the cast skin of one species with the adult of another.

FAMILY: SIPHLONURIDAE

GENUS: *SIPHLONURUS*

Common Names: Gray Drake, Black Drake, Yellow Drake

Emergence and Distribution

```
J    F    M    A    M    J    J    A    S    O    N    D
               1————15         15————15
               Coastal         Rockies
```

Four species of *Siphlonurus* are known from the West. *Siphlonurus occidentalis,* the Gray Drake or Black Drake, is the most widespread and abundant species. In California, Oregon, Washington, and British Columbia they begin emerging in the spring or early summer. In the Rocky Mountain region they are late emergers, with hatches occurring from late July to early October.

We have seen heavy hatches of *Siphlonurus* in Oregon in early June. Ernest Schwiebert, in *Nymphs,* tells of fishing over them on the Yellowstone River in September, and lists the emergence period as late July to early October. The bar graph shows periods of peak emergence.

The wide range and extended emergence dates of *Siphlonurus* are typical for western insects. The angler who is prepared to identify and match a hatch wherever he finds it will have a great advantage over the angler who depends on emergence tables and pattern lists.

Nymph Characteristics

*a.   Gill plates large; double on abdominal segments 1 and 2 or 1 through 7.

*b.   Antennae short; less than 2½ times width of head.

  c.   Three tails of equal length; fringed with interlocking hairs.

  d.   Color: Body usually light to dark gray with darker markings on abdomen. One species pale yellow.

**e.   Size: Nymphs large, up to 22mm (7/8 in.) excluding tails.

    *The most important features, those which help in immediate recognition of the insect described, are starred in this and all following characteristics charts.

    **All lengths given throughout the book, unless otherwise noted, are body lengths only, excluding antennae and tails.

Dun Characteristics

  a.   Wings light smokey-gray.

  b.   Two tails.

  c.   Color: Ranges from yellow-olive to almost black, usually with distinct markings on abdomen.

  d.   Size: Large, body up to 22mm (7/8 in.).

Spinner Characteristics

  a.   Males with large eyes which meet on top of head.

  b.   Wings clear.

  c.   Two tails.

  d.   Color: Ranges from yellow-olive to almost black, usually with distinct markings on abdomen.

  e.   Size: Large, body up to 22mm (7/8 in.).

Habitat

Siphlonurus nymphs are most abundant in slow water. Quiet pools and backwaters of streams are prime habitat, but they also live along the margins of lakes. These streamlined nymphs are usually found in weed beds, around the stems of plants and grasses growing from the water, or along undercut banks where tangles of roots dangle in gentle currents. They may also occur over open rock and mud bottoms.

Siphlonurus nymphs usually migrate from flowing water to quiet areas as they mature. The first hatch we encountered, on southern Oregon's Williamson River, was overwhelming. Clouds of spinners swarmed over the river. The nymphs, however, could not be found. We swept nets through beds of weeds, grass growing along the edges of the stream, and beneath undercut banks. The nets always came up empty.

A swale leading away from the river had a few inches of water in it, inundating some thick pasture grass. We absent-mindedly dipped a net in it; the bottom came up squirming with hundreds of mature *Siphlonurus* nymphs. They had migrated to such shallow water that fish could not follow them.

It is also common to find *Siphlonurus* in isolated pools left along streams as spring floods recede. Most of the time, though, the nymphs are found where fish can feed on them.

Habits

Siphlonurus nymphs are excellent swimmers. Their three tails, with interlocking hairs, form an effective paddle. The nymphs dart in five- to ten-inch bursts across silty bottoms or among vegetation. They eat a variety of foods. Algae, insect remains, and soft-bodied midge larvae are all part of their diet. We once had a large Big Yellow May (*Hexagenia limbata*) nymph die in our aquarium. Before it was dead *Siphlonurus* nymphs were browsing on its gills. The next morning they had consumed half of the body.

Mature *Siphlonurus* nymphs can be recognized by their large, dark wing pads. They are found in quiet water where plant stems, rocks, or debris stick out of the water. Emerging nymphs crawl out on these several inches before molting into the dun. In *Hatches,* Caucci and Nastasi also report seeing *Siphlonurus* emerge in the surface film.

Emergence may occur in the morning, early afternoon, or after dark. While on Oregon's Williamson River, during a good hatch, we searched from morning until night trying to find the emerging duns. We saw none. They were apparently emerging at night. The duns are not available to feeding fish except in the rare case when they emerge during the day in open water or are blown into the water. After emergence, the duns molt to spinners in two to four days.

Spinner flights usually form from mid-morning to late evening. The swarms can be unbelievable, with hundreds of thousands of insects in the air at one time. After copulation the females drop to the water, usually several times, releasing a cluster of eggs each time. When all eggs have been laid the females fall spent to the water. At the peak of a hatch, the water is often covered by dead or dying females. Large rafts of them pile up in eddies like ice flows in the Arctic. At such times there is little hope of fish choosing even the best artificial amid so many naturals.

Siphlonurus have a one year life cycle.

Imitation

The following *Siphlonurus* patterns are effective on the waters where they were developed. They will probably work just as well on other western waters. However, two things must be kept in mind. First, there are four western species of *Siphlonurus,* each a slightly different color. Second, the color within a species may vary from watershed to watershed, and might even differ between individuals collected from the same lake or stream.

The listed dressings should be tied and tried, but they should also be considered ideas on which to base size and color variations to match insects collected in your own fishing.

Nymphs

Siphlonurus nymph imitations should be tied on 2X or 3X long shank hooks, ranging from sizes 10 to 14. The most common size for mature specimens is 10. Colors range from pale yellow through light to dark gray. These swimming nymphs are streamlined; dressings imitating them should be slender and tapered.

GRAY DRAKE (*Barry Parker*)

Hook: Mustad 9672 (3X long), No. 10.
Thread: Gray.
Tail: Woodduck flank.
Rib: Fine gold or copper wire.
Body: Muskrat fur.
Wingcase: Woodduck flank.
Legs: Woodduck flank.

The Gray Drake is tied by Barry Parker for Idaho hatches. He points out the need for accurate imitation of *Siphlonurus* nymphs because of their slow-water habitat.

BLACK DRAKE (*Polly Rosborough*)

Hook: Mustad 38941 (3X long), No. 10.
Thread: Gray.
Tail: Speckled guinea fibers, short.
Body: Beaver belly fur, with guard hairs.
Legs: Speckled guinea fibers, tied in at each side.
Wingcase: Small bunch of natural black ostrich flues.

Polly Rosborough describes this pattern in *Tying and Fishing the Fuzzy Nymphs,* one of the most valuable references available to western fly fishermen.

The Gray Drake and Black Drake are tied to imitate *Siphlonurus occidentalis.* Other *Siphlonurus* species are not as widespread but are just as important where they are found in good numbers. *S. spectabilis,* imitated by Rosborough's Yellow Drake, is restricted to the Pacific states. His Near Enough, tied with a gray fox fur body, is also a fine *Siphlonurus* imitation. Both of these dressings and the detailed steps in tying them are outlined in Polly's book.

Presentation

Presentation of *Siphlonurus* nymph imitations should be keyed to the habits and habitat of the natural nymphs. Their agile swimming indicates the need to give action to the fly. This can be done by casting down and across stream, letting the current activate the fly. You may need to add a little life, especially in still water, with pulsing movements of the rod tip, or with short strips of line. Most fish feed on these nymphs in the slack water or eddies along the margins of streams and lakes. The flies should not be weighted. They can usually be fished with a dry line and eight- to twelve-foot leaders.

Duns

Siphlonurus emerge by crawling out of the water on plant stems, sticks, or rocks; therefore, the duns are seldom available to fish. However, they are large and cruising trout will move long distances to take strays. Their imitations will be worth carrying when duns are getting on the water. They should be tied on standard dry fly hooks in sizes 10 through 14. The species range in color from yellow-olive to dark gray.

GRAY WULFF (Lee Wulff)

Hook: Mustad 94840 (1X fine), Nos. 10-12.
Thread: Gray.
Wings: Brown bucktail, upright and divided.
Tail: Brown bucktail.
Body: Blue-gray wool yarn.
Hackle: Blue dun.

The Gray Wulff is the most popular *Siphlonurus* dun pattern. If it is used only for this hatch it can be dressed sparsely.

GRAY DRAKE DUN (Swisher and Richards)

Hook: Mustad 94833 (3X fine), No. 12.
Thread: Gray.
Tails: Drak gray hackle fibers.
Body: Gray deer hair, elongated.
Rib: Dark brown thread.
Wings: Two partridge breast feathers dyed dark gray.
Hackle: Short dark dun hackle clipped in V.

The Gray Drake Dun is from Swisher and Richard's *Selective Trout.* The slow water preferred by *Siphlonurus* may make an imitative pattern such as this necessary.

Presentation

Dun patterns should be presented without drag, in such a manner that the fish will see the fly before it sees the leader. This may require fishing downstream, with slackline casts.

Spinners

Spinners are more likely to be available to fish than are duns. However, during the peak hatching period spinner falls are often too heavy to fish: so many naturals are on the water that presenting an artificial is futile. The following patterns are offered for areas with light falls, for fishing in the hour or so before spinners coat the currents, or for the early and late stages of the hatch.

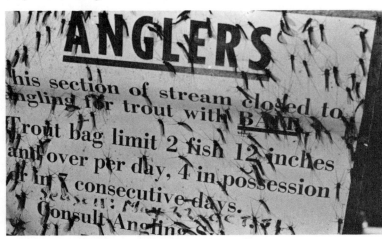

BLACK DRAKE SPINNER (Polly Rosborough)

Hook: Mustad 94840 (1X fine), Nos. 8-10.
Thread: Black.
Tail: Purplish dun gray hackle fibers.
Rib: Gray thread.
Body: Purplish brown synthetic yarn.
Hackle: Purplish dun gray.

Polly's patterns call for a lot of dyed hackle and body materials. You should study the exact colors of the naturals on your own waters before getting out the dying pots to match them. You might find different colors are called for; you might not need to dye at all.

GRAY DRAKE SPINNER (Swisher and Richards)

Hook: Mustad 94833 (3X fine), No. 12.
Thread: Gray.
Tails: Dark brown hackle fibers.
Body: Dark grayish-brown muskrat fur.
Wings: Light gray hen hackle tips, spent.
Hackle: None.

This delicate pattern is a fine model for any of the *Siphlonurus* spinners. It should be well dressed with floatant before it is cast.

Presentation

Like the duns, these spinner patterns should be presented with drag-free drifts. During heavy spinner falls this requires spotting a fish carefully and presenting the fly to it precisely, usually from a position slightly upstream and across from the rises.

Siphlonurus are important insects throughout the West. Heavy hatches occur wherever suitable habitat is found. These hatches can be fished successfully with one of the given patterns, or a minor variation, at any time during their June through September emergence.

FAMILY: SIPHLONURIDAE

GENUS: *AMELETUS*

Common Name: None.

Emergence and Distribution

```
*J   F   M   A   M   J   J   A   S   O   N   D
    15————————————————————————————15
        1———15            1———30
```

*Areas where graph is doubled indicate periods of likely peak emergence.

Ameletus is a distinctly western genus of mayflies. Sixteen species are recorded from the West, only four from the rest of the country. We have seen emergences in the opening and closing weeks of the trout season, and often in between. Due to the large number of species and wide variety of habitats found in the West, hatches of *Ameletus* occur from February through October.

Nymph Characteristics

- *a. Lower mouthparts (maxillae) have crown or comb-shaped spines.
- b. Antennae short, less than 2½ times width of head.
- *c. Small, single, oval gills on abdominal segments 1 through 7; leading edges of gills outlined with dark, sclerotized band.

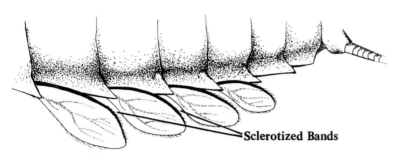

Sclerotized Bands

Figure 11. Detail of *Ameletus* sp. gills.

- d. Three tails fringed with interlocking hairs. One to several dark bands across tails.
- e. Color: Body from light brown to reddish- or purplish-brown.
- f. Size: Body length 6-14mm (¼ - ½ in.).

Dun Characteristics:

- a. Males with large eyes which meet on top of head.
- b. Two tails.
- c. Color: Brown, yellowish-brown, or pale olive. Sometimes with distinct markings on abdomen.
- d. Size: Length 10-14mm (approx. ½ in.).

Spinner Characteristics

- a. Males with large eyes which meet on top of head.
- b. Two tails.
- c. Wings clear.
- d. Color: Similar to dun; body brown, yellowish-brown, or pale olive.
- e. Size: Length 10-14mm (approx. ½ in.)

Habitat

Ameletus are distributed throughout the western states, but fishable numbers occur sporadically across this range. Some of the best populations are found in high mountain streams of the Rockies, where they have been collected at altitudes up to 11,000 feet.

Ameletus nymphs are commonly found in small, rapid streams, near but not in fast water. They rest on clean stones, vegetation, or debris. We have collected them from small coastal streams and from large desert rivers. They often inhabit deep undercut banks, away from the main current, the same places inhabited by large trout. *Ameletus* are not found in lakes.

Habits

Ameletus nymphs can swim with minnow-like speed. Disturbances of their habitat will often send them scurrying for better cover. Their active swimming behavior makes them readily available to trout.

Ameletus have a one-year life cycle. The nymphs feed on algae or other plant material. When mature they select a quiet area near the water's edge to emerge. The nymphs crawl from the water on plant stems, twigs, rocks, or logs, like their sister genus, *Siphlonurus.* It may take fifteen minutes for the dun to free itself from the nymphal shuck. Because they emerge ¿ ove water the duns are seldom available to fish.

Spinner flights of *Ameletus* have not been recorded in either fishing or scientific literature. Mating may take place far from the water or high above it. There is still much to be learned about this interesting western genus.

Imitation

Ameletus have been mentioned in only one fly fishing book, Charles R. Meck's *Meeting and Fishing the Hatches,* and then only briefly. We have collected them from nearly all western running waters. From tiny Pacific rain forest streams to waters such as the big Deschutes, there were always a few *Ameletus* along the margins and beneath undercut banks. But we did not find them in fishable numbers, and had almost reached the point of mentioning them only to keep anglers from confusing them with more important mayfly swimmers.

In September of 1978 we were invited to fish an Oregon spring creek. It flowed glass-clear through stands of lodgepole and ponderosa pine. Bleached deadfalls criss-crossed the stream, with trout rising among the tangled branches. We caught few. Toward the end of the last day we noticed some nymphal shucks along the water line of a fallen log. A closer look showed neat rows of cast skins lining most of the logs. We got our collecting nets and poked them under the logs, swished them through trailing weedbeds, and swept them along undercut banks. The nets wriggled with minnow-like *Ameletus* nymphs. We had finally found them in fishable water, good numbers, and big enough to interest the largest trout. But we still needed more information on patterns and presentation. A coincidence brought it to us.

A few days after the trip we stopped at Dave McNeese's fly shop in Salem, Oregon. Polly Rosborough was there. We mentioned the *Ameletus* hatch to Dave, who is an excellent photographer. He went to the back of the store, searched through some slide boxes, and brought back a picture.

"Is that it?" he asked.

The robust shape, black-banded tails, and purplish-amber body were all correct. The single-plated gills stood out on the nymph's abdomen, making it easy to recognize as an *Ameletus.*

"Yes, that's it," we told Dave.

"Let me see it!" Polly reached over to take the slide from Dave. He looked puzzled for a moment.

"That's my *Isonychia bicolor,*" he said, and a big piece of the western fly fishing puzzle fell into place. Polly mentions *Isonychia bicolor* in *Tying and Fishing the Fuzzy Nymphs.* According to scientific literature, *I. bicolor* does not occur in the western states.

Fly fishing literature has overlooked the *Ameletus.* Polly, using the best sources available, placed this important species with the group it closely resembled: the genus *Isonychia.* Polly's original Bicolor Walker pattern, and his *Isonychia bicolor* patterns, probably match *Ameletus.* Polly is not alone. Caucci and Nastasi's *Hatches,* the definitive book about mayflies for the angler, has a picture of an *Ameletus* labelled as a western species of *Siphlonurus.* It appears this important mayfly genus has not been ignored entirely by fly fishing writers. It has just been identified incorrectly.

Nymphs

The sparse information available about *Ameletus* offers little help in the search for imitations. We feel that Polly Rosborough's *Isonychia bicolor* nymph is an imitation of an *Ameletus* species. If you find these nymphs to be important in your waters we suggest you try Polly's pattern or create your own variation of it.

> *ISONYCHIA BICOLOR (Polly Rosborough)*
> *Hook: Mustad 38941 (3X long), Nos. 8-10.*
> *Thread: Brown.*
> *Tail: Dyed dark brown, ringneck pheasant body feather*
> *fibers.*
> *Rib: Yellow thread.*
> *Body: Fiery brown synthetic yarn.*
> *Legs: Dyed dark brown, ringneck pheasant body feather*
> *fibers tied in at throat.*
> *Gills: Tuft of marabou, one shade lighter than body, 2/3*
> *length of body, tied in at end of body, under wingcase.*
> *Wingcase: Dyed seal brown hen hackle tip, 1/3 body length.*

Polly states that the body color of the natural varies from purplish-brown to fiery brown, that imitations are successful within that range and that body color is less important than size, shape, and action of the fly in the water. In our experience this statement is true not only for *Ameletus,* but for most other nymphs as well.

Presentation

Ameletus nymph imitations should be presented along undercut banks and the margins of streams. They should be given swimming action either by the current or with a pulsing of the rod tip, just as for *Siphlonurus.*

Duns

The sporadic hatching of *Ameletus,* combined with their habit of crawling out to emerge, casts doubt on the usefulness of dun patterns for this genus. We have found none in the literature, nor have we found a need to create any. If you find that fish are taking *Ameletus* duns on your waters, we would suggest working out patterns along the lines of the Catskill school of dry flies, or trying no-hackles for smoother water.

Spinners

We offer no patterns for *Ameletus* spinners. According to Edmunds, Jensen, and Berner's scientific work, *The Mayflies of North and Central America, Ameletus* mating flights have never been observed. We have seen only sporadic returns of ovipositing females.

Ameletus mayflies will be the subject of much research in the next few years. Their importance is not fully understood yet, but we now know their imitations are effective in some western waters.

FAMILY: ISONYCHIIDAE

GENUS: *ISONYCHIA*

Common Name: Great Western Lead-Wing.
Emergence and Distribution

J	F	M	A	M	J	J	A	S	O	N	D

```
25————————————————30
25————15   15————30
Rockies      Coastal
```

There are four species of *Isonychia* recorded from the West. *I. sicca campestris* and *I. velma* are the most common. Emergence of *Isonychia* in the Yellowstone area begins in late May and continues until the first week of July. In the Pacific Northwest and coastal states emergence is later in the year, normally beginning in late August and continuing through October.

Isonychia populations are usually sparse. Their small numbers, however, are often made up for by their large size: wherever they exist, trout will feed on them. Because they crawl out to emerge, similar to *Siphlonurus* and *Ameletus,* the nymphs are more important than either the dun or spinner.

Nymph Characteristics
*a.   Forelegs with double row of long hairs on femur and tibia.
*b.   Gills plate-like on abdominal segments 1 through 7. Fibrilliform gill tufts at base of gillplates and base of forelegs.

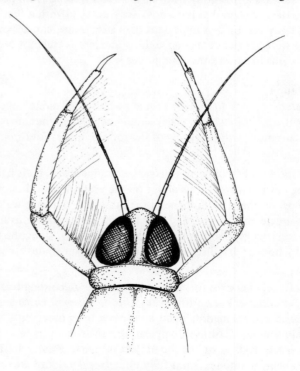

Figure 12a. *Isonychia* **nymph.**

Figure 12b. *Isonychia* **dun.**

c.   Three tails of equal length, fringed with fine interlocking hairs.
d.   Color: Body reddish-brown or purplish-brown to gray.
e.   Size: Mature nymphs range from 12 to 22mm (½ - 7/8 in.).

Dun Characteristics

*a.   Remnants of gill tufts remain at base of forelegs.
b.   Wings dark gray.
c.   Two tails.
d.   Color: Ranges from reddish- or purplish-brown to gray.
e.   Size: Large insects; body, excluding tails, 12 to 22mm (1/2 - 7/8 in.).

Spinner Characteristics

a.   Males with large eyes meeting on top of the head.
b.   Wings clear.
c.   Two tails.
d.   Color: Similar to dun; reddish- or purplish-brown to gray.
e.   Size: Similar to dun; body, excluding tails, 12 to 22mm (1/2 - 7/8 in.)

Habitat

Isonychia occur in sporadic populations throughout the Rocky Mountains, the Pacific coast states, and California. Where they are found in fair numbers their size gives them summer and late fall importance.

The nymphs prefer riffles in small to large streams. They often perch on tangled branches or other debris that trails in fast water. Rocks or flat ledges in swift currents may also harbor good populations of *Isonychia* nymphs.

Habits

Isonychia nymphs are extremely strong swimmers. Their tails, with interlocking hairs, form a large surface area and provide the major thrust. The nymphs can swim upstream in surprisingly fast currents; they evade collecting nets with speed and agility.

The long hairs on the forelegs of the nymph form a filter-feeding basket. The nymph perches on a stick or rock, faces into the current, and holds this basket in front of its head. Diatoms, algae, and tiny animal life is filtered from the current and browsed off the hairs.

Isonychia nymphs mature in about one year. They crawl a few inches out of the water on rocks or plant stems to emerge. This occurs in late afternoon, evening, or just after dark. The restless movement of nymphs prior to emergence provides the best fishing opportunity.

Isonychia duns are rarely available to fish. After twenty to thirty hours these subimagoes molt into sexually mature imagoes. Mating spinners generally gather in large swarms in late evening, although we have observed small numbers active in the middle of the day. Fertilized females release a spherical egg mass several feet above the water or dip to the water's surface to release it.

Imitation

There are few *Isonychia* patterns discussed in western fishing literature. We have chosen those which reflect the different fishing philosophies and tying styles of their creators.

Nymph

Isonychia nymph imitations should be tied on 3X long shank hooks, in sizes 6 through 10. Colors range from purplish-brown to gray. The dressings for these powerful swimmers should be blockier than the other swimmer patterns.

> *VELMA MAY (Charles Brooks)*
> *Hook:* No. 10, 3X long.
> *Thread:* Olive.
> *Weight:* Lead wire, 12-20 turns.
> *Tail:* Grizzly hackle fibers dyed dark green.
> *Body:* Mottled brown wool.
> *Rib:* Purple wool, one strand, and gray ostrich herl.
> *Overrib:* Gold wire.
> *Hackle:* Grizzly, dyed dark green.

*Note: Brooks does not use Mustad hooks. He recommends English hooks but seldom gives the manufacturer's designation for them.

This pattern was given by Charles Brooks in *Nymph Fishing for Larger Trout*. Brooks weights the fly heavily, reflecting the rough Yellowstone-area waters he fishes and his preference for putting his flies on the bottom. If you find *Isonychia* nymphs in heavy, fast water, consideration should be given to this weighted imitation.

> *ISONYCHIA VELMA NYMPH (Polly Rosborough)*
> *Hook:* Mustad 38941 (3X long), Nos. 6-8.
> *Thread:* Brown.
> *Tail:* Three fibers of dyed purple ringneck pheasant center
>   tail feather.
> *Rib:* Gold wire, 8 turns.
> *Body:* Deep purplish-brown synthetic yarn.
> *Legs:* Medium brown ringneck pheasant body plumage tied in
>   at throat.
> *Gills:* Purplish-brown marabou tied in over the body and
>   extending 2/3 the length of the body.
> *Wingcase:* Dyed purplish-brown ringneck pheasant body feather,
>   Church Window, tied over the gills and extending 1/3 the
>   length of the body.

Polly's patterns are shaped by the nature of his southern Oregon streams. These waters are less boisterous than most western rivers: his unweighted flies fish them perfectly. We recommend his patterns for *Isonychia* nymphs wherever they are found in moderate to gentle water.

Presentation

Presentation of *Isonychia* nymphs should mimic their bold swimming. They should be given long strips with the line hand in slow water or rhythmic action of the rod tip in fast water. In some situations it is best to tumble them along the bottom with no action except that given by the current.

Duns

The *Isonychia* habit of crawling out on rocks or plant stems to emerge negates the effectiveness of dun imitations. To our knowledge none have been created for western hatches.

Spinners

A search of our reference books reveals only one spinner pattern for the western *Isonychia,* Polly Rosborough's *I. velma* spinner pattern.

> *ISONYCHIA VELMA SPINNER (Polly Rosborough)*
> *Hook: Mustad 38941 (3X long), No. 8.*
> *Thread: Brown.*
> *Tail: Eight or ten purplish-dun hackle fibers, one-half inch long.*
> *Rib: Deep yellow thread, 7 turns.*
> *Body: Burgundy acrylic yarn.*
> *Thorax: Lemon-yellow yarn.*
> *Wings: Natural sooty-black neck hackle tips, spent.*
> *Hackle: Two long chartreuse, web-free saddle hackles.*

Presentation

Trout are not likely to be selective to this scattered genus, but they will not likely pass up Polly's imitation if it is well presented during the period of *Isonychia velma* activity.

Isonychia patterns make excellent searching flies wherever the naturals are present in the water. The nymphs are especially effective. They can be fished almost streamer-fashion to cover a lot of water. The largest fish are likely to be turned by them, especially when a few of the naturals are active.

FAMILY: BAETIDAE

GENUS: *BAETIS*

Common Name:  Blue-winged Olive.

Emergence and Distribution

J F M A M J J A S O N D
15——————————————15

Baetis is a large and widely distributed genus, found in all of the western states. Edmunds, Jensen, and Berner, in *The Mayflies of North and Central America,* list seventeen western species.

Hatches can occur throughout the year, depending on the species, geographic area, and weather conditions. Several species have two or three generations per year; adults of these species emerge in the spring, summer, and again in late fall. The number of generations depends on the species and the water temperature of a particular stream. Because of the large number of species, multiple generations, and varying habitats, it is impossible to predict the hatches of *Baetis* without careful study of specific waters. Their abundance and diversity make them important in every western state.

Because of their small size, *Baetis* are often overlooked by fishermen. Fish seldom make the same mistake. Many writers have noted that trout prefer to eat certain insects. When a hatch of tiny *Baetis* occurs simultaneously with that of a larger insect, trout may ignore the bigger meal and become selective to the *Baetis*.

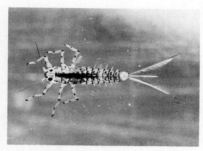

Nymph Characteristics

*a. Antennae long, two or more times longer than width of the head.

*b. Three tails fringed with fine interlocking hairs; middle tail shorter than outer two. One species, *B. bicaudatus*, with only two tails.

c. Small, single gill plates on abdominal segments 1 through 7.

d. Color: Varies widely, ranging from light tan, cream, or olive to olive-brown or dark brown.

e. Size: Body length, excluding tails, 3-12mm (1/8 - 3/8 in.)

Dun Characteristics

*a. Eyes of male large; each eye divided into two halves.

*b. Hind wings very small; long and narrow.

c. Two tails.

d. Color: Shades of light or dark olive, brown, or gray. Wings slate gray or blue dun.

e. Size: Small; length, excluding tails, 3-10mm (1/8 - 3/8 in.).

Spinner Characteristics

*a. Eyes of male large, divided, and turbinate.

*b. Hind wings very small; long and narrow.

c. Wings clear.

d. Two tails.

e. Color: Male with abdominal segments 2 through 6 often clear and translucent white or brown; female uniform color, normally light brown to reddish-brown.

f. Size: Small; length, excluding tails, 3-10mm (1/8 - 3/8 in.).

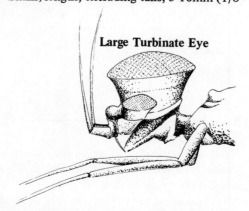

Large Turbinate Eye

Figure 13. Head of male *Baetis* sp.

Habitat

Baetis nymphs are found in most flowing-water habitats. They live in quiet pools, slow eddies, and white-water rapids, but are most common in shallow riffles. Nymphs may be found on or under rocks, debris or underwater vegetation. They are especially abundant in the trailing weeds of rich alkaline streams. In mountainous areas *Baetis* nymphs may be the only mayfly present at high altitudes.

Habits

Baetis nymphs swim rapidly; quick flips of the tails propel them in short bursts of three to five inches. When the nymphs stop swimming they immediately cling to the substrate, facing upstream, often in the full force of the current. Rapid darts from one spot to another are common for these active little swimmers. Such active behavior causes them to be a common component of stream drift. Thus they are often available to feeding trout.

Baetis nymphs feed on plant or small detrital material. Their food is scraped from the surfaces of leaves or rocks. The nymphs go through as many as twenty-seven instars. Mature nymphs can be recognized by their dark, well developed wing pads.

To emerge, the nymphs release their hold on the substrate and float or swim to the surface. The subimago bursts quickly out of the nymphal cuticle in the surface film. The dun normally leaves the surface immediately, but on cold days we have seen them float up to fifty feet before getting airborne. Emergence can occur any time during the day, depending on the species and time of year. During the warmest months it usually takes place in the cool hours of the day; during colder months in the warmer hours.

The subimagoes molt to imagoes in seven to twelve hours after emergence. Mating flights usually occur in late morning or early afternoon, although swarms have also been observed in late afternoon and evening. After copulation the females of many species land on protruding rocks or sticks and crawl under water, laying their eggs in rows on the submerged part of the objects. Other species lay their eggs on the water's surface. The female dies soon after all eggs are laid.

Imitation

One beauty of the *Baetis* is the ease with which they can be matched. Despite the large number of species, they come in a range of colors that can be copied with variations of a few patterns. Because they are small these patterns can be kept simple.

Nymphs

Baetis nymphs range in size from 14 to 24. The most common sizes are 16 and 18. Colors cover a wide spectrum, from tan, cream, and pale olive to gray and dark brown. As with most of the swimmers, their imitations should be slender and nicely tapered.

> *BAETIS SOFT HACKLE (Rick Hafele)*
> *Hook: Mustad 9671 (2X long), Nos. 14-20.*
> *Thread: Gray.*
> *Tails: Blue dun backle fibers.*
> *Body: Gray seal fur.*
> *Hackle: Blue dun ben backle.*

This nymph was tied to match a *Baetis* hatch on Oregon's desert Malheur River. Our trip was in late fall; the days were warm with a weak sun, but the nights were below freezing. The first day we fished a nice hatch of *Baetis,* and collected several duns. A stomach sample, however, gave evidence the fish were concentrating on the nymphs.

That night, while the Hafele half of the team designed and tied a few of the listed pattern, the Hughes half was content to warm his hands around a steaming mug of hot water and honey laced with blackberry brandy. The next day the results showed quickly, and it was Hafele who had the hot hand. The same pattern tied with olive and brownish-olive bodies will cover most of the *Baetis* spectrum. These little soft-hackled flies will almost always take fish when the nymphs are rising to the surface at emergence.

BAETIS NYMPH (Swisher and Richards)
Hook: Mustad 9671 (2X long), Nos. 14-24.
Tails: Woodduck or merganser flank dyed olive.
Body: Dark brown or medium olive and medium brown rabbit
   fur mixed.
Wingpads: Black ostrich herl clump or black crow quill segment.
Legs: Woodduck or merganser dyed olive.

This is a more traditional nymph dressing. It copies the natural more accurately than a soft-hackle. The body fur options, offered by Swisher and Richards in *Selective Trout,* cover most *Baetis* nymph colors. They wisely point out that species identification of the *Baetis* should be left to taxonomists, and that the group is well matched with size and color variations of one pattern.

PALE GRAY-WINGED OLIVE NYMPH (Ernest Schwiebert)
Hook: Orvis Premium (1X long), Nos. 18-20.
Thread: Tan 6/0 nylon.
Tails: Light olive-dyed gray partridge fibers.
Body: Light brownish-olive dubbing.
Gills: Pale olive-gray goose quill ribbing.
Thorax: Light brownish-olive dubbing.
Wingcases: Medium olive-grayish feather section tied down
   over thorax.
Legs: Light olive-dyed gray partridge fibers.
Head: Tan 6/0 nylon.

This exact imitation is offered by Schwiebert in *Nymphs.* He gives several other *Baetis* patterns, with bodies from pale olive to dark brownish olive. It is wise to keep this color range in mind, for the same species will vary in color from stream to stream.

John Atherton, in *The Fly and the Fish,* originated the theory that fish do not reject a fly because they see the wrong color; they reject it because they do not see the right color. Atherton, an artist, felt that by mixing different colors of dubbing together we enhanced our chances of offering the right color to the fish. It is well to bear this theory in mind. Blending several colors of dubbing to achieve the desired shade may be more effective than dying a single patch of fur the correct color.

Presentation

Baetis nymph patterns are most effective when fished over feeding fish just before a hatch or during the early stages of emergence. The prehatch restlessness of these swimmers makes them available for some time before the duns appear on the surface. During the hour or so before surface activity begins the nymph should be allowed to sink, then be brought up through the water by lifting the rod tip. When surface activity begins we have had our best luck presenting the nymphs on long leaders, with upstream casts, just as we would fish a dry fly to rising fish. The small imitations should be allowed to sink just under the surface film. It might be necessary to dress all but the last few inches of leader. This not only keeps the fly near the surface, but helps in detecting subtle takes. The angler must watch closely for signs of a strike: a slight hesitation of the leader or the line tip, a swirl in the area of the fly, or a flash under water. Short casts and accurate presentations are required to fish nymphs successfully with dry fly tackle and techniques.

Duns

When the emergence is strong, and fish are feeding on the surface, dun patterns become more effective than nymphs. This is the first genus we have discussed in which the dun stage is important to fishermen.

Baetis duns range in size from 14 through 24. The most common sizes are 16 and 18. The color spectrum is similar to that of the nymph, with pale-olives, dark-olives, and brownish-olives most common.

The patterns we will list are designed specifically to match *Baetis* hatches. You should bear in mind, however, that a color selection of standard midge patterns, with hackle fiber tails, fur bodies, and two to three turns of stiff hackle at the collar, will suffice in many *Baetis* situations.

LITTLE OLIVE (Ed Koch)
Hook: Mustad 94833 (3X fine), Nos. 18-22.
Thread: Olive nymph thread.
Tail: Blue dun hackle fibers.
Body: Blend of olive and tan spun fur.
Wings: Blue dun hackle points.
Thorax: Same as body.
Hackle: Blue dun, four turns.
Head: Olive nymph thread.

This dressing, listed in Ed Koch's *Fishing the Midge,* is tied in the traditional, or Catskill, style of dry flies. Its sparse hackle makes it perfectly suited to typical *Baetis* waters. Koch advocates the use of winged patterns even for very small flies, especially in the quieter waters often inhabited by *Baetis.* Many color variations can be based on his Little Olive pattern.

The duns of *Baetis* can often be fished successfully with other traditional patterns, such as the Adams and Light Cahill, especially in cases where the fish are not selective. Selectivity, however, is not always brought on by fishing pressure; we have fished some relatively remote western waters where the fish were pretty fussy.

BAETIS NO-HACKLE (Swisher and Richards)
Hook: Mustad 94833 (3X fine), Nos. 14-24.
Thread: Olive.
Tails: Light gray hackle fibers, split.
Body: Medium olive or medium olive and medium brown
*   rabbit fur mixed.*

Wings: Light or medium gray hen hackle fibers, clump.
Hackle: None (or light gray, parachute).

This no-hackle pattern offers the most exact duplication of the natural mayfly body, tails, and wings. It also gives the best silhouette in the surface film. Complete directions for tying the flies originated by Swisher and Richards are given in *Tying the Swisher and Richards Flies.* These two authors have developed many tying concepts in *Selective Trout* and *Fly Fishing Strategy.* The booklet describing how to tie their flies is a necessary adjunct to the study of their fine books.

Presentation

Because they often hatch in smooth-flowing waters, *Baetis* duns present a special challenge. On such heavily fished waters as Henry's Fork of the Snake River in Idaho hatches of these tiny insects can be especially frustrating. Expert anglers there have recently been using surface film emerger patterns.

Surface film emergers have split tails, dubbed bodies, sparse hackles clipped top and bottom, and a ball of polypropylene yarn on top of the body in place of the wings. They float flush in the film. The polypro ball represents the tangled wings of a natural that has failed to escape its shuck, or is just starting to emerge from it.

These emerger patterns, and the listed dun patterns, should be presented softly and precisely in the feeding lanes of rising fish. It is important to patiently scout the lie and rise-rhythms of one fish rather than haphazardly fishing the water.

If you can wade into the proper position to cast quartering downstream your fly will be more likely to reach the fish ahead of your leader or line. The closer you cast above the trout's lie the less chance stray currents have to impart unseen drag.

Spinners

We have not experienced fishable spinner falls of *Baetis.* We do not doubt, however, that they are important on many western rivers. The same pattern used for the dun stage may work for the spinner during a specific hatch. If not one of the following patterns should be tried.

BAETIS COMPARA-SPINNER (Caucci and Nastasi)
Hook: Mustad 94833 (3X fine), Nos. 16-18.
Thread: Match body color.
Tails: Medium or dark gray hackle fibers, split.
Body: Dark olive or dark reddish-brown dubbing.
Wings: Light gray hackles, two, tied in at thorax; these should
be oversized; clip the top and bottom fibers in a V so all
that remains are the fibers sticking out to the sides.

The compara-spinners, from Caucci and Nastasi's *Hatches,* can be tied quickly and should be kept in mind as a concept whenever a mayfly spinner fall is encountered.

BAETIS SPINNER (Swisher and Richards)
Hook: Mustad 94833 (3X fine), Nos. 14-24.
Thread: Brown.
Tails: Light gray hackle fibers, split.
Body: Medium or dark brown rabbit fur.
Wings: Light gray hen hackle tips, spent.
Hackle: None.

The realism of this pattern, from *Selective Trout,* makes it useful in all slow-water spinner situations. Bear in mind that body, wing, and tail colors will often have to be varied to suit the spinner fall you are matching.

Baetis provide a fishing opportunity unique among the mayflies. Many female spinners crawl under water on logs, rocks, or plant stems to oviposit their eggs. When finished they either return to the surface or are washed into the current, where they are eagerly taken by trout. Two patterns imitate the spinners in this condition. They are traditional wet flies from Ernest Schwiebert's *Matching the Hatch.*

> **BLUE QUILL SPINNER (Ernest Schwiebert)**
> *Hook: Mustad 94840 (1X fine), Nos. 16-20.*
> *Thread: White.*
> *Tails: Two long gray fibers.*
> *Body: Bleached peacock quill.*
> *Hackle: Pale bluish gray hen hackle.*
> *Wings: Gray mallard primary, tied down-wing and lacquered.*
>
> **GINGER QUILL SPINNER (Ernest Schwiebert)**
> *Hook: Mustad 94840 (1X fine), Nos. 16-20.*
> *Thread: White.*
> *Tails: Two long woodduck fibers.*
> *Body: Ginger hackle quill, stripped.*
> *Hackle: Pale ginger hen hackle.*
> *Wings: Gray mallard primary, tied down-wing and lacquered.*

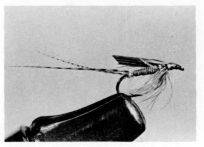

Presentation

If you find yourself doing poorly during *Baetis* spinner falls we recommend trying a traditional wet fly, fished with a traditional wet fly presentation.

Some of the most important recent literature on fly fishing has elevated the *Baetis* mayflies to their proper place on the list of major hatches. The refinement of tying techniques, the availability of gossamer threads and fine-wire hooks, and the new interest in delicate tackle should encourage western trout fishermen to seek out opportunities to fish over these prolific mayflies.

FAMILY: BAETIDAE

GENUS: *CALLIBAETIS*

Common Name: Speckle-wing Quills.

Emergence and Distribution

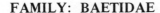

```
J   F   M   A   M   J   J   A   S   O   N   D
            1————————————————————15
            1——15    15——30    1——15
```

There are fifteen species of *Callibaetis* mayflies in the western region of the United States and Canada. They are distributed through the entire area, with fishable populations in all of the states and provinces.

Many species have two or three generations per year. The first adults usually emerge in early spring, followed by second and third broods in mid-summer and fall. In colder northern areas, and at high altitudes, *Callibaetis* are likely to have only two generations in a season. Where the warm summer break is short they may have only one. In most of the West, however, good hatches occur throughout the season.

There is often some overlap between peak periods of emergence. The spring brood may still be tapering off when the first of the summer hatch appears. *Callibaetis* are capable of causing a fishable rise on most days of the fishing season.

The importance of the *Callibaetis* mayflies has been largely overlooked. There are two reasons: they are most important in the West, and they are primarily lake and pond dwellers. There are only a few representative species in the East and Midwest, where most writing has focused, and there are few found in rivers and streams, often the preferred habitat of fly fishermen.

Nymph Characteristics

*a. Antennae long, two or more times longer than width of head.
*b. Large gills on abdominal segments 1 through 7. Gills on segments 1 through 4 or 1 through 7 with a small recurved flap producing the appearance of double gills.

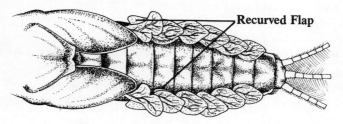

Figure 14. Gills of *Callibaetis* nymph.

c. Three tails of equal length, fringed with fine interlocking hairs.
d. Color: Body light to dark gray, tan, grayish-brown, or pale green.
e. Size: Length, excluding tails, 6-12mm (1/4 - 1/2 in.).

Dun Characteristics

*a. Eyes of male large and divided.
b. Wings mottled; hind wings small.
c. Two tails.
d. Color: Body brownish-olive to gray on back; usually light tan to olive underneath.
e. Size: Length, excluding tails, 6-12mm (1/4 - 1/2 in.)

Spinner Characteristics

*a. Eyes of male large, divided, and slightly turbinate.
*b. Front wings of female clear with speckled brown or gray markings; male front wings entirely clear or occasionally mottled.
c. Two tails.
d. Color: Body finely marked in gray or brown; lighter underneath.
e. Size: Length, excluding tails, 6-12mm (1/4 - 1/2 in.).

Habitat

On western lakes, ponds, and impoundments *Callibaetis* are usually the most important mayflies. As anglers begin to see that some of our finest fly fishing exists in these waters, the study of their insect life takes on a new fascination.

Callibaetis also occur in backwashes and along the slack margins of some streams. They inhabit many spring rivers, and some high, meandering, mountain meadow streams. They prefer still water but tolerate very slow currents, especially where they flow through weedbeds.

Callibaetis nymphs can survive high water temperatures, as well as both acid and alkaline water. They are almost always found in or near vegetation, and are commonly associated with shorelines in lakes or ponds. Where habitat is favorable they occur in great numbers.

Habits

These still or slow water nymphs swim and rest among tangled plant stems and debris along the margins of lakes, ponds, and meadow streams. Quick flips of their tails propel them in six-inch bursts. They arch their abdomens gracefully and fan their gills rhythmically when at rest.

The nymphs eat primarily diatoms and algae, and are a major converter of plant to animal tissue in lake ecosystems. They grow rapidly, molting nine to sixteen times during their development. In as little as six weeks after hatching from the egg the nymphs can have dark wing pads and be ready to emerge.

Prior to emergence the nymphs swim up and down between the surface and the safety of tangled plants. This restless activity can stir savage feeding by trout. Finally the nymphs make a steady, rapid swim to the surface, where the subimago bursts free from the nymphal shuck and is airborne in seconds. Trout often concentrate on the easily captured nymphs, ignoring the escaping duns. Emergence usually occurs in afternoon or early evening, with the duns molting to spinners seven to nine hours later.

Large mating swarms congregate from early morning to mid-afternoon. The swarms may be four to twenty feet above the water, or over open meadows near the water. The males rise and fall several feet at a time; the females fly into the swarm, where copulation occurs. The fertilized females then return to resting spots along the shore for about five days, until the eggs are ready to hatch. Females with mature eggs begin to oviposit in mid-afternoon, dipping the tip of their abdomen to the water to release four to five hundred eggs. The eggs hatch almost immediately after being deposited in the water, and the nymphs begin feeding at once.

Imitation

Some of the most exciting fishing on still waters comes during heavy hatches of *Callibaetis*. These multi-brooded mayflies present a unique opportunity and a unique problem. The same species is often available in early spring; mid-summer, and late fall; they can be fished over for a good part of the season. But each generation requires less time to mature and is slightly smaller than the preceding one.

The watchful angler fishing over a *Callibaetis* hatch will keep a close watch on the size of his flies related to the size of the emerging insects. In spring he might fish with a No. 12; the summer emergence might require a No. 14; the fall hatch might diminish to a No. 16. If the angler is not aware of this, and fishes through the season with the No. 12 that was successful in spring, he will find his success tapering off as the season progresses.

Nymphs

Callibaetis nymphs vary in color from light tan through grayish-brown to pale olive. Their imitations should be tied on 2X or 3X long shank hooks in sizes 12 through 18. They should be slender and neatly tapered.

We have had surprising success using such soft-hackled flies as the Pheasant-tail and March Brown Spider to match *Callibaetis* nymphs. These patterns, from Sylvester Neme's *The Soft-Hackled Fly,* are dressed for running water. We discovered their effectiveness on lakes after getting into a hatch when we had no closer imitations.

> *GOLD RIBBED HARE'S EAR*
> *Hook: Mustad 9671 (2X long), Nos. 12-18.*
> *Thread: Tan.*
> *Tail: Guard hairs from an English hare's ear.*
> *Rib: Narrow gold tinsel.*
> *Body: Tan fur from an English hare's mask.*
> *Wingcase: Brown turkey quill.*
> *Legs: Picked body fur.*

This traditional nymph dressing is an excellent producer during most *Callibaetis* hatches. It is wise to select a dressing one size smaller than the nymph that is emerging; fish will accept it more readily.

> *TIMBERLINE (Randall Kaufmann)*
> *Hook: Mustad 9672 (3X long), Nos. 12-16.*
> *Thread: Brown.*
> *Weight: 3-5 turns lead wire diameter of hook shank.*
> *Tail: 3 moose body hair fibers tied short.*
> *Rib: Copper wire.*
> *Body: Hare's ear fur with guard hairs.*
> *Wingcase: Dark side of ringneck pheasant tail.*
> *Thorax: As body, but thicker.*
> *Legs: Sparse ringneck pheasant tail fibers.*

This pattern comes from Randall Kaufmann's *American Nymph Fly Tying Manual.* The slight weighting called for in the Timberline is valuable in more than one respect. It will help the fly penetrate the surface film and sink quickly. When casting to visible, cruising trout, it is important that the fly reach the level of the fish before the fish has passed it. The weight also allows the nymph to be fished deep on a long leader and floating line. During a *Callibaetis* emergence it is quite common for trout to ignore hatching duns in favor of ascending nymphs. Their feeding may be so far below the surface that no evidence of it is seen. In this case allowing the nymph to sink a few feet, then sweeping it up with a long, steady raising of the rod tip will bring the artificial to the surface in a long swim, in the manner of the rising natural. During their ascent the nymphs generally do not pause; stopping the fly during the retrieve will often cause following fish to turn away.

MEDIUM SPECKLE-WING QUILL NYMPH (Ernest Schwiebert)
Hook: Orvis Premium (1X long), Nos. 16-18.
Thread: Light brown 6/0 nylon.
Tails: Light brown pheasant tail fibers.
Body: Light brown dubbing mixed with guard hairs.
Gills: Pale yellowish brown goose quill ribbing.
Thorax: Light brown dubbing mixed with guard hairs.
Wingcases: Light mottled brown feather section tied down over thorax.
Legs: Light brown partridge hackle fibers.
Head: Light brown nylon.

This imitative pattern is given in Schwiebert's *Nymphs* for *Callibaetis pacificus,* a widespread western species. We have not found it necessary to copy the naturals this closely. However, for those who find a need for exact imitation, or for those to whom fly tying itself is a large part of the challenge, this dressing is offered as an excellent imitation and a model on which to base variations to match specimens from your own waters.

Presentation

We mentioned fishing a weighted nymph by pulling it in a sweeping motion toward the surface. We also often present them on a long leader and dry line, letting them sink along vegetation or tangled limbs and deadfalls, then hand twist retrieving them very slowly. When necessary we use wet-tip or even full sinking lines to get them to the depth we want. Most often, however, we fish them relatively shallow during or just prior to an emergence.

Duns

Callibaetis duns usually escape the water quickly. However, on windy or cold days they have trouble getting airborne and trout often focus on them rather than the nymphs. We have also found them important during heavy hatches, when the fish are greedy and willingly accept either nymphs or duns.

Callibaetis dun patterns should be dressed on 1X or 3X fine wire hooks, in sizes 12 through 18. Body colors range from pale olive to light brown. The wings range from pale tan to dark slate-brown.

LIGHT CAHILL
Hook: Mustad 94840 (1X fine), Nos. 12-16.
Thread: Tan.
Wings: Woodduck flank fibers, upright and divided.
Tail: Light ginger hackle fibers.
Body: Cream badger underfur.
Hackle: Light ginger.

This traditional pattern is selected to illustrate the important point that body color for an imitation of the dun must copy the belly color, not the back color, of the natural. The common myth that the *Calli-baetis* is a Blue Dun is usually debunked by a close look at the live insect. There are species which are bluish, and that can be matched with a Blue Dun. Most, however, range from creamish-olive to olive-brown, with the belly color always a lighter shade than the wing and back colors. The cream of the Light Cahill imitates this well.

CALLIBAETIS COMPARA-DUN (Caucci and Nastasi)
Hook: Mustad 94833 (3X fine), Nos. 12-18.
Thread: Olive to tan.
Tails: Ginger or brown hackle fibers, split.
Body: Mixed dubbing to match belly color of natural.
Wing: Natural tan to slate-brown hair from mask of deer.

The compara-dun patterns given by Caucci and Nastasi are excellent for still-water imitations. They float well yet present a natural silhouette to the fish. In the range of colors and sizes given they are our favorite *Callibaetis* dressings.

CALLIBAETIS NO-HACKLE DUN (Swisher and Richards)
Hook: Mustad 94833 (3X fine), Nos. 12-16.
Thread: Olive.
Tails: Cream hackle fibers, split.
Body: Medium brown and medium olive rabbit fur mixed.
Wings: Slate-gray hen hackle fibers, clump.
Hackle: None, or cream, parachute.

The body color selected by Swisher and Richards for their *Callibaetis* dun agrees with our own collecting. It must be varied from area to area to match the body color of the natural dun.

Presentation

If rises are sporadic, it might be best to cast to any rise that can be reached. If the pattern of a cruising fish can be determined by previous rises the fly should be presented where the next rise will appear. If a lot of fish are rising in a small area it is best to cast the fly into the area and wait for a fish to come to it, rather than picking it up and casting to each rise. There will be less disturbance to put the trout down.

Spinners

We have not found *Callibaetis* spinners important. The males dance over the water in afternoon and evening swarms; females, with their distinctive mottled forewings, may cover the water where the wind pushes them against logs or shoreline debris. But the trout seem to ignore them. We have seen an occasional spinner taken, but never a consistent rise to them. There are two possible explanations: either the trout are already gorged on the nymphs and duns of the emergence, which usually is earlier in the day than the mating flight, or there is simply not enough nourishment left in the spent females to make them worth an effort.

Although we have not found *Callibaetis* spinners important, such a situation could arise, especially in the spring when the first generation insects are large. If you find trout feeding on spinners we suggest imitations based on Caucci and Nastasi's compara-spinner concept, with split fiber tails, dubbed bodies, and wings of wound hackle clipped on the top and bottom.

MAYFLY CRAWLERS

Mayfly crawler nymphs, unlike the streamlined swimmers, are generally robust. They are flatter and more rectangular in outline. The nymphs have three tails with sparse whorls of hair; these hairs do not interlock to form a paddle-like surface. Adult crawlers have three tails, making them easy to distinguish from the two-tailed adults of the swimming genera.

Crawlers are much more abundant in running water than in still water. Some species prefer slow sections of streams where silt and debris accumulate; others are found only in fast, well oxygenated riffles.

Crawler nymphs are not active and do not swim well; they crawl across the substrate. When dislodged from it they struggle with slow undulations of the abdomen, swimming feebly until contact is once again made with the bottom, or until they are eaten by a trout. Most of their diet consists of algae and detrital material.

FAMILY: EPHEMERELLIDAE

GENUS: *EPHEMERELLA*

Common Names: Lead-winged Olive, Pale Morning Dun, Green Drake.

Emergence and Distribution

J   F   M   A   M   J   J   A   S   O   N   D
1————————————20

Ephemerella is the only genus of the family Ephemerellidae found in North America. It is a large and diverse genus, with thirty-five species recorded in the area from the Rocky Mountains to the Pacific Ocean and from New Mexico north into Canada.

In the East and Midwest, such famous hatches as the Hendricksons (*E. subvaria*) herald the beginning of spring. Good western hatches of *Ephemerella* do not normally begin until June. Emergences can be expected from then until late fall.

Some of the best fishing of the season comes with the prolific hatches of various *Ephemerella* species. As a guide to this confusing genus, a few of the major species are listed below with their general dates of emergence. The exact time emergence begins depends on geographic location, character of the particular stream, and yearly weather conditions.

Common Name	Species	Emergence
Western Green Drakes	*E. doddsi*	*June 1 - July 15*
	E. grandis ingens *(formerly E. glacialis)*	
	E. grandis grandis	
Blue-winged Red Quill	*E. hecuba*	*July 1 - Aug. 30*
Pale Morning Dun	*E. inermis*	*June 1 - Aug. 30*
	E. infrequens	
Slate-winged Olive	*E. coloradensis*	*July 1 - Oct. 1*

The Green Drakes have been called the most important hatch of the western season. *E. doddsi* is most abundant in the coastal mountain streams of the Pacific Northwest. From the Cascades east to the Rockies *E. grandis ingens* (previously known as *E. glacialis*) predominates. In the Rockies *E. grandis grandis* (previously known as simply *E. grandis*) is the dominant species. These are large mayflies. The duns have bodies in shades of green with grayish, lead-colored wings. The nymphs are typically dark reddish-brown.

Another important group of *Ephemerella* found in all western states is formed by the *E. infrequens* and *E. inermis* species. These are smaller than the Green Drakes, and their pale yellow colors have brought them the name Pale Morning Duns.

Nymph Characteristics
*a. Head, thorax, and/or abdomen often with dorsal tubercles, or spines.
*b. Gills small, located dorsally on segments 3 through 7, or 4 through 7 only. Gills on segment 4 may be operculate, covering other gills.
c. Body shape variable, from greatly flattened to round.
d. Three tails equal length; with spines, whorls of hairs, or both.
e. Color: Variable; generally dark shades of brown to olive-brown.
f. Size: Mature nymphs range from 5 to 19mm (1/8 - 3/4 in.).

Dun Characteristics
*a. Wings dark slate-gray to pale yellowish-dun. Hind wings with distinct, slightly rounded costal projection.

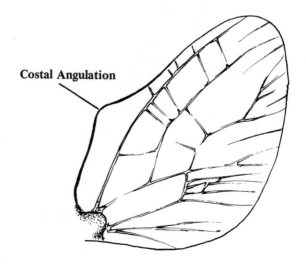

Costal Angulation

Figure 15. Hindwing of *Ephemerella* adult.

b. Three tails, one-half to three-quarters body length.
c. Color: Body ranges from bright olive-green to pale cream or yellowish-tan.
d. Size: Body length ranges from 6 to 19mm (1/8 - 3/4 in.).

Spinner Characteristics
a. Hind wings with distinct, slightly rounded costal projections. Wings clear.
b. Three tails.
c. Color: Body colors variable, ranging from brown to dark olive-green to pale cream or tan.
d. Size: Body length 6-19mm (1/8 - 3/4 in.).

Habitat

Because of its diversity, members of this genus are found in almost all running-water ecotypes. Some species even occur in lakes, always along shorelines where there is prominent wave action. In streams the nymphs occur in slow, silty pools or backwaters, near banks at the base of plants and rooted vegetation, in medium currents where tangled branches or other debris accumulate, and in torrential rapids broken with rocks and boulders. With such wide geographic distribution and environmental adaptations, *Ephemerella* is perhaps the most cosmopolitan of the mayfly genera.

Habits

Ephemerella nymphs are feeble swimmers. When dislodged they move with an erratic up and down wiggle of the abdomen. They generally prefer to stay well hidden in rock crevices, thick moss, or at the base of algae and rooted plants. Those occurring in swift water are often dislodged, drifting freely until the current brings them to a new holding place. *Ephemerella doddsi* has a sucker-like membrane on the underside of its abdomen that holds it firmly to flat rocks in fast water.

Emergence is a critical time in the life cycle of *Ephemerella*. Fast water species often migrate to sheltered areas before emerging. They become available to feeding fish during the migration. Their vulnerability is increased as some nymphs swim clumsily from the bottom to the surface, perhaps several times, before emerging in the surface film. Some species are buoyed to the surface by trapped gasses, while others emerge a foot or more under water and make the final ascent to the surface in the dun stage. Emerger patterns fished in the early stages of a hatch are often very effective.

Emergence is most common from late afternoon until after dark. The subimaginal wings must dry before the insect can fly. Duns often float a long distance before leaving the water. These long drifts over smooth currents produce some of the best classic dry fly fishing of the mayfly hatches. In many situations the fish have plenty of opportunity to be choosy; exact imitation is often an advantage.

Once free from the surface the subimagoes fly to nearby vegetation and molt to imagoes in twenty to thirty hours. Mating swarms are generally small, occurring from afternoon until dark. After mating, the females oviposit a compact, spherical mass of eggs by dipping the abdomen to the surface film. Spent females often die on the surface, providing excellent spinner fishing.

Imitation

The *Ephemerella* species are dominant hatches wherever and whenever they occur. The Green Drake hatch on Henry's Fork of the Snake River in Idaho is so famous that anglers come from all over the world to fish it. On crowded days fishermen are only a cast apart, but fish continue to rise greedily. Everybody gets to fish over plenty of willing, but highly selective, trout. Both proper pattern selection and careful presentation become critical.

Ephemerella are too diverse to give imitations for each important species. The list of dressings for them covers the two most important groups: the Western Green Drakes and the Pale Morning Duns.

Nymphs

Ephemerella nymphs are generally dark. Their blocky shape calls for shorter shank hooks than swimmer nymph imitations. Crawler patterns are usually tied on standard, 1X, or 2X long hooks. Bodies should be thicker and with less taper than swimmer dressings.

Ephemerella nymphs range in size from the large Green Drakes, imitated with size 8 and 10 flies, to the smaller Pale Morning Duns, imitated with dressings tied on size 16 and 20 hooks.

Many popular searching patterns work well for the Green Drakes. These include the Zug Bug, Gray Nymph, Gold Ribbed Hare's Ear, and Teeny Nymph. The latter, tied with natural pheasant tail fibers, is an excellent imitation of the Green Drake nymphs.

> *IDA MAY (Charles Brooks)*
> *Hook: Nos. 8-10, 1X long.*
> *Thread: Black Nymo.*
> *Tail: Grizzly hackle fibers dyed dark green.*
> *Rib: Peacock herl and gold wire.*
> *Body: Black fuzzy yarn or fur.*
> *Hackle: Grizzly dyed dark green.*

The Ida May is from Charles Brooks' *Nymph Fishing for Larger Trout.* Weighting, at the option of the tier, is with several turns of lead wire equal in diameter to the hook shank. Weighting of *Ephemerella* nymph patterns is worth considering. These crawlers have little swimming ability; when dislodged they drift helplessly along the bottom. Weight helps get imitations down with the naturals.

> *WESTERN GREEN DRAKE NYMPH (Caucci and Nastasi)*
> *Hook: Mustad 9671 (2X long), No. 8.*
> *Thread: Olive.*
> *Tails: Dark brown wet hackle barbules.*
> *Body: Dark brown dubbing.*
> *Wing pads: Black dyed mallard primary.*
> *Legs: Dark brown wet hackle.*

This pattern, from *Hatches,* duplicates the form of the natural perfectly. The size and color can be varied to suit insects on your favorite waters.

GREAT LEAD-WING OLIVE DRAKE NYMPH
(Ernest Schwiebert)
Hook: Orvis Premium (1X long), Nos. 8-10.
Thread: Dark olive 6/0 nylon.
Tails: Darkly barred woodduck.
Body: Dark brownish-mottled dubbing, with light olive
*   lacquer sternites.*
Gills: Medium olive gray marabou secured with fine gold
*   wire.*
Thorax: Dark brownish-mottled dubbing with a light olive
*   sternum.*
Wingcases: Dark mottled olive-brown feather section tied
*   down over thorax.*
Legs: Dark partridge dyed medium olive.
Head: Dark olive 6/0 nylon.

This pattern from Schwiebert's *Nymphs* is offered for the perfectionist. It is tied specifically for the *Ephemerella grandis* (now *E. grandis grandis*) species. His book offers similar ties for most other important western species of *Ephemerella.*

PALE MORNING DUN NYMPH (Swisher and Richards)
Hook: Mustad 3906B (1X long), Nos. 16-20.
Thread: Brown or olive.
Tails: Dark brown partridge.
Body: Medium brown fur or dark brown and medium
*   olive fur mixed.*
Wing pads: Dark brown or olive-brown.
Legs: Dark brown partridge.

Nymphs of the Pale Morning Dun should be fished near the bottom and without action, just as Green Drake imitations are fished.

Presentation

Ephemerella nymph imitations should be fished dead-drift. The amount of lead needed to get them to the bottom varies with water depth and current speed. In many cases an unweighted fly will sink sufficiently if cast upstream far enough. Many tiers prefer to leave their flies unweighted, wrapping lead wire around the leader, or adding split shot, when weight is needed.

Emergers

The underwater emergence of most *Ephemerella* makes imitation with emerger patterns very effective during the early stages of a hatch. These are similar to the listed nymph patterns, but have short wings added to represent the uncased wings of the dun as it swims or is buoyed the last few inches to the surface. Emergers are fished shallow, and should be tied on light wire hooks. There are several ways to suggest the wings of the natural: two hackle points can be tied short over the body of the fly; a small clump of fur, with both the underfur and guard hairs left in, can be tied behind the head of the fly and left to unfurl over the body; or a small piece of nylon stocking can be rolled and tied in over the body. Schwiebert suggests tying in a pair of mallard wing quill segments, just as for a traditional wet fly, keeping these wings 40% of the length of a normal wet fly wing.

Emerger patterns should be fished dead drift just under the surface, or flush in the surface film. They can also be presented as wet flies, across and downstream with an action that brings them swimming toward the surface like the natural.

Duns

Emerging *Ephemerella* duns float on the surface for a long time before their wings dry and they can escape to streamside cover. These long floats cause the fish to key on the dun stage during a hatch. To those of us who prefer to fish dry when fish are willing to accept our flies on the surface, duns are the most important stage of an *Ephemerella* hatch.

The duns are diverse. They range in color from yellow Pale Morning Duns to bright green Western Green Drakes. Some species, notably *E. coloradensis,* are brown with an olive cast.

Ephemerella duns change color quickly after emerging. While doing some emergence trap work on *E. doddsi* in a coastal stream, we found all the duns had dark brown bodies. However, our patterns met little success until we caught a freshly emerged dun: it was a pale yellowish-olive, with just a tinge of brown. Within an hour or two brown became the dominant color. To imitate *Ephemerella* duns accurately one must observe a dun within minutes of emergence.

Size also varies radically within the genus. It includes some of the smallest and some of the largest mayflies. Dun patterns are tied on hooks from size 8 to 18.

> ***GREEN DRAKE WULFF***
> *Hook: Mustad 94840 (1X fine), Nos. 8-12.*
> *Thread: Olive.*
> *Tail: Natural grayish-brown bucktail.*
> *Body: Olive dubbing.*
> *Wings: Natural grayish-brown bucktail.*
> *Hackle: Brown and grizzly, mixed.*

This Wulff pattern floats well in rough water, and will often be the fly of choice simply because a more exact copy of the natural will not float in the fast water where the naturals often emerge.

> ***GREEN DRAKE COMPARA-DUN*** *(Caucci and Nastasi)*
> *Hook: Mustad 94833 (3X fine).*
> *Thread: Olive.*
> *Wings: Dark gray deer hair.*
> *Tails: Dark brown dry hackle barbules, split.*
> *Body: Brownish-olive.*

This Green Drake pattern is offered in *Hatches* as matching the *E. grandis grandis, E. grandis ingens (glacialis),* and *E. doddsi* hatches. With variations in hook size and color the pattern is an excellent type for any *Ephemerella* dun.

> ***WESTERN GREEN PARADRAKE*** *(Swisher and Richards)*
> *Hook: Mustad 94833 (3X fine), Nos. 10-12.*
> *Thread: Brown.*
> *Tails: Olive hackle fibers.*
> *Body: Medium green dyed elk hair extended body, ribbed*
>   *with dark brown thread.*
> *Wings: Dark elk hair, clump.*
> *Hackle: Olive, parachute, sparse and short.*

This exact imitation of the Western Green Drake floats flush in the surface film. The elk hair body and parachute hackle will float the fly on calm waters, including the tailouts and edges of riffles where the fast-water *Ephemerella* normally emerge.

The Paradrake was designed to fish the Green Drake emergence on the Henry's Fork of the Snake. These are among the most selective trout in the world; this pattern can be used anywhere the selectiveness of the fish demand an exact imitation.

> *PALE MORNING COMPARA-DUN (Caucci and Nastasi)*
> *Hook: Mustad 94833 (3X fine), Nos. 16-18.*
> *Thread: Olive.*
> *Tails: Medium gray dry hackle barbules, split.*
> *Body: Olive dubbing mixed with tinge of yellow.*
> *Wing: Light to medium deer hair.*

Because *Ephemerella infrequens* and *E. inermis,* the Pale Morning Duns, generally hatch in relatively smooth waters, we usually use non-hackled patterns for them. Caucci and Nastasi suggest that any compara-dun can be improved upon for fast-water fishing with the addition of a hackle wound half in front and half behind the deer hair wing of the standard compara-dun. You may want to add such a hackle if the water you fish is too rough for the compara-dun pattern as listed.

Presentation

When fishing dun patterns for the *Ephemerella* we have found it just as important to present the fly properly as to choose the correct imitation. During a major hatch of *E. coloradensis* on a smooth Oregon spring creek we found we could do well even with hackled patterns, if we presented them so they would reach the trout before the leader. By wading downstream, and spotting rising fish far ahead, we could work into position and cast down to them. Serpentine S-turns of slack in our line would feed the fly, without drag, into the feeding lane of the trout. The most exact imitations failed us when presented upstream, in the traditional dry fly manner.

Spinners

Ovipositing females return to the river for egg laying a short time after the mid-day emergence of the duns. Some species seem to allow a polite hour between the emergence of the last straggling dun and the appearance of the first ovipositing spinner. This is an excellent time to eat lunch, repair your leader, dress your line with floatant, and change to a spinner pattern.

Most *Ephemerella* spinners are darker than duns. They tend to dark-olives and browns. Imitations are tied on the same range of hook sizes used for the duns: Nos. 8-18.

> *GREAT RED QUILL SPINNER (Ernest Schwiebert)*
> *Hook: Mustad 94840 (1X fine), Nos. 10-12.*
> *Thread: Olive.*
> *Tails: Three pheasant tail fibers.*
> *Ribbing: Dark brown cotton thread.*
> *Body: Rabbit and red fox fur dubbing.*
> *Wings: White hackle points tied spent.*
> *Hackle: Pale bluish-gray dun.*

Schweibert gives this pattern in *Matching the Hatch*. It imitates the female spinners of the Green Drakes.

> **GREEN DRAKE COMPARA-SPINNER (Caucci and Nastasi)**
> **Hook:** *Mustad 94831 (2X long, 2X fine), No. 8.*
> **Thread:** *Olive.*
> **Tails:** *Dark gray or brown dry hackle barbules, split.*
> **Body:** *Dark brownish-olive.*
> **Wings:** *Light gray and ginger dry hackle.*

The compara-spinner is excellent for smooth-water spinner falls. We have used it for the *Ephemerella* as well as for other mayfly genera.

> **GREEN DRAKE SPINNER (Swisher and Richards)**
> **Hook:** *Mustad 94833 (3X fine), Nos. 10-12.*
> **Thread:** *Brown.*
> **Tails:** *Bronze blue dun hackle fibers, split.*
> **Body:** *Reddish-brown rabbit fur ribbed with light gray muskrat fur.*
> **Wings:** *Pale gray hen-hackle tips.*
> **Hackle:** *None.*

The Green Drake Spinner, by Swisher and Richards, is another pattern that can be altered in size and color to meet many hatches of *Ephemerella.*

> **PALE MORNING DUN SPINNER (Swisher and Richards)**
> **Hook:** *Mustad 94833 (3X fine), Nos. 16-18.*
> **Thread:** *Brown.*
> **Tails:** *Bronze blue dun hackle fibers.*
> **Body:** *Reddish-brown and yellow fur, mixed.*
> **Wings:** *Bronze blue dun hackle.*

This is an excellent spinner pattern for the Pale Morning Duns. The hackle can be clipped top and bottom for smooth water, or left unclipped for fast-water spinner falls.

Presentation

Depending on the roughness of the water and the selectiveness of the fish, spinner patterns can be presented with traditional upstream casts or with slack-line, downstream casts.

The different stages of the *Ephemerella* mayflies—nymph, emerger, dun, and spinner—can all be important. Because they are often large and fish are often selective to them, careful attention must be paid to pattern selection and presentation.

FAMILY: LEPTOPHLEBIIDAE

GENUS: *LEPTOPHLEBIA*

Common Name: Western Black Quill.

Emergence and Distribution

J	F	M	A	M	J	J	A	S	O	N	D
				1———25							
				1———25							

Leptophlebia are primarily spring emergers. The nymphs grow rapidly in the late summer and fall, then overwinter as nearly mature nymphs. In the spring mature nymphs migrate to side pools or shallow marshy areas. Some crawl out to emerge, but most emerge in the surface film of these quiet backwaters. Emergence occurs throughout the day, with the peak in mid-afternoon. The three western species emerge in most areas from May through June.

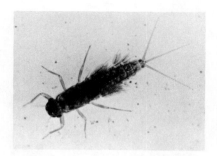

The importance of *Leptophlebia* to fly fishermen has been called marginal by many writers. We have not found them of great importance in our own fishing. However, we do know of western trout waters that harbor good populations of these crawlers. Throughout the foothills of the Sierras, Cascades, and Rockies there are drainages that begin with swamps and meandering marsh creeks; the open meadows and slow areas of these streams are perfect habitat for large trout and *Leptophlebia* nymphs.

Nymph Characteristics
*a. Head squarish; body slightly flattened.
*b. Gill lamellae double on abdominal segments 2 through 7; each gill terminating in a long filament.
  c. Three tails equal length; either with fine, sparse hairs, or hairs absent.
  d. Color: Ranges from light yellowish-brown to dark chestnut brown.
  e. Size: Body length 7-15 mm (1/4 - 5/8 in.).

Dun Characteristics
  a. Wings dark slate-gray.
*b. Hind wings large and elliptical.
  c. Three tails, dark in color.
  d. Color: Body yellowish-brown through gray to dark chocolate brown.
  e. Size: Body length 6-14mm (1/4 - 1/2 in.).

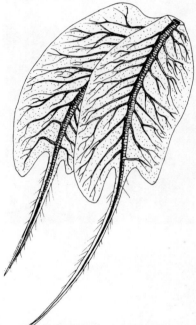

Figure 16a. Gills of *Leptophlebia* nymph.

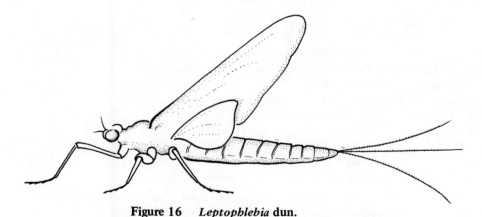

Figure 16 *Leptophlebia* dun.

Spinner Characteristics
  a. Wings clear or with brown markings.
  b. Three tails, body length or longer.
  c. Color: Body light brown to dark slate-gray.
  d. Size: Body length 6-14mm (1/4 - 1/2 in.).

Habitat

Most *Leptophlebia* nymphs live in the slow eddies or pools along the banks of medium to large streams. Some are found in ponds and lakes. The nymphs will often be concentrated in areas where leaf debris or other detritus collects. Prior to emergence they migrate to shallow, marginal waters. These migrations can consist of hundreds of nymphs, and travel a mile or more, like a school of minnows.

The sluggish rivers heavily populated by *Leptophlebia* are more common in the East and Midwest, explaining their relative abundance in those states. We have found these mayflies only in isolated populations in the West, but they are sometimes highly concentrated. Their long migrations can provide excellent fishing opportunities.

Habits

Leptophlebia behave in true crawler fashion. They remain hidden in leaf litter or detritus, exposing themselves only at night when they move to the upper surface of the substrate to scavenge plant and animal remains. When necessary, they swim awkwardly, with side-to-side undulations of the abdomen. This cautious behavior changes prior to emergence. The nymphs then crawl or swim boldly during the day, and often make several trips from the bottom to the surface before emerging.

After emergence the duns molt into spinners in eighteen to thirty hours. Small groups of spinners swarm and mate from mid-afternoon until dark. When mating is complete the females return to the water and lay their eggs by sporadically dipping the tip of their abdomen to the water's surface.

Imitation

Most western fishermen will not find situations where *Leptophlebia* are important to their fishing. However, the angler able to recognize these mayflies and fish their imitations may be prepared to solve a situation which offers trophy fishing.

Nymphs

Leptophlebia nymphs are not as chunky as the *Ephemerella*. Their imitations should be slender, and tied on 2X or 3X long shank hooks. Typical colors are tan to dark brown. Sizes range from 10 to 16,

> **GOLD RIBBED HARE'S EAR**
> *Hook: Mustad 9671 (2X long), Nos. 12-14.*
> *Thread: Tan.*
> *Tail: Guard hairs from the base of an English hare's ear.*
> *Rib: Fine gold wire.*
> *Abdomen: Tan hair from a hare's mask.*
> *Thorax: Dark brown fur, with guard hairs, from a hare's mask.*
> *Wingcase: Mottled brown turkey quill section.*

This pattern suggests the form and color of so many aquatic insects that we always carry it in a full range of sizes. It is probably all an angler will need in the way of a *Leptophlebia* nymph imitation.

> **WESTERN BLACK QUILL NYMPH (Ernest Schwiebert)**
> *Hook: Mustad 9672 (3X long), Nos. 12-14.*
> *Thread: Light brown 6/0 nylon.*
> *Tails: Pale barred woodduck fibers.*

> *Body: Medium grayish hare's ear dubbing mixed with guard*
> *hairs on light olive silk.*
> *Gills: Grayish-olive marabou laid thickly on either side of the*
> *body and secured with fine gold wire.*
> *Thorax: Medium grayish dubbing on light olive silk.*
> *Wingcases: Grayish-brown feather section tied over thorax.*
> *Legs: Grayish-olive hackle fibers.*
> *Head: Light brown nylon.*

The Western Black Quill Nymph is an exact imitation from Schwiebert's *Nymphs*. It imitates a western *Leptophlebia* species. This dressing or a variation of it will serve to imitate any of the western species.

Presentation

Imitations of the *Leptophlebia* nymphs should be presented in shallow water along the edges of ponds and marshy streams. Usually there will be some sign of cruising fish; often your presentation will be made to trout visibly searching the shallows for restless *Leptophlebia* nymphs. A slow hand-twist retrieve should be used when fishing water where the fish cannot be seen.

Duns

Leptophlebia duns are usually dark. They can be fished successfully with such traditional patterns as the Adams and Blue Dun in sizes 10 through 14.

> *BLACK QUILL (Ernest Schwiebert)*
> *Hook: Mustad 94840 (1X fine), Nos. 10-14.*
> *Thread: Black.*
> *Tail: Dark blackish-gray dun hackle fibers.*
> *Body: Stripped badger hackle quill.*
> *Wing: Black hackle points.*
> *Hackle: Dark blackish-gray dun.*

This pattern reflects the dark coloration of western *Leptophlebia* duns. The hackle stem body depicts the distinct segmentation of the natural.

> *LEPTOPHLEBIA COMPARA-DUN (Caucci and Nastasi)*
> *Hook: Mustad 94833 (3X fine), Nos. 10-14.*
> *Thread: Black.*
> *Tails: Dark gray hackle fibers.*
> *Body: Two parts medium brown, one part black, one part*
> *red dubbing mixed.*
> *Wing: Dark gray deer hair.*

The compara-dun offers the best outline of the natural. Although you might need to vary the dubbing mixture, this style of fly may be your best choice because the natural emerges in shallow, almost still, water and rests for a long time before flying away.

Presentation

Dun dressings will be presented in the slowest water. They must be fished with the finest tackle and softest presentations.

Spinners

We have not fished over any *Leptophlebia* spinner falls. The following western pattern is from Schwiebert's *Matching the Hatch.*

BLACK QUILL SPINNER (Ernest Schwiebert)
Hook: Mustad 94833 (3X fine), Nos. 10-14.
Thread: Black.
Tails: Three brown mallard fibers.
Body: Badger hackle quill, stripped.
Wings: Medium bluish-gray hackle points tied spent.
Hackle: Very dark bluish-gray, trimmed off on top and
*   bottom.*

The Black Quill Spinner should work well for most western *Leptophlebia* spinner falls. If necessary, we suggest you vary it or use a comparaspinner pattern with dubbed body and trimmed hackle wings to imitate the spinners you find important.

FAMILY: LEPTOPHLEBIIDAE

GENUS: *PARALEPTOPHLEBIA*

Common Names: Blue Quill, Red Quill, Blue Dun.

Emergence and Distribution

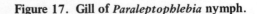

J	F	M	A	M	J	J	A	S	O	N	D

1————————————————————10

This genus is a dominant member of the mayfly fauna in most western streams. There are twenty species of *Paraleptophlebia* in the West. Emergence is spread over the spring, summer, and fall months.

Some species, for example *P. gregalis,* emerge as early as March, with heavy hatches common in April and May. These species overwinter as nearly mature nymphs. Other species, such as *P. debilis,* overwinter in the egg stage, with eclosion in spring; the nymphs grow rapidly, emerging in late summer and fall. Some hatches, such as *P. bicornuta,* extend into October and November, providing excellent fall fishing.

Paraleptophlebia species have adapted to faster currents than their *Leptophlebia* cousins. There are hatches on the most famous western rivers, from Oregon's McKenzie to Idaho's Henry's Fork, and Montana's Rock Creek. There are hatches from New Mexico to Alberta and California to British Columbia.

Figure 17. Gill of *Paraleptophlebia* **nymph.**

Nymph Characteristics
*a. Body slightly flattened; square shaped head.
*b. Single, tuning-fork shaped gills on abdominal segments
    1 through 7.
c. Three tails equal length; as long as or longer than body.
d. Color: Body normally uniform in color; shades of olive-
    brown to dark brown.
e. Size: Body length 6-12mm (1/4 - 1/2 in.).

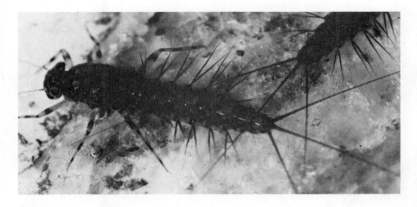

Dun Characteristics
*a. Hind wings rounded and well developed.
 b. Wings light smoky-gray.
 c. Three tails of equal length.
 d. Color: Body light blue dun to deep reddish-brown.
 e. Size: Body length 6-12mm (1/4 - 1/2 in.).

Spinner Characteristics
 a. Three tails, equal in length.
 b. Wings clear, occasionally tinted with amber.
 c. Color: Body of female reddish- to purplish-brown; males with thorax and tip of abdomen brown, the middle of the abdomen white or clear.
 d. Size: Body length 6-12mm (1/4 - 1/2 in.).

Habitat
Paraleptophlebia are distributed in large numbers throughout the entire western region. In small Pacific coastal streams they are a staple in the diet of scrappy cutthroats. On famous inland rivers, such as the Yellowstone or Henry's Fork, they are often the preferred morsel of ultra selective tippet smashers.

This genus favors running water. Early instar nymphs are common in fairly fast riffles, usually resting on moss, debris, or coarse gravel. As the nymphs mature they move to slower water. These larger nymphs are found in areas where leaf and other detritus accumulates, or along undercut banks, where they rest on exposed roots and tangled branches. They rest on the trailing plants in rich streams with heavy vegetation and moderate currents.

Paraleptophlebia are most common in small- to medium-sized streams. Good populations are also found on may large rivers.

Habits
The nymphs of *Paraleptophlebia* are poor swimmers. Their awkward side-to-side undulations do not result in much forward motion. When caught in the currents they may drift a long distance before regaining a hold on the substrate. This lack of swimming ability, and their common occurence in the drift, combine to make them important components of trout diets.

The nymphs move to slower water as they mature, anticipating emergence. When ready to emerge they crawl several inches above the water on sticks, rocks, plant stems, or other projections before the subimagoes work free of the nymphal shucks. On Henry's Fork we have seen nymphs

emerge on plant growth just under the surface. The duns quickly pop to the surface, then ride the currents several feet before their wings are dry. Emergence is usually sporadic throughout the day.

The dun stage lasts from twelve to forty-eight hours before the final molt. In early spring or late fall spinners are most active in the mid-afternoon or early evening. Summer mating flights occur in the evening just as the sun leaves the water. The females fly into a dancing cloud of males, and are seized by a male. Copulation is completed in the time it takes the pair to fall only two or three feet. The female immediately dips to the water several times, releasing a packet of eggs each time. Both males and females die shortly after mating.

Imitation

Paraleptophlebia become very important where they emerge in open water. For example, there are excellent September hatches on the Yellowstone and Henry's Fork. Imitations are most useful in smooth currents; in rougher rivers the nymphs migrate to the shallows and the duns emerge after the nymphs crawl out of the water. Neither stage is readily available to feeding trout.

Nymphs

Few nymph imitations have been created for the *Paraleptophlebia*. In most situations a Gold Ribbed Hare's Ear in size 14 or 16 is an excellent imitation. Patterns tied especially for these nymphs should be dressed on 1X or 2X long hooks in sizes 12 through 18. The bodies should be slender and slightly tapered. Colors are usually olive-brown to dark brown.

> WESTERN BLUE QUILL NYMPH (Ernest Schwiebert)
> *Hook: Orvis Premium (1X long), Nos. 14-16.*
> *Thread: Dark tannish-gray 6/0 nylon.*
> *Tails: Dark barred woodduck fibers.*
> *Body: Dark grayish-brown dubbing tightly spun on brown silk.*
> *Gills: Pale grayish marabou secured with fine gold wire.*
> *Thorax: Dark grayish-brown dubbing on brown silk.*
> *Wingcases: Dark grayish-brown feather section tied over thorax.*
> *Legs: Dark grayish-brown hackle.*
> *Head: Dark tan nylon.*

This nymph imitates species found in the coastal states, from California to British Columbia. The Little Western Red Quill is found in the Rocky Mountain watersheds. Its nymph is tied on Nos. 16-18 hooks, and has a reddish-brown body. Both are excellent imitative patterns and should be considered when you are matching a hatch of western *Paraleptophlebia.*

Presentation

Nymph patterns may be fished with dry fly tactics to dimpling or tailing fish. They also may be cast to cruisers along the shallow edges of streams. In a moderate current they can be fished with wet fly tactics: down and across stream casts, a short drift while the fly sinks, then a gentle movement of the rod tip to activate the imitation as it makes its swing.

Emergers

In *Nymphs* Schwiebert suggests there are times when the naturals are taken just under the surface film. Charles Brooks, in *Nymph Fishing for Larger Trout,* offers an emerger pattern that presents the imitation suspended from the surface.

> *NATANT NYLON NYMPH (Charles Brooks)*
> *Hook: Mustad 94831 (2X long, 2X fine), Nos. 14-18.*
> *Thread: Brown or tan 5/0 Nymo.*
> *Tails: Grouse or grizzly fibers, sparse and short.*
> *Rib: Gold wire.*
> *Body: Black, brown, gray, or tan wool.*
> *Wing: Square of nylon stocking enclosing gray or tan*
> *polypro yarn.*
> *Legs: Grizzly or grouse.*

Brooks recommends suspending this fly from the surface by using paste floatant on the wing ball. We have found emerger patterns effective on rivers like the Henry's Fork of the Snake during *Paraleptophlebia* hatches.

Duns

Paraleptophlebia duns are important smooth-water patterns. They range in color from blue dun to reddish-brown, in size from 12 to 18.

> *RED QUILL*
> *Hook: Mustad 94840 (1X fine), Nos. 12-18.*
> *Thread: Brown.*
> *Tail: Brown backle fibers.*
> *Body: Natural reddish-brown neck hackle stem.*
> *Wings: Dyed gray hackle tips, upright and divided.*
> *Hackle: Brown.*

This is the accepted pattern for the September *Paraleptophlebia* hatch on Henry's Fork. It is used in size 16.

> *DARK BLUE QUILL (Ernest Schwiebert)*
> *Hook: 94840 (1X fine), Nos. 16-18.*
> *Thread: Black.*
> *Tails: Dark bluish-gray hackle fibers.*
> *Body: Unbleached stripped peacock herl.*
> *Wings: Black hackle points.*
> *Hackle: Very dark bluish-gray dun.*

This tie is similar to the Red Quill. It represents darker species of western *Paraleptophlebia*.

> **PARALEPTOPHLEBIA COMPARA-DUN (Caucci and Nastasi)**
> **Hook:** Mustad 94831 (2X long, 2X fine), No. 16
> **Thread:** Black.
> **Tails:** Brown dry hackle barbules, split.
> **Body:** Reddish-brown dubbing.
> **Wings:** Medium gray deer hair.

This compara-dun gives a more exact silhouette of the natural. Its use may be called for when fish are feeding selectively on the unruffled water of our spring rivers. A pattern using grayish-brown fur for the body will match the darker species of this genus.

Presentation

Paraleptophlebia duns emerge in mid-current if the flow is not heavy and the water not broken by riffles. Their imitations should be fished along the lines of drift selected by feeding trout. On the popular Yellowstone area rivers it is necessary to present the fly on the nose of the fish, with the fly preceding the leader. The fish are educated; only an accurate presentation of the correct imitation is likely to fool them.

Spinners

Spinner falls of *Paraleptophlebia* can be heavy and important to the angler. They range in color from reddish-brown to white, in size from 14 to 18.

> **BLUE QUILL SPINNER (Ernest Schwiebert)**
> **Hook:** Mustad 94833 (3X fine), Nos. 16-18.
> **Thread:** White.
> **Tails:** Two long gray fibers.
> **Body:** Bleached peacock quill.
> **Wings:** White hackle points, tied spent.
> **Hackle:** Pale bluish-gray dun clipped top and bottom.

The Blue Quill Spinner represents the darker *Paraleptophlebia* species.

> **FEMALE RED QUILL SPINNER (Frank Klune)**
> **Hook:** Mustad 94833 (3X fine), Nos. 16-18.
> **Thread:** Brown.
> **Tails:** Two long pheasant tail fibers.
> **Body:** Bleached peacock quill with tan tip at tails.
> **Wings:** White hackle points tied spent.
> **Hackle:** Medium brown, clipped top and bottom.

The Female Red Quill Spinner and the Blue Quill Spinner are from Schwiebert's *Matching the Hatch*. These two patterns should arm the angler to meet any western *Paraleptophlebia* spinner falls.

Paraleptophlebia are found in good numbers throughout the western region. Wherever they emerge in open water, instead of crawling out along the shoreline, they are important hatches.

FAMILY: TRICORYTHODIDAE

GENUS: *TRICORYTHODES*

Common Name: White-winged curse.

Emergence and Distribution

J F M A M J J A S O N D
15————————————————10

There are six species of *Tricorythodes* in the Southwest, from New Mexico north to Nevada and west through California. One species, *T. minutus,* is the most widespread, emerging from the northern Rockies to the Pacific Northwest.

Emergence of these minute mayflies extends over a long period, lasting from early summer through late fall. Life cycles for many species are not well known. It is suspected the winter is spent in the egg stage, with eclosion occurring in the spring and early summer. The nymphs mature rapidly; when conditions are perfect they can be ready to emerge in about five weeks. Such rapid growth often allows two generations in a summer, the first emerging in June or July, the second in August, September, or October. Thus the emergence of a single species can extend over several months.

Nymph Characteristics
  *a. Gills on second abdominal segment triangular in shape and cover gills on segments 3 through 7.
  b. Three tails, with center tail equal to or longer than outer tails.
  c. Color: Body light to dark brown.
  *d. Size: Minute; 3-10mm (1/8 - 3/8 in.)

Operculate Gill on 1st Segment

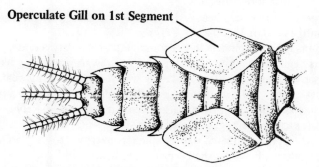

Figure 18. Operculate gills of *Tricorythodes* nymph.

Dun Characteristics
  *a. Hind wings absent; front wings large, whitish-gray.
  b. Three tails.
  c. Color: Female usually with light green abdomen and dark brown thorax; male with both abdomen and thorax dark brown.
  d. Size: Body length only 3-6mm (1/8 - 1/4 in.).

Spinner Characteristics
- *a. Front wings clear; hind wings absent.
- b. Three tails.
- c. Color: Female with pale to dark green abdomen and dark brown thorax; male with dark brown or black abdomen and thorax.
- d. Size: Body length only 3-6mm (1/8 - 1/4 in.).

Habitat

Tricorythodes nymphs are restricted to streams, dominantly in slow water sections. They are common in silty areas that are unsuitable for most other mayflies. Streambeds of fine sand or gravel and areas of thick moss or rooted vegetation also harbor good populations of these tiny nymphs.

Tricorythodes are found in streams of all sizes, from small creeks to large rivers. They are often overlooked because of their minute size, but they can be a major trout food in waters of marginal quality for other mayflies.

Habits

Tricorythodes nymphs are very feeble swimmers, moving with the familiar slow undulations of the abdomen. They normally remain on the substrate and move entirely by crawling. They are herbivorous, feeding on diatoms, algae, and other plant material. Their crawling behavior, coupled with their minute size, makes nymph imitations difficult to fish.

Tricorythodes become more available to fish when emergence approaches and the nymphs become more active. Emergence may occur in several ways. Many species emerge under water and the dun floats to the surface. Others float to the surface as nymphs where the subimagoes quickly burst free. In other cases the nymph crawls up rocks or plant stems to just above the water line before the dun escapes the nymphal shuck. We have observed *T. minutus* emerging both in the surface film and on rocks just above the surface.

Emergence can be very heavy. It normally starts early in the morning, lasting until 10:30 or 11:00 a.m.

The duns molt to spinners in a few minutes to about two hours. Mating flights begin almost immediately, with great swarms hovering like suspended snowflakes several feet above the water. These swarms peak between 9:00 and 11:00 a.m., although in November we have observed them as late as 2:00 p.m. After mating, the females immediately drop to the water to lay their eggs. These great spinner falls often present the best fishing. Trying to match size 24 spinners over two to four pound selective trout can bewilder the best of fishermen.

Imitation

It is difficult to find specific *Tricorythodes* patterns in fishing literature. The western angler is left a little on his own. The following dressings provide a framework on which to build imitations of those species you find in your own area.

Nymphs

Tricorythodes nymphs are perhaps the least important stage to the angler. They are tied on tiny No. 20 to No. 26 hooks. Their dubbed bodies should be relatively stout.

TRICORYTHODES NYMPH
Hook: Mustad 94842 (up eye), Nos. 20-26.
Thread: Brown.
Tails: Three pheasant center tail fibers, short.
Body: Tan to brown dubbing, tapered.
Legs: Picked out dubbing.

This simple pattern may offer the trout all they need to see in an imitation of these tiny nymphs. Three or four turns of fine lead wire may be needed if you plan to fish the nymph more than a few inches below the surface.

TRICORYTHODES FALLAX NYMPH (Ernest Schwiebert)
Hook: Mustad 94840 (1X fine), No. 20.
Thread: Brown.
Tails: Brown mottled mallard fibers.
Body: Brown dubbing.
Ribbing: Chocolate-dyed goose-quill herl fiber.
Gills: Brown-mottled feather section coated with vinyl
    lacquer.
Thorax: Rich reddish-brown dubbing.
Wingcases: Dark brown-mottled feather sections.
Legs: Dark brown-mottled mallard.
Head: Brown.

This pattern is from Schwiebert's study of the genus in a two-part article in *Fly Fisherman Magazine* (Vol. 8, No. 6 and 7, 1977). We leave it to the enterprising tier-angler to modify or simplify Schwiebert's pattern to strike a balance between the selectivity of the fish and the amount of time spent at the tying bench.

Emergers

As mentioned, some *Tricorythodes* cast the nymphal shuck under water, reaching the surface with the dun wings trailing above the thorax. Stomach samples have shown this is a preferred stage of the hatch. Schwiebert suggests imitating emergers by adding marabou above the body of the nymph. He also notes that ostrich herl flues may be clipped short over the thorax, or the fluff from the base of a hackle feather can give the unfurling wing effect. Swisher and Richards add that short hackle tips can be tied in over the body to imitate the wings of the natural as it ascends the last few inches to the surface. All of the above ideas should be kept in mind when tying flies to fish the early stages of a *Tricorythodes* hatch.

Presentation

Tricorythodes nymphs should be fished dead-drift to fish feeding under the surface. When rises are visible it is wise to present an emerger in or just under the surface film.

Duns

Simple midge patterns, with hackle fiber tails, dubbed or floss bodies, and two or three turns of stiff hackle may make the best dun patterns. If the hackle is trimmed on the bottom the fly will float flush in the film, like a compara-dun.

BLACK MIDGE AND OLIVE MIDGE
Hook: Mustad 94842 (up eye), Nos. 22-24.
Thread: Black or olive.
Tails: Blue dun hackle fibers or white hackle fibers.
Body: Black tying thread or pale olive beaver belly fur.
Hackle: Light blue dun or cream.

These two midge patterns cover a wide range of *Tricorythodes* hatches; a few simple variations of body and hackle color will match any of the western species.

TRICORYTHODES FALLAX DUN (Ernest Schwiebert)
Hook: Mustad 94840 (1X fine), No. 22.
Thread: Brown.
Tails: Smoky grayish-dun hackle fibers.
Body: Medium reddish-brown.
Wings: Pale gray hackle points.
Hackle: Brown furnace.
Head: Brown.

This pattern is for the western species *T. fallax.* We recommend that you look closely at your natural and be prepared to offer the fish alternative ties with either black or pale-olive bodies and white hackle point wings.

Presentation

Presentation becomes very critical over selective trout. The fly must reach the trout before the leader. An upstream cast will be futile unless it is presented from an angle that allows the fly to pass over the fish first. The fly should be lifted gently from the water after each cast and shown to the trout again and again. Often they will not take until the tenth or perhaps twentieth cast, especially if naturals are abundant.

Spinners

The Black and Olive Midge dun patterns may be used for *Tricorythodes* spinners. The hackle should be clipped on the top and bottom to leave only those fibers on each side which represent the spent wings of the natural. This clipping can be left until the streamside situation calls for it. We find throughout this guide that a small selection of midge patterns in four or five colors, on hook sizes 18 through 24, will allow us to match many hatches.

TRICORYTHODES FALLAX SPINNER (Ernest Schwiebert)
Hook: Mustad 94840 (1X fine), No. 22.
Thread: Brown.
Tails: Smoky grayish-dun hackle fibers.
Body: Dark reddish-brown.
Wings: White hen-hackle points tied spent.
Hackle: Brown furnace.
Head: Brown.

This pattern, or one like it with a black or pale-olive body, will imitate most western *Tricorythodes.* If the water is smooth the hackle can be clipped in a V both top and bottom, to leave a few supporting fibers along the wings while allowing the fly to float flush in the surface film.

TRICORYTHODES FALLAX NO-HACKLE SPINNER
(Ernest Schwiebert)

Hook: Mustad 94840 (1X fine), No. 22.
Thread: Brown.
Tails: Smoky grayish-dun hackle fibers, split.
Body: Dark reddish-brown.
Wings: White polypropylene yarn fibers tied spent.
Thorax: Dark mahogany-brown.
Hackle: None.

We have found that a similar dressing with olive abdomen and thorax represents a widespread Pacific Northwest species.

The following wet fly imitates the spinner after it has been swept under the water.

WET BLUE DUN
Hook: Mustad 94840 (1X fine), Nos. 20-24.
Thread: Gray.
Tails: Blue dun hackle fibers.
Body: Muskrat fur.
Hackle: Blue dun, sparse.
Wings: Natural gray quill sections.

Presentation

This and other traditional wet flies are effective when the water is roughened by a wind-riffle, or in areas where it is not practical to fish tiny dry flies.

Spinners are regarded by many as the most important stage of *Tricorythodes* hatches. Western anglers may also encounter situations when nymph, emerger, and dun patterns are effective.

MAYFLY CLINGERS

Mayfly clinger nymphs are adapted to life in fast water. They are characterized by flattened bodies, flat shovel-shaped heads, well developed lateral gills, and eyes which are located in the top surface of the head rather than to the sides. Their flat shape allows them to cling closely to the substrate, avoiding the main force of the current.

Adult clingers have a typical mayfly outline. Their front wings are heavily veined and have two pairs of cubital intercalary veins. All clinger adults have two tails, and have five distinct segments in the hind tarsi. The adult head retains some of the flat shovel-shape of the nymph. This helps distinguish clingers from the two-tailed swimmers, which have delicate, round heads.

Clingers are found only in streams and rivers. They thrive in fast, even torrential rapids, but also occur in slicks and eddies near fast water. They are well adapted to holding on in this habitat, but are occasionally dislodged from the bottom. They are poor swimmers, and float downstream until contact is again made with the substrate.

The clinger group consists of five genera, all in the family Heptageniidae: *Epeorus, Heptagenia, Rhithrogena, Cinygmula,* and *Cinygma.*

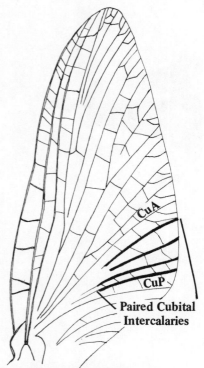

Figure 19. Forewing of
Heptageniidae adult.

FAMILY: HEPTAGENIIDAE

GENUS: *EPEORUS*

Common Name: Little Yellow May.

Emergence and Distribution

J F M A M J J A S O N D
        15————————————31

    There are nine known species of *Epeorus* across the West. Emergence begins in early spring and continues through the summer. We have witnessed excellent hatches in the Northwest in May. Emergences in the Rocky Mountains usually occur in June and July, depending on elevation. Some species are common at high elevations, where they emerge as late as August.

    Epeorus are typical of the clinger group. They present unique problems of imitation to the tier, but the need for exact imitation is lessened by the fast-water habitat of the naturals. They usually live in broken currents; trout must either take or refuse the artificial with little time to look it over. Therefore, patterns for nymph, dun, and spinner can all be tied on a more impressionistic level.

Nymph Characteristics

  *a. Two tails, body length or longer. *Epeorus* is the only mayfly genus with two tails in the nymph stage.

  b. Head and body flattened, with head 1-1/3 to 1-1/2 times as wide as it is long.

  c. Large lateral gills on abdominal segments 1 through 7, sometimes overlapping and producing a suction cup effect.

  d. Color: Light brown to dark chocolate brown. Wingpads of mature nymphs black.

  e. Size: Body length 7-18mm (1/4 - 3/4 in.).

Dun Characteristics

  a. Head retains wide, flat appearance of nymph.

  b. Wings well developed; pale tan to yellow in color.

  c. Two tails approximately body length.

  d. Color: From pale cream or olive to distinct yellow.

  e. Size: Body length 7-18mm (1/4 - 3/4 in.).

Spinner Characteristics

  a. Eyes of male large, almost touching on top of head; often black.

  b. Forelegs of male body length or longer.

  c. Wings clear, with distinct veins.

  d. Two tails longer than the body.

  e. Color: Body normally light cream or yellow.

  f. Size: Body length 7-18mm (1/4 - 3/4 in.).

Habitat

Epeorus nymphs require cold, clean, well oxygenated water to survive. Their typical habitat is in fast, often turbulent riffles. They cling to the bottoms and sides of smooth, fist-sized or larger, rocks, avoiding the

strongest currents. They may also be found on tangled branches or logs that are caught in fast riffles.

The different species of *Epeorus* are found in small to large streams from sea level to 10,000 feet. They are abundant throughout the western region because of the large number of cold, fast streams.

Habits

Epeorus nymphs are poor swimmers. Because of their fast water habitat a dislodged nymph will be carried some distance downstream before it can re-attach itself to the substrate. But few *Epeorus* nymphs are found in the drift, attesting to their tenacious grip. Just prior to emergence, however, the nymphs crawl restlessly to the upper surfaces of rocks. This exposes them to the full force of the current, and many are dislodged.

At emergence the subimagoes of many species leave the nymphal shuck while still under water. The subimago, with its wings folded back over the abdomen, is then buoyed to the surface by a bubble of gas. In other species the nymph rises to the surface and the subimago emerges in the surface film. While rising to the surface, whether as duns or nymphs, they are easy prey for waiting fish. Emerger patterns fished to imitate this behavior provide excellent sport. Emergence of most species occurs between early morning and late afternoon.

Subimagoes leave the water quickly in warm, dry weather. If it is cold and wet, however, the duns may float several feet before getting airborne. After about one day the subimagoes molt to imagoes and mating flights begin to form. Swarms of some *Epeorus* are small, occurring in the early morning or late evening hours. Other species form large swarms just as the sun leaves the water. After mating, the females dip to the water over fast riffles, releasing eggs each time the abdomen touches the surface.

Imitation

Epeorus nymph imitations are rarely effective because of the firm grip the naturals have on the substrate. After heavy rainfalls they are tumbled in the currents more often, but fishing is seldom productive during such spates.

Emergers are much more important. Rising duns and nymphs are taken easily by feeding fish. Soft-hackle and flymph patterns imitate them perfectly.

The floating dun can also be important, especially on cold, wet days when they have difficulty leaving the water. High floating patterns are perfect for picking pockets in fast runs and riffles during an *Epeorus* hatch.

Spinner flights of most species are small and sporadic. Some, however, form large swarms, and are important to the fisherman.

Nymphs

Most *Epeorus* nymph fishing can be done with traditional searching patterns such as the Gold Ribbed Hare's Ear or the dark Zug Bug. These should be tied on Nos. 12 to 16, 1X or 2X long hooks, and weighted.

> *EPEORUS NYMPH (Poul Jorgensen)*
> *Hook: Mustad 38941 (3X long), Nos. 10-16.*
> *Thread: Olive.*
> *Tails: Two pheasant center tail fibers.*
> *Abdomen: Medium brown Seal-ex dubbing with a touch of olive.*
> *Gills: Abdomen picked out at sides.*
> *Thorax and Legs: Medium brown fur with guard hairs left in.*

This style is exceptional in its representation of the flat shape of the clinging mayfly nymphs. It comes from Poul Jorgensen's *Modern Fly Dressings for the Practical Angler*. He makes a very wide body by spinning the material on a thread loop, then roughing it up with a hobby saw. After wrapping the body he trims the top and bottom, leaving the wide, flat appearance of the natural. Not only is this concept excellent, it is easy and quick to tie. With minor variations in size and color this style pattern will imitate any of the clinging mayfly nymphs.

Presentation

Epeorus nymphs have little or no swimming ability. Their imitations should be tumbled along the bottom.

Emergers

Epeorus emerge in the open currents. They do not crawl out on rocks or plant stems. They are usually buoyed to the surface by a bubble of gas that forms under the cuticle. Some rise to the surface as duns, with their wings trailing; others rise as nymphs and emerge to the dun stage in the surface film.

Soft-hackle patterns and flymphs, which imitate the working of the wings and legs of the ascending natural, are the most effective emerger patterns. They should be dressed on light wire hooks in a range of colors from light tan through dark brown, and from pale to light yellow.

> *PARTRIDGE AND YELLOW SOFT-HACKLE*
> *(Sylvester Nemes)*
> *Hook: Mustad 94840 (1X fine), Nos. 10-16.*
> *Thread: Yellow.*
> *Body: Yellow floss, thin.*
> *Thorax: Hare's mask fur.*
> *Hackle: Gray or brown partridge.*

This pattern, from Sylvester Neme's *The Soft-Hackled Fly,* is suggestive of the emerging *Epeorus.* The soft hackle fibers compress around the fur thorax when activated by the currents, giving the fly the wide front and quick taper of the natural. The working of the soft hackles as the fly is caught and released by turbulence represents the legs and unfolding wings of the emerging dun.

Nemes recommends fishing his soft-hackle patterns just under the surface film. Mends of a double taper dry line are used to keep the fly moving at the pace of the current, without pull from the line or leader.

HARE'S EAR FLYMPH (Leisenring and Hidy)
Hook: Mustad 94840 (1X fine), Nos. 10-16.
Thread: Primrose yellow.
Tails: Two or three woodduck flank fibers.
Rib: Very narrow flat gold tinsel.
Body: Fur from the lobe or base of a hare's ear spun on
    primrose yellow silk.
Hackle: None.
Wings: English woodcock secondaries with buff tips.
Legs: Pick out body dubbing.

"Flymphs," Pete Hidy told us, "represent the stage of a hatching insect which some people call an emerger. It has left the bottom and is rising to the surface. It is no longer a nymph and not yet an adult: it is a flymph."

Hidy is co-author of the classic book, *The Art of Tying the Wet Fly and Fishing the Flymph,* written with James Leisenring in 1941 and released in a new edition in 1971. Hidy is the most devoted student of the flymph, and the stage of aquatic insect life it imitates. This book is one of value to all fly fishermen. Its pages demand careful study and the dressings it lists call for patient tying techniques. We spent a day with Mr. Hidy, and learned to tie the flies the way he ties them. We have found more and more situations in which the pages of *The Art of Tying the Wet Fly and Fishing the Flymph* contain the solution to fishing problems.

"I want to show you something," Mr. Hidy told us. He fixed one of his flymphs on the point of a sewing needle, then submerged it in a glass of water. The fuzzy body fibers and hackles entrained shiny bubbles of air.

"Look at that hydrofuge," he said. We thought of the *Epeorus* mayflies, rising through the water with the same bubbles trapped under their cuticles.

Other Hidy and Leisenring flymphs effective for *Epeorus* include the Watery Dun, Tup's Nymph, Light Snipe and Yellow, and Pale Watery Dun Wingless.

Presentation

Soft-hackles should be presented with the mending tactics recommended by Nemes. They make excellent searching patterns. Flymphs are very effective when cast to rising trout.

"Cast just above and beyond the fish," Hidy instructed us. "Give the fly a little pull to pop it under water, then let the current swing it across the position of the fish." We have tried his methods, and his dressings, during *Epeorus* hatches. They bring bold takes from the most selective fish.

Duns

Epeorus duns break through the surface film and ride the current briefly before their wings are dry enough for flight. During this drift they are taken readily by trout. Dressings for them should be tied on light wire hooks in sizes 10 through 16. Typical colors are ginger, cream, and pale yellow.

Patterns for the dun stage must be selected with the fast-water habitat of the natural in mind: they should be chosen for their floatability as well as their representation of the natural. Ginger and Light Ginger Bi-visible patterns can be effective for *Epeorus* duns. They suggest the presence of an insect on the water through the dimples made on the surface by the points of their hackles. In very fast water, this is often enough to fool trout, and bi-visibles are often the only flies that will float.

> *GRIZZLY WULFF (Lee Wulff)*
> *Hook: Mustad 94840 (1X fine), Nos. 10-16.*
> *Thread: Brown.*
> *Wings: Red fox squirrel tail, upright and divided.*
> *Tails: Red fox squirrel tail.*
> *Body: Yellow floss.*
> *Hackle: Brown and grizzly mixed.*

The Wulff series contains some of the best floating, and fish taking, flies available. While they are not often considered imitations for specific hatches, they do give the impression of many mayfly duns. The Grizzly Wulff, with its yellow body, is an excellent impressionistic pattern for many fast water *Epeorus* duns.

> *GORDON QUILL (Theordore Gordon)*
> *Hook: Mustad 94833 (3X fine), Nos. 10-14.*
> *Thread: Olive.*
> *Wing: Woodduck flank fibers, bunched.*
> *Tails: Woodduck fibers.*
> *Body: Light peacock quill, counter-wound with fine gold*
> *   wire.*
> *Hackle: Blue dun.*

This pattern was originated by Theordore Gordon, the dean of American dry fly fishermen, before the turn of the century. Although it is tied for an eastern species, it will also fish well for many of our western *Epeorus.* The Light Cahill, another traditional pattern, represents some species with cream colored bodies.

Presentation

Epeorus dun patterns do not need to be fished with the same fine tactics as some of the previously discussed genera. Although it is always best to present a dry fly so the leader does not cross the fish first, in rough water the best floats are obtained with upstream casts. If drag is not a problem, cast at an angle to the current rather than straight upstream: the float will be longer and the leader will not pass directly in front of the fly.

Spinners

We recommend the dun pattern be used to imitate the spinner of the same species. It will not be an exact copy, but it will usually be close enough to take trout. If the dun pattern gets refusals, a pattern along the following lines should be tried.

> *RED QUILL SPINNER (Charles Wetzel)*
> *Hook: Mustad 94840 (1X fine), Nos. 10-16.*
> *Thread: Brown.*
> *Tails: Two long pheasant tail fibers.*
> *Body: Bleached peacock quill.*
> *Wings: White hackle points tied spent.*
> *Hackle: Medium reddish-brown.*

This pattern, or a variation of it with a pale fur body, effectively imitates *Epeorus* spinners. With the full hackle listed it will float well. If the spinner fall occurs over flats or pools the hackle may be trimmed to let the body float flush in the surface film.

Emergers and duns are the most important stages of *Epeorus* hatches. Soft-hackled wet flies, flymphs, and traditional dry flies match them well in their rough-water habitat.

FAMILY: HEPTAGENIIDAE

GENUS: *HEPTAGENIA*

Common Name: Pale Evening Dun.

Emergence and Distribution

J   F   M   A   M   J   J   A   S   O   N   D
              20————31

Ten species of *Heptagenia* inhabit the region from the Rockies to the Pacific Coast. Hatches occur from April through October over this range. In our experience, as well as in reports by other authors, the best hatches occur in June and July.

Heptagenia are of minor importance in the East and Midwest, but hatches of *Heptagenia* in the West are often consistent and large enough to provoke excited feeding by trout. Western anglers should be prepared to recognize and match them during their mid-summer emergences.

Nymph Characteristics
 *a. Labrum 1/2 to 3/4 the width of the head.
 *b. Body and head flat; head 1-1/3 to 1-1/2 times as wide as it is long.
 *c. Three tails, body length.
  d. Color: Ranges from light olive-brown to dark brown.
  e. Size: Body length 6-12mm (1/4 - 1/2 in.).

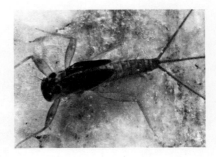

Labrum.

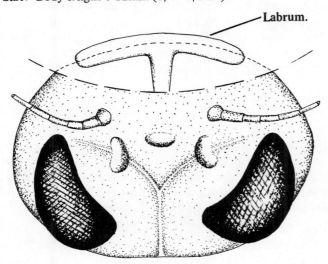

Figure 20. Cut-a-way view of *Heptagenia* head.

Dun Characteristics
  *a. Head retains flattened, wide appearance of nymph.
  b. Wings well developed, with many veins; pale cream in color.
  c. Two tails approximately body length.
  d. Color: Body creamish-white to reddish-brown.
  e. Size: Body length 5-15mm (1/4 - 5/8 in.).

Spinner Characteristics
  a. Eyes of male large, touching or nearly so on top of head.
  b. Wings clear.
  c. Two tails body length or longer.
  d. Color: Body pale cream or tan.
  e. Size: Body length 5-15mm (1/4 - 5/8 in.).

Habitat

Like the *Epeorus*, *Heptagenia* nymphs are adapted for clinging to the substrate in fast water. Unlike *Epeorus*, however, *Heptagenia* commonly inhabit the slower pools and eddies adjacent to riffles. They are often found in shallow riffles, under stones or debris near the bank. This is especially true of mature nymphs, which migrate to slower water before emerging. *Heptagenia* inhabit waters from small mountain streams to larger valley rivers.

Habits

Heptagenia nymphs are active, scurrying quickly to the undersides of rocks or wood debris if it is disturbed. Their flattened bodies are well adapted to fast-water habitats where they cling tenaciously to the substrate. As a result, young and maturing nymphs are seldom found drifting in the current. If they are dislodged, their swimming ability is limited to quick flips of the abdomen that help them return to the substrate.

Heptagenia nymphs are typically found in slower water than *Epeorus* nymphs and they normally migrate to quieter water adjacent to riffles prior to emergence. These migrations expose nymphs to hungry fish; the best fishing opportunities, however, occur during a hatch.

At emergence some species release their grip on the substrate and trapped gases buoy them to the surface film, where the subimago bursts free. Other species leave the nymphal shuck under water and the dun rises to the surface, buoyed by a bubble of gas, with the wings folded back over the abdomen. Fishing with rising nymphal patterns or winged emerger patterns to match this behavior can be exceptional. One must observe closely to determine which type of emergence behavior is taking place.

Hatches generally occur in the afternoon or evening. On warm days the duns fly quickly off the water. If the weather is cool or stormy, however, they may remain on the surface several feet before flying away, stimulating good surface feeding.

The subimagoes molt to imagoes in approximately two days. Mating swarms form in the late afternoon or early evening. Gravid females then fly close to the water, touching the surface sporadically. With each touch a few eggs are released until all of them have been dispersed.

Imitation

Heptagenia display some of the same behavior discussed under *Epeorus*. Many of the same patterns, especially the flymphs, will work for this genus.

The *Heptagenia* habit of migrating to quiet areas before emergence often takes them out of fishable waters. Just as often, though, trout and other selective feeders such as whitefish will follow them to the shallows and feed on them as they emerge. Much of our fishing over this genus has been in the quiet water along the edges of riffles and runs.

Nymphs

Nymph patterns can be effective during migrations of the nymphs. The often mentioned Gold Ribbed Hare's Ear, tied on hook sizes 12 through 16, is one of the best. Closer imitations, with light olive-brown to dark brown bodies, should be based on the following patterns.

> *CLINGER NYMPH (Poul Jorgensen)*
> *Hook: Mustad 9671 (2X long), Nos. 12-16.*
> *Thread: Tan.*
> *Tails: Light brown partridge fibers.*
> *Body: Tan or brown synthetic or fur.*
> *Thorax: Rabbit fur, with guard hairs.*

Jorgensen offers three ways to add a wingcase to his clinger patterns. The first is to clip the guard hairs and some fur from the excess thorax dubbing on top of the fly. The wingcase is then "painted" with a water-proof marking pen. It should be slightly darker than the thorax and body. The second method is to tie in a turkey or duck quill segment at the head of the abdomen, then tie it down over the thorax in the standard fashion. His third method calls for cutting a wingcase from a strip of cream colored latex, then tying it in at the head of the fly. The latex is then colored with a waterproof pen so it is slightly darker than the thorax.

In any of the variations of this pattern, be sure to use the roughed-up dubbing method, trimming top and bottom, to get the wide, flat appearance of a clinger nymph.

> *LITTLE GRAY-WINGED DUN NYMPH*
> *(Ernest Schwiebert)*
> *Hook: Mustad 9671 (2X long), Nos. 14-16.*
> *Thread: Dark brown 6/0 nylon.*
> *Tails: Dark brown mallard fibers.*
> *Body: Dark brown dubbing mixed with guard hairs.*
> *Wingcases: Dark mottled brown feather tied down over*
> *   thorax.*
> *Legs: Dark brown-dyed partridge hackle.*
> *Head: Dark brown dubbing.*

Schwiebert, in *Nymphs*, lists this pattern for *Heptagenia criddlei*. The nymph is found in Rocky Mountain waters from Colorado to Montana, and west into Oregon, Washington, and the Canadian provinces. Emergence occurs over a period from early June to mid-July. It is well to remember that the addition of unfurling wings may help take fish.

Presentation

Presentation of *Heptagenia* nymphs, especially on large rivers, often puts the angler in the unique position of wading out to waist deep water and turning to cast over rising fish in the shallows through which he waded. Casts to rises should be dead-drift, just as with a dry fly. Forty-five degree downstream casts, with a little time to allow the nymph to sink briefly before it is raised like an ascending natural, may also be effective.

Duns

Heptagenia duns usually emerge in quieter water than *Epeorus.* Where they are found in rough water a Ginger or Light Ginger Bi-visible pattern in sizes 12 to 16 can be effective. The duns range in color from creamish-white to reddish-brown. The most common species are ginger and pale yellow. Imitations should be tied on fine wire hooks in sizes 12 through 16.

LIGHT CAHILL
Hook: Mustad 94840 (1X fine), Nos. 12-16.
Thread: Tan.
Wings: Woodduck flank fibers, upright and divided.
Tails: Light ginger hackle fibers.
Body: Cream badger underfur.
Hackle: Light ginger hackle fibers.

This traditional eastern tie is one that will move West quickly as we begin to study our hatches. There are many species among the *Heptagenia* and its sister genera which are well matched by this cream-colored pattern. Variations in this and other Catskill school dry flies should form the basis for our experiments over feeding fish in the West.

HEPTAGENIA COMPARA-DUN (Caucci and Nastasi)
Hook: Mustad 94833 (3X fine), Nos. 12-16.
Thread: Tan.
Tails: Light ginger hackle fibers, split.
Body: Cream and yellow dubbing, mixed.
Wings: Deer hair dyed creamish-yellow.

When the nymphs have migrated to quiet shallows and backwaters before emergence, exact imitations such as compara-duns and no-hackles may be needed to take fish. They will float well and give the proper silhouette of the natural.

Presentation

Heptagenia dun imitations should be presented softly over fish rising in riffles or along the quiet margins of the stream. Close attention should be paid to the rise-forms of feeding fish. Often they appear to be taking duns but are actually feeding under the surface. A carefully cast flymph will then be more effective than a dry fly.

Spinners

To suggest the spinners of *Heptagenia* we recommend you try one of the dun patterns. If that fails, a more exact copy is called for.

HEPTAGENIA COMPARA-SPINNER (Caucci and Nastasi)
Hook: Mustad 94833 (3X fine), Nos. 14-18.
Thread: Tan.
Tails: Cream hackle fibers, split.
Body: Cream fur.
Wings: Cream, or light ginger, mixed with white, trimmed
  top and bottom.

This is a variation of the compara-spinner. You may find it beneficial to alter the colors according to your own collections of *Heptagenia* spinners.

Emerger and dun stages of *Heptagenia* are the most important to the angler. This is true throughout the clinging mayfly group.

FAMILY: HEPTAGENIIDAE

GENUS: *RHITHROGENA*

Common Names: Red Quill, March Brown.

Emergence and Distribution

```
J   F   M   A   M   J   J   A   S   O   N   D
    1 ———————————————————————— 15
        1 ———— 30
```

Rhithrogena is a genus well represented in the West, with seven species distributed from New Mexico north to Alberta and west to the Pacific Coast. They are primarily spring and early summer emergers. One species, *R. morrisoni,* the Western March Brown, produces an excellent hatch in the Northwest in late February, March, and early April. Farther inland, where colder winters are the rule, they may not emerge until early summer. Other species of *Rhithrogena,* such as *R. hageni,* emerge in June, July, and August.

Rhithrogena have largely disappeared as fishable hatches in the East. This is related to their demand for unpolluted waters, and is seen as a foreboding of what could happen in the West.

Nymph Characteristics
*a. Gills large, first and last pairs overlap under abdomen, forming a sucker-like disc.
b. Front of head with slight median emargination, or center notch.
c. Three tails body length or slightly shorter.
d. Color: Body ranges from olive-brown to dark brown with the underside often lighter in color.
e. Size: Body length 5-12mm (1/4 - 1/2 in.).

Dun Characteristics
a. Head retains wide, flat appearance of nymph.
b. Wings well developed; mottled-brown.
c. Two tails approximately body length.
d. Color: Body light- to reddish-brown on back; underside much lighter, olive, cream, tan, or light brown.
e. Size: Body length 6-15mm (1/4 - 5/8 in.).

Spinner Characteristics
a. Eyes of male large and touching on top of head.
b. Wings clear and heavily veined.
c. Two tails body length or longer.
d. Color: Body reddish-brown on top, tan to light brown ventrally.
e. Size: Body length 6-15mm (1/4 - 5/8 in.).

Habitat
The unique gills of *Rhithrogena* nymphs form an effective sucker-like disc, enabling them to cling with suction cup tightness to smooth stones and rocks. The tenacity of their grip will be clear the first time you try to pull one of these nymphs from a wet rock. With the help of this unique adaptation they often live in the fastest currents of the stream. It is also

common to find *Rhithrogena,* esepcially mature nymphs, in medium-fast slicks adjacent to swift runs. They often migrate to this slower water before emerging.

Rhithrogena can be found in small, tumbling creeks to large, swift-flowing rivers. They occur in streams from sea level to over 10,000 feet. With such a broad distribution, it is very likely you will have a chance to fish over hatches of this swift-water mayfly.

Habits

Flat *Rhithrogena* nymphs hide in small crevices or under stones, clinging tightly in the fastest currents, avoiding the main force of the water. They are seldom dislodged from the bottom. If dislodged, they are poor swimmers and tumble helplessly until they can again clasp the substrate.

Nymphs feed on the thin diatom and agal layer so common on the tops of stones in shallow runs. In the evening, or on overcast days, they will move to the tops of stones to feed. This foraging activity can expose them to the main force of the current, causing more to be cast into the drift.

The nymphs mature in about seven months. Our observations suggest that some species migrate to slower areas above and below riffles several weeks prior to emergence. During these migrations nymphs are washed off the bottom; this is a good time to fish nymphal imitations.

When ready to emerge the nymphs release their limpet-like grip on the bottom and rise quickly to the surface. Imitating this emergence activity produces some of the best fishing opportunities; trout will consistently feed a few inches under the surface on the helpless rising nymphs. Emergence is most common in the afternoon or evening.

Subimagoes pop free of the nymphal shuck quickly in the surface film. During hatches early in the year, when the air temperature is low, the duns may float twenty or more feet before takeoff. This often provokes fish, which have just completed an appetizer of emerging nymphs, to start a main course of juicy duns. Dry fly fishing can be excellent at this time.

After approximately two days the newly emerged subimagoes molt to imagoes. Mating swarms form in late afternoon or evening, often just following the day's emergence. The females fly into the swarms and mating occurs quickly. After copulation the females drop to the surface, releasing their eggs each time the abdomen touches the water. While we have seen good mating swarms, we have not observed fish feeding on spinners.

The *Rhithrogena* life cycle lasts one year.

Imitation

Rhithrogena nymph imitations can be important during pre-hatch migrations of the naturals. Flymphs or emerger patterns have been effective for us during *Rhithrogena* hatches when both nymph and dun dressings failed to take fish.

The dun can be the most exciting stage of the hatch, especially during early hatches when cold weather keeps the naturals on the water for a long time. We have seen little feeding to *Rhithrogena* spinners, although it probably does happen.

Nymphs

Nymphs of *Rhithrogena* mayflies can usually be imitated adequately with traditional patterns such as the Gold Ribbed Hare's Ear. They should be tied on 2X long hooks, usually in sizes 12 through 16.

> **RHITHROGENA CLINGER NYMPH (Poul Jorgensen)**
> *Hook: Mustad 9671 (2X long), Nos. 12-16.*
> *Thread: Brown.*
> *Tails: Three pheasant tail fibers.*
> *Abdomen: Light reddish-brown fur or synthetic.*
> *Thorax and Wingpads: Dark reddish-brown rabbit fur and*
> *   guard hairs.*

This color variation of the Jorgensen clinger pattern, from *Modern Fly Dressings for the Practical Angler,* should be tied with a flat body and wide, dark thorax and wingcases. The wing pads should be darkened with a waterproof marker or tied in with a goose or dark turkey quill segment.

Presentation

The traditional patterns and the Clinger Nymph should be fished dead-drift along the bottom, to imitate the tumbling natural. A few turns of lead wire under the body should be considered when you are dressing *Rhithrogena* nymph imitations.

Emergers

Patterns imitating the nymph as it ascends to the surface are more effective during a hatch than weighted nymphs. Traditional ties, for example the Hare's Ear, often serve well. Soft-hackled flies and flymphs are usually better.

> **MARCH BROWN SOFT-HACKLE**
> *Hook: Mustad 94840 (1X fine), Nos. 12-16.*
> *Thread: Brown.*
> *Tails: Three pheasant tail fibers.*
> *Body: Dark brown hare's mask fur.*
> *Hackle: Brown partridge.*

This simple tie has served us well during many *Rhithrogena* hatches.

> **MARCH BROWN FLYMPH**
> *Hook: Partridge long may up eye, Nos. 14-16.*
> *Thread: Pearsall's gossamer silk, crimson.*
> *Tails: 2-3 pheasant center tail fibers.*
> *Body: Dark hare's ear fur spun on crimson silk.*
> *Hackle: Furnace or brown hen.*

We worked out this pattern for the *R. morrisoni* hatch in the Willamette Valley. It is still being changed as we fish over the hatch from one season to the next. It should, however, lay the groundwork for similar experiments over other *Rhithrogena* hatches. The Partridge hooks and Pearsall's silk are available from Veniards of England, listed in the back of the book.

Presentation

Emerger patterns should be cast across stream or up and across. Their drift should be followed closely with the rod tip. We have found takes to both soft-hackles and flymphs are usually solid, leaving no doubt in the angler's mind that a fish has struck his fly. There are days, however, when fish sip them. The only indication of a strike might be a movement of the line tip or a slight bellying of the line in the current.

Duns

Traditional duns such as the American March Brown can be effective for early *Rhithrogena* hatches. We have also fished an April hatch that was matched with size 16 Little Olive duns, as listed in the *Baetis* section.

> **AMERICAN MARCH BROWN (Preston Jennings)**
> *Hook: Mustad 94840 (1X fine), Nos. 10-14.*
> *Thread: Orange.*
> *Wings: Woodduck flank fibers.*
> *Tail: Dark brown hackle.*
> *Rib: Brown thread.*
> *Body: Tannish-red fur.*
> *Hackle: Brown and grizzly, mixed.*

This pattern was originally tied for an eastern hatch, but matches our Western March Brown well. Slight variations in shade, such as a tan body fur, might be in order for some hatches. A Red Quill or Brown Bi-visible may also be called for, depending on the roughness of the water, and the need for better floatation.

> **MARCH BROWN COMPARA-DUN**
> *Hook: Mustad 94833 (3X fine), Nos. 12-14.*
> *Thread: Tan.*
> *Tails: Nutria or beaver guard hair fibers, split.*
> *Body: Tan hare's ear or synthetic.*
> *Wings: Tan deer body hair.*

This pattern was designed from the compara-dun style for the *R. morrisoni* by Richard Bunse of Falls City, Oregon. He has fished over the hatch for years in early spring on the tributaries of the Willamette. Often his quarry are free rising whitefish, whose tiny mouths and selective ways make them more of a challenge than trout.

Presentation

Rhithrogena duns should be fished as carefully as other mayfly imitations: wherever possible the imitation should be cast so it covers a rising fish ahead of the line and leader, and without drag.

Spinners

We have not seen fish rising to *Rhithrogena* spinner falls, although such rises may occur. We have found no patterns for this stage of the insect in fly fishing literature, nor have we created any of our own. The ties given for *Epeorus* can be modified in size and color to meet the needs of a *Rhithrogena* fall if you find them important.

FAMILY: HEPTAGENIIDAE

GENUS: *CINYGMULA*

GENUS: *CINYGMA*

Common Name: *Cinygmula*–Blue-Winged Red Quill; *Cinygma*–None.

These two genera are very similar to the *Heptagenia*. Their populations are usually sporadic, but they can be important in localized areas.

Cinygmula nymphs, the more common of the two, live in the medium to fast water of mountain streams and occasionally occur in high lakes. They have been recorded at elevations up to 11,000 feet in Colorado and Utah.

Eight of the nine known species of *Cinygmula* are found in the West. Depending on location and the species, emergence may occur between April and October. In *Nymphs,* Schwiebert mentions that *Cinygmula ramaleyi* emerge in June from Colorado streams at 8,000 feet. We have collected *Cinygmula* adults from Oregon coastal streams in June and July.

There are only four known species of *Cinygma,* all of which are restricted to the western region, from the Rocky Mountains to the Pacific Coast. This genus is usually found in high elevation streams but may be found down to sea level in the Pacific Northwest. Nymphs are found most frequently on logs and wood debris.

Little is known about the life cycle of the *Cinygma.* We have seen adults in the Northwest from April through July. Emergence probably occurs later in the year at higher elevations.

The nymphal characteristics of *Cinygmula* and *Cinyma* are listed below. Adult characteristics are not given because of their similarity with *Heptagenia.* To distinguish adults it is necessary to use a microscope and consult a scientific key.

Cynygmula Nymph Characteristics
*a. Front of head with distinct emargination, or notch.
b. Plate-like gills of equal length on abdominal segments 1 through 7.
c. Three tails.
d. Color: Body light to dark brown, often with lighter markings.
e. Size: Body length 7-11mm (1/4 - 1/2 in.).

Cinygma Nymph Characteristics
*a. Front of head completely rounded; labrum less than 1/8th width of head.
*b. Gills on first segment half as long as those on segments 2 through 7.
c. Three tails.
d. Color: Body typically dark brown.
e. Size: Body length 10-12mm (approximately 1/2 in.).

We have encountered these two minor genera of the clinging mayflies over a widespread area but seldom in fishable numbers. The hatches of *Cinygma* we have fished were perfectly matched with *Heptagenia* patterns. The nymphs and duns are so similar to *Heptagenia* that once we did not notice we were fishing over *Cinygma* until we got around to keying them out some weeks later.

Within the Heptageniidae family of mayflies the nymphs are all adapted to fast water by their flattened shape. As long as the angler bears in mind the differences in size and color, any of them can be fished with the same style patterns. Traditional nymphs and Jorgensen clingers will work well for the nymphs of *Cinygmula* and *Cinygma* as well as for the better known genera. Traditional dun patterns, compara-duns, and no-hackles will allow the angler to successfully fish spinner falls. Emerging duns often provide the best fishing when imitated with soft-hackles and flymphs.

MAYFLY BURROWERS

The burrowing mayflies comprise a single family, the Ephemeridae. Within this family two genera, each represented by one species, occur commonly in the West: *Ephemera simulans* and *Hexagenia limbata*.

Burrowers are found in both rivers and lakes. Their main requirement is a suitable substrate in which to burrow their U-shaped, four to five inch deep tunnels. The bottom must be soft enough to burrow in but not so soft the tubes collapse. Tremendous populations have been recorded where conditions are perfect: estimates range as high as 23.6 billion nymphs from a single pool in the upper Mississippi River. The nymphs can tolerate relatively low oxygen levels but are susceptible to pollution. They are gone from many areas in the Great Lakes and the Mississippi River that once had huge hatches.

Large size and great abundance make them a major fish food where habitat is favorable. During their hatches the biggest fish will often feed with reckless abandon, providing some of the best fishing of the year.

FAMILY: EPHEMERIDAE

GENUS: *HEXAGENIA*

Species: *Hexagenia limbata.*

Common Names: Sandfly, Fishfly, Mayfly, Big Yellow May.

Emergence and Distribution

J   F   M   A   M   J   J   A   S   O   N   D

1————————————15

Hexagenia limbata produces the famous "Michigan Caddis" hatch of the north-central states. Peak emergence there is near the end of June. In the western region, climate and elevation differences spread emergence out from May to the middle of October. Water temperature is probably the major factor controlling emergence: lakes and streams which warm early in the year produce May hatches; colder systems follow through the summer and fall months.

The huge mayflies of the *Hexagenia* genus have two habits which keep them hidden from anglers: they burrow in the mud of lake and stream bottoms as nymphs, and they emerge as adults at twilight and into the night. The nymphs are difficult to find even for a person who knows what kind of bottom they like. The adults are not noticed because fishermen have usually gone home before they emerge.

The wide western distribution and sometimes heavy population densities of this insect are surprising when compared to the little we know about it. Night fishing is legal in the Midwest, unlike most of the West. A confusion of patterns has been developed to match *Hexagenia limbata* on midwestern waters.

Nymph Characteristics
*a. Head with large mandibular tusks; forelegs designed for burrowing.
*b. Frontal process widest at its base, with apex truncate, conical, or rounded.
*c. Gills on segment one small and forked; those on segments 2 through 7 large and fringed, overlapping on top of abdomen.
 d. Three tails heavily fringed with fine hairs.
 e. Color: Body pale yellowish-brown.
 f. Size: Large; body length 12-37mm (1/2 - 1-1/1 in.).

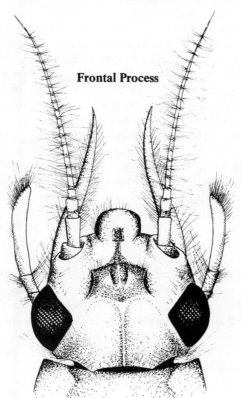

Frontal Process

Figure 21. Head of *Hexagenia limbata* nymph.

Dun Characteristics
 a. Wings large and well developed; pale brown in color.
 b. Two tails.
 c. Color: Body from light tan to bright yellow with distinct dark markings.
*d. Size: Body large; 16-37mm (3/4 - 1-1/2 in.) excluding tails.

Spinner Characteristics
    a. Wings clear or tinged with brown; some veins may be darkened.
    b. Two tails, body length or longer.
    c. Color: Body of female tan to yellowish-brown; male yellowish-brown to reddish-brown.
    d. Size: Body large; 16-37mm (3/4 - 1-1/2 in.).

Habitat

The large nymphs of *Hexagenia limbata* burrow U-shaped tubes four or five inches deep. The substrate must be soft, silty mud firm enough to prevent the collapse of the tubes.

Nymphs are abundant in both lakes and rivers, wherever the proper substrate is found. They occur at depths ranging from a few inches to fifty feet, but are most prevalent in water one to ten feet deep. Where nymphs are abundant the small tubular openings of their burrows are visible on the mud bottom.

Habits

Nymphal development normally requires one to two years, with the rate of development largely dependent on water temperature. During development the nymphs remain in their burrows. They circulate water through their tubes by waving their gills rhythmically over the abdomen. They leave their burrows only at night to feed across the bottom. If disturbed they re-enter their burrows or quickly dig into the mud. This secluded behavior effectively protects the nymphs from feeding fish.

Emergence of *Hexagenia limbata* usually occurs at nightfall. The nymphs leave their protective burrows and swim quickly and smoothly to the surface, with strong up-and-down undulations of the body. When they rise through several feet of water they are easy prey for feeding fish. The largest fish often concentrate on rising nymphs even when many adults are on the water.

As the nymphs hit the surface film the duns burst free of the shuck. Their large size and force of emergence sometimes produces an audible "pop". The duns float several seconds on the surface before getting airborne. Fish feed ravenously on these large, grasshopper-sized mayflies.

Duns that avoid the ravages of feeding fish fly to nearby vegetation and molt into spinners after one or two days. Large mating flights form, usually just after emergence tapers off. Copulation occurs thirty to sixty feet above the surface. Mating requires about thirty seconds, after which the females drop to the water's surface to oviposit. Each female lays from 2,000 to 8,000 eggs, then dies on the water. The ovipositing females are also heavily fed upon by fish.

Imitation

Polly Rosborough studied *Hexagenia limbata,* and published patterns to match it, in *Tying and Fishing the Fuzzy Nymphs.* His fishing is done on the rivers of southern Oregon and northern California; his patterns are effective in matching this hatch from California to British Columbia and New Mexico to Alberta.

Nymphs

The burrowing nymphs are long, slender, and have little taper from front to back. Their imitations should be tied on 2X or 3X long hooks. The bodies should be slender and untapered.

BIG YELLOW MAY (Polly Rosborough)
Hook: Mustad 38941 (3X long), Nos. 6-8.
Thread: Yellow.
Tail: Barred lemon woodduck fibers.
Shellback: Dyed lemon woodduck barred teal flank feather.
Ribbing: Yellow synthetic yarn.
Legs: Dyed lemon woodduck teal fibers tied in at the throat.
Wingcase: A small bunch of dyed lemon woodduck barred
  teal fibers tied in over the body and extending one-half
  the length of the body.
Note: *Dyed teal fibers for shellback should have a lighter cast than*
  those for the wingcase and legs.

Presentation

This pattern was developed by Polly to meet the demands of slow, meadow-stream rivers. *Hexagenia* nymphs should be fished across and down stream, with the pulsating swimming motion of the natural imitated with a similar motion of the rod tip.

A surprising number of western lakes, from the coast to the Flathead in Montana, have good populations of *Hexagenia*. In still waters the nymphs should be allowed to sink to the bottom, then be raised toward the surface with an upsweeping of the rod.

Duns

It is illegal to fish after dark in many western states. The duns emerge so close to dark that it is often not possible to fish over them. On cloudy days, however, emergence starts earlier. In states where night fishing is legal anglers should do a little exploring to find these hatches and fish the duns after nightfall.

We received a letter from Carl Christianson, of Coos Bay, Oregon, in response to one of our articles in *Flyfishing the West*. He has fished over *Hexagenia limbata* hatches in coastal lakes for some years, and settled on the Bucktail Caddis as an imitation after careful experimentation. Because the hatch is so short, with so little time to fish it before dark, he wanted a fly he would not have to change after a fish or two. Carl found the fish took the caddis pattern readily enough. Its ability to float after several fish made it the best choice. We could not ask for sounder reasoning; we only hope the name "Bucktail Caddis" does not get attached to the natural mayfly as the "Michigan Caddis" has in the Midwest. Polly's name for it—Big Yellow May—seems perfect to us.

BIG YELLOW MAY DUN (Polly Rosborough)
Hook: Mustad 38941 (3X long), No. 8.
Thread: Yellow.
Wings: Pale yellow hackle tips tied upright and divided.
Tail: Barred lemon woodduck fibers.
Shellback: Barred lemon dyed teal flank fibers.
Rib: Yellow thread.
Body: Yellow synthetic yarn with a good full taper.
Hackle: Yellow and light ginger, mixed.
Note: *Use ten full turns of high quality saddle hackle to properly float*
  this fly.

A stout tippet is needed to turn over this bulky fly. Because the natural is big enough, and the hatches heavy enough, to get the lunkers working, you may need that husky leader to play the fish.

Presentation

The dun imitation should be presented to working fish with a traditional drag-free float. If this fails to draw fish the fly should be given a slight twitching motion on subsequent casts. This small movement might convince the trout a natural is struggling to leave the surface.

Spinners

It is nearly dark when the spinners begin to fall. A few minutes fishing may be sandwiched into the last legal moments of the fishing day. In states where night fishing is legal this fishing period may last an hour or more. Always be sure to carry a flashlight in the back of your vest when following this elusive hatch.

A Grizzly Wulff in size 6, with its yellow floss body, can be used during these spinner falls. Its dressing was given in the *Epeorus* section.

> **BIG YELLOW MAY SPINNER (Polly Rosborough)**
> *Hook: Mustad 38941 (3X long), No. 8.*
> *Thread: Tan.*
> *Tails: Yellow and ginger hackle fibers, mixed.*
> *Body: Yellow synthetic yarn.*
> *Wings: Dyed yellow deer hair, semi-spent.*
> *Hackle: Yellow and ginger, mixed.*

This heavily hackled pattern floats well and presents a good outline of the natural at rest on the water.

Presentation

Polly Rosborough has worked out a system for fishing the *Hexagenia limbata* hatch with his Big Yellow May nymph, dun, and spinner patterns He begins fishing in the pre-hatch period with a nymph and a three-pound test tippet. As soon as the hatch starts and duns appear, he switches to a pre-tied leader with a dun attached. The change is sped by the use of connecting loops; in no time he is back to fishing. The effectiveness of the dun lasts about half an hour, Polly tells us, then he switches again, taking off the entire leader and quickly looping on a five-pound leader and a spinner imitation. With this he fishes out the last legal light.

This system lets Polly change flies and step up his tippet size without tying any knots in the heat of battle. It is a good system wherever *Hexagenia* are found.

FAMILY: EPHEMERIDAE

GENUS: *EPHEMERA*

Species: *Ephemera simulans.*

Common Name: Brown Drake.

Emergence and Distribution

J F M A M J J A S O N D
1————15

Ephemera simulans emerges in the summer months. Peak activity is usually in July. Temperature is the dominant factor controlling emergence: depending on altitude, latitude, and the number of cold springs feeding a river, emergence may occur as early as May or as late as October.

Ephemera simulans is distributed from the Rocky Mountains to the Pacific Coast. It dwindles west of the Cascades, however, and the best populations are found in the Rocky Mountain states.

Nymph Characteristics

*a. Head with prominent mandibular tusks; forelegs designed for burrowing.

*b. Frontal process forked, widest at apex.

c. Gills on segment 1 small and forked; gills on segments 2 through 7 large, fringed, overlapping on top of abdomen.

d. Three tails fringed with fine hairs.

e. Color: Body pale yellowish-brown.

f. Size: Body 12-20mm (1/2 - 3/4 in.).

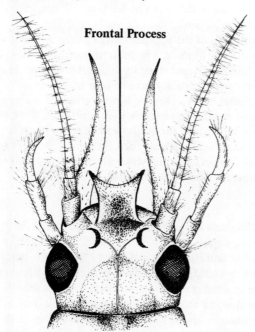

Frontal Process

Figure 22. Head of *Ephemera simulans* nymph.

Dun Characteristics

a. Wings well developed; pale brown with dark markings.

b. Three tails.

c. Color: Body yellowish-tan to brown with dark markings on the back of the abdominal segments.

d. Size: Body large, 10-15mm (3/8 - 5/8 in.).

Spinner Characteristics

a. Wings with dark markings.

b. Three well developed tails.

c. Color: Body yellowish-tan to brown with dark markings on the back of the abdominal segments.

d. Size: Body large, 10-15mm (3/8 - 5/8 in.).

Habitat

Nymphs of *E. simulans* are abundant in rivers and lakes. They burrow several inches to almost a foot into silty sand or fine gravel bottoms. They are not found in the muddy clay bottoms preferred by *Hexagenia limbata.* In rivers they may be found in moderate currents, but they predominate in slow backwaters, eddies, or margins. In lakes they are found along the shoreline in water from a few inches to fifteen feet deep.

Habits

The behavior of *E. simulans* is very similar to *H. limbata.* During the day the nymphs remain well hidden in their burrows. As evening approaches they begin feeding on the bottom. Unlike the scavenger feeding *H. limbata,* the nymphs of *E. simulans* are thought to be mostly carnivorous, capturing insects and other small animals. They normally mature in a single year; two years may be required in areas where the water remains cold.

At emergence the nymphs leave their burrows and swim for the surface. They are vulnerable and are fed upon heavily. They swim quickly with up-and-down undulations of the body. Emergence occurs in late evening, often after dusk.

Duns burst free of the nymphal shuck at the surface. Although they are smaller than *H. limbata,* a large hatch of *E. simulans* is an impressive sight. The newly emerged duns fly to nearby vegetation and molt into spinners after approximately twenty-four hours.

Mating flights begin during or shortly after the emergence of the duns. Large swarms of males congregate over vegetation along the shoreline. When a female flies into the swarm a male seizes her from below and copulation occurs. The female then flies over the water to oviposit. Many females lie spent on the water after releasing their eggs, causing strong, deliberate rises by feeding fish.

Imitation

Brown Drakes emerge during the same period as the Western Green Drakes (*Ephemerella*). They do not usually begin until twilight. According to Swisher and Richards, in *Selective Trout,* the hatches may overlap. The fish will switch from the Green Drake to the Brown Drake, leaving the fisherman frustrated if he does not notice the change and switch patterns. The size and color of the two insects look similar from a distance: only close observation of a captured natural will solve the problem.

Nymphs

Ephemera simulans nymphs are long, slender, and only slightly tapered. Their imitations should be tied on 2X or 3X long hooks, usually in sizes 10 and 12.

> ***BROWN DRAKE NYMPH** (Barry Parker)*
> *Hook: Mustad 9672 (3X long), No. 10.*
> *Thread: Tan.*
> *Tails: Woodduck (or imitation).*
> *Body: Tan fur dubbing.*
> *Wingcase: Woodduck (or imitation).*
> *Legs: Woodduck (or imitation).*

This pattern was developed to imitate a heavy mid-June hatch of Brown Drakes on Idaho's Silver Creek.

BROWN DRAKE NYMPH (Swisher and Richards)
Hook: Mustad 9672 (3X long), Nos. 10-12.
Thread: Tan.
Tails: Light tan partridge, short.
Body: Creamy tan German fitch and medium brown rabbit
  fur mixed.
Wingpads: Dark brown ostrich clump.
Legs: Light tan partridge.

This pattern may also be dressed on a 3X fine hook, and fished in the surface film during the early stages of a hatch. When trout are taking duns, however, fishing full floating patterns will be easier, especially in the deepening twilight when Brown Drakes usually hatch.

Presentation

Ephemera nymphs leave their burrows and swim swiftly to the surface for emergence. Nymph patterns should be fished to simulate this fast rise to the surface by using the current or lifting the rod tip to bring the fly up quickly.

The nymph is available to fish longer than the dun or spinner. The importance of nymph patterns is greater than that of dun patterns in most situations. This is especially true when the quarry is large trout, which tend to confine their feeding to the ascending nymphs while smaller fish feed on the surface.

Duns

Dun patterns can be important in the last minutes of legal light. During the height of the hatch even the largest fish may switch to feed on them. They are usually tied on dry fly hooks in sizes 8 through 12.

BROWN WULFF (Lee Wulff)
Hook: Mustad 94840 (1X fine), Nos. 8-12.
Thread: Black.
Wings: Brown calf tail or bucktail, tied upright and divided.
Tails: Brown calf or bucktail.
Body: Brown or cream fur or yarn.
Hackle: Brown.

The Wulff series of patterns are good suggestions for many of our large western mayfly hatches. They can be altered quite readily in color and size to suggest the natural over which you are fishing.

BROWN DRAKE (Swisher and Richards)
Hook: Mustad 94840 (1X fine), Nos. 10-12.
Thread: Tan.
Tails: Ginger hackle fibers, split.
Body: Yellow, light gray, and brown rabbit fur, mixed.
Wings: Dark deer body hair, clump.
Hackle: Brown and grizzly, parachute.

This excellent parachute pattern offers good floatation and suspends the fly body in the surface film for a proper outline of the natural.

Spinners

To fish the spinner fall we would suggest the use of one of the dun patterns, or a spent-wing modification of it, until it is found that a more exact imitation is needed. This stage may be overshadowed by the dun during some *Ephemera* hatches. If you find fish feeding selectively on the spinners, however, the following pattern should be tried.

BROWN DRAKE SPINNER *(Swisher and Richards)*
Hook: Mustad 94833 (3X fine), Nos. 10-12.
Thread: Tan.
Tails: Ginger hackle fibers, split.
Body: Yellow and light brown rabbit fur, mixed.
Wings: Brown and grizzly hackle, full or clipped top and
  bottom.

This imitation, or a similar compara-spinner, will serve to match spinner falls of the Brown Drakes.

Chapter Three

Stoneflies Order: Plecoptera

Fossil evidence suggests that a fly fisherman walking along a lonely stream 260 million years ago would have recognized some of the insects as stoneflies. Like present stonefly nymphs, these prototypes had three well developed thoracic segments, two stout tails and antennae, and a pair of claws at the tip of each leg. Ancient adult stoneflies also resembled modern adults, with four large, heavily veined wings held flat on top of their abdomens when not flying. It is difficult to say what patterns our fly fishing forefathers would have used, though, since the evolution of fur and feathers was still about 200 million years in the future.

With only a few exceptions present day stonefly nymphs are found in flowing waters. They require high levels of dissolved oxygen: riffle sections of cold streams produce the best populations. Conditions which increase stream temperatures or reduce oxygen levels seriously affect stonefly populations. This makes them valuable indicators of water quality. The wide variety of cold mountain streams in the West results in a rich stonefly fauna, with approximately 150 known species.

The life cycle of stoneflies is similar to that of mayflies. Both have incomplete metamorphosis, with no pupal stage. After oviposition the sticky eggs adhere to the substrate, and normally incubate for two or three weeks before hatching. The eggs of some species, however, hatch after only a few minutes; the eggs of others incubate for two or three months.

Newly hatched nymphs begin feeding immediately. Depending on the species they eat algae, plant detritus, or other insects. As the nymphs grow they must periodically molt, shedding their exoskeleton. Most stonefly nymphs molt twenty to thirty times.

Food supply and stream temperature are the major factors affecting growth and development. In *The Stoneflies (Plecoptera) of the Pacific Northwest* Stanley Jewett, Jr. states that optimum temperatures are between 5° and 12°C (40-55°F). Under favorable conditions most stonefly nymphs mature in a year or less, although some species require two or three years.

Stonefly nymphs generally crawl among the rocks and gravel of swift riffles, and often become dislodged. They are poor swimmers, drifting downstream with little or no movement until they again touch the substrate. The number of nymphs in the drift usually increases prior to emergence due to their pre-hatch migration from riffles to slower water. To emerge stonefly nymphs crawl out on rocks and vegetation. This is most common in the late evening, with the transformation from nymph to adult often taking several minutes.

Stoneflies have a single adult stage; they do not molt like adult mayflies. Also unlike mayflies, adult stoneflies have functional mouthparts. Some species feed on flowers or plant foliage; other species do not feed at all.

Several days to a week or more after emergence adults mate. Mating occurs on streamside foliage rather than in the air. Most species mate during the day, but some nocturnal species mate at night.

Shortly after mating the females lay their eggs. They normally oviposit in one of two ways: by flying over the water and releasing a spherical mass of eggs each time the tip of the abdomen touches the water, or by crawling under water and depositing the eggs directly on the substrate. Most oviposit while flying. The number of eggs laid per female varies from a few hundred up to 1,400.

Adult stoneflies are most vulnerable to feeding fish during oviposition. They are concentrated along the rivers at this time, and their clumsy flight causes many to fall into the water. The time of day these flights occur depends on the weather and the species. Generally they are heaviest in the evening.

Recent revision in the classification of stoneflies requires some clarification of the system we are using in *The Complete Book of Western Hatches*. In the publication *The Stoneflies (Plecoptera) of the Rocky Mountains*, R. W. Bauman, *et. al.* (1977) elevated most of the previous subgenera to full genus standing. Using this classification system the names of many well known genera are different. For example, *Acroneuria californica*, the Golden Stone, becomes *Calineuria californica*. The correctness of such changes must be decided by professional taxonomists. However, to prevent any more confusion over scientific names we will follow the older, more familiar, classification system used in *The Stoneflies (Plecoptera) of the Pacific Northwest*, by Stanley Jewett. Only time will determine the acceptance of one system over the other.

SMALL BROWN STONE COMPLEX

Family	Genus	Common Name
Nemouridae	*Nemoura*	Little Brown Stone
Leuctriidae	*Leuctra*	Needle Fly
Capniidae	*Capnia*	Winter Stone
Taeniopterygidae	*Brachyptera*	Little Red Stone

Emergence and Distribution

Nemoura

J F M A M J J A S O N D
1————————————15

Leuctra

J F M A M J J A S O N D
1———————————31 1————15

Capnia

J F M A M J J A S O N D
1—————31   1————30

Brachyptera

J F M A M J J A S O N D
15————————————31

Small brown stoneflies are available most of the year, but especially in early spring, from February to May. Two genera, *Nemoura* and *Brachyptera,* are abundant in the spring. The other two genera, *Leuctra* and *Capnia,* while common in the spring, are also found in the fall and early winter. *Capnia* are very common in the middle of winter; they often crawl about the snow on sunny days in January and February. Depending on latitude and altitude the main activity of these four groups may start earlier or later in the year than indicated.

These four genera are widely distributed throughout the West. Baumann *et. al.* (1977) states: ". . . members of this family (Nemouridae) are the most common stoneflies in most habitats in the Rocky Mountains." The Pacific Coast area also has large populations. Of the four genera, species of *Brachyptera* are relatively uncommon in most areas. *Capnia* may be abundant but not noticed because of their winter emergence. You are most likely to enounter species of the genus *Nemoura.*

Representative species of these smaller stoneflies are found in virtually every western trout stream. Their importance, however, is in keeping with their size. They are often overshadowed by emergences of larger insects. But imitations of them can prove valuable at certain times.

Nemoura: Little Brown Stones.

Nymph Characteristics

*a. Ventral side of neck region often with one to several finger-like gill filaments.

*b. Wingpads angled sharply away from the thorax.

c. Bodies stout, often with small hairs or spines on legs and upper thorax.

d. Second tarsal segment shorter than first.

e. Color: Light to dark brown.

f. Size: Body length 7-13mm (1/4 - 1/2 in.).

Figure 24.

1st   2nd   3rd

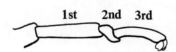

Leg of Nemouridae

1st   2nd   3rd

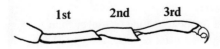

Leg of Taeniopterygidae

Adult Characteristics
*a. Wings smoky gray, usually with dark markings; when at rest wings lie flat on top of the abdomen.
*b. Second tarsal segment shorter than first.
*c. Tails very short, one segmented and difficult to see.
d. Nymphal gill remnants sometimes present at base of head.
e. Color: Body dark brown to black.
f. Size: Body 9-13mm (3/8 - 1/2 in.).

Leuctra: Needle Fly.

Nymph Characteristics
*a. No external gills.
*b. Narrow wingpads parallel to body.
*c. Body slender; lacks hairs and spines.
d. Second tarsal segment shorter than first.
e. Color: Light to dark brown.
f. Size: Body 7-13mm (1/4 - 1/2 in.).

Adult Characteristics
*a. When at rest wings roll slightly around abdomen, giving adult a very narrow, needle-like appearance. Wings uniform smoky gray to light brown without dark markings.
*b. Second tarsal segment shorter than first.
*c. Tails very short, one segmented, and difficult to see.
d. No gill remnants.
e. Color: Body dark brown to black.
f. Size: Body 9-13mm (3/8 - 1/2 in.).

Capnia: Winter Stone.

Nymph Characteristics
*a. Body without hairs or spines; usually stouter than *Leuctra.*
b. Narrow wingpads parallel to body.
c. No external gills.
d. Second tarsal segment shorter than first.
e. Color: Dark brown to black.
f. Size: Body 7-10mm (1/4 - 3/8 in.)

Adult Characteristics
*a. Second tarsal segment shorter than first.
*b. Tails long, many segmented, and easily seen.
c. No gill remnants.
d. Wings uniform smoky gray to brown; when at rest wings lie flat on top of abdomen.
e. Color: Body black.
f. Size: Body 7-10mm (1/4 - 3/8 in.).

Brachyptera: Little Red Stone

Nymph Characteristics
*a. Second tarsal segment as long or longer than the first.
b. No external gills in neck region.
c. Wingpads sharply angled away from the thorax.
d. Body stout, with some hairs.
e. Color: Dark brown to black.
f. Size: Length 7-13mm (1/4 - 1/2 in.).

Adult Characteristics

*a. Wings smoky gray, sometimes with dark markings; when at rest wings lie flat on top of abdomen.

*b. Second tarsal segment as long as or longer than first.

*c. Tails short, one segmented and difficult to see.

d. No gill remnants in neck region.

e. Color: Body reddish-brown to black.

f. Size: Body 7-13mm (1/4 - 1/2 in.).

Habitat

The habitats utilized by the nymphs of the Little Brown Stone complex are very similar. Streams of small to medium size harbor the best populations, but several species are also abundant in large rivers. Medium to medium-fast currents are generally preferred. Substrates consisting of leaves, sticks, or other organic debris provide excellent habitat for these stoneflies. Also the bottoms of stones and rocks that provide shelter from the main force of the current are often selected habitats. Whatever the current speed or substrate, good populations will only occur where the water is well oxygenated.

Prior to emergence the nymphs often migrate from slicks and riffles to slow eddies or pools close to the bank. Many species also emerge on the tops of protruding rocks in shallow riffles. Bridge abutments are frequently used as emergence sites.

Habits

Except for small differences in the length of the life cycle or timing of emergence the habits of these four genera are similar and can be discussed as a single group. Like most stoneflies the nymphs are poor swimmers. Their choice of habitat protects them from the full force of the current. As a result few are dislodged and available to fish. Those which are dislodged drift with little motion until they again contact the bottom.

The nymphs feed mainly on detritus, and are fully grown in one year or less. The mature nymphs then migrate to emergence sites. They crawl out on rocks and other objects sticking out of the water before molting to adults. During emergence activity fish feed on the restless nymphs. The extent of feeding will depend on the number of insects actively moving to emerge. Generally emergence occurs sporadically throughout the day rather than in short, concentrated time periods. This varies with the time of year and the species emerging. Emergence during the early spring and winter is heaviest in the afternoon; summer emergence may occur in the morning, afternoon, or evening.

The adults are poor flyers. They are more inclined to run than fly when disturbed. Because of their poor flying ability they often fall or are blown into the water: fishing adult patterns under overhanging vegetation can be very effective. Most species emerge in early spring and are active during the warmest part of the day. A close look among streamside vegetation may be necessary, however, to locate the small adults.

Mating occurs on the foliage or rocks near the emergence site. Soon after mating the females return to the water to lay their eggs. Rarely does one see large swarms of ovipositing females; they return to the river sporadically throughout the day.

The adult life span is not known for most species. It probably lasts one to two weeks. The total life cycle for these stoneflies is roughly one year.

Imitation

Although the insects in the small brown stone complex are a major food in the diet of trout, we feel they are seldom taken selectively. The average fisherman is not likely to find need for exact imitations of these stoneflies, nymph or adult. Most of the patterns listed are suggestive.

Nymphs

Small brown stone nymphs are long and slender. Patterns suggesting them should be tied with bodies only slightly tapered. Colors range from light to dark brown. Patterns like the Gold Ribbed Hare's Ear and the Teeny Nymph in sizes 10 through 16 are excellent matches in most situations.

> *FEBRUARY RED SOFT-HACKLE*
> *Hook: Mustad 9671 (2X long), Nos. 12-16.*
> *Thread: Dark red.*
> *Body: Dark red or brownish-red floss.*
> *Hackle: Brown partridge.*
>
> *PARTRIDGE AND ORANGE (Sylvester Nemes)*
> *Hook: Mustad 94840 (1X fine), Nos. 10-16.*
> *Thread: Orange.*
> *Body: Orange or burnt orange floss.*
> *Hackle: Brown partridge.*

The February Red is an old British pattern fished on the rough border rivers between Scotland and England. The Partridge and Orange is a pattern detailed by Sylvester Nemes in *The Soft-Hackled Fly.* Both are useful imitations of the small stoneflies. Other dark soft-hackle patterns imitate color variations within this complex of smaller Plecoptera. We almost always carry a small fly box with row after row of various soft-hackle patterns. Since Neme's book came out in 1975 we have been finding his patterns useful in many selective situations. Often the careful study of insects allows for such simplification, helping us to realize that a single pattern style may be fished for many different groups.

> *LITTLE BROWN STONE (Polly Rosborough)*
> *Hook: Mustad 38941 (3X long), Nos. 10-12.*
> *Thread: Brown.*
> *Tail: 4-6 fibers from the neck ruff of a ringneck.*
> *Body: Seal-brown yarn.*
> *Wingcase: Purplish ringneck pheasant neck feather tied in at*
>   *head and extending 1/3 over the body.*
> *Legs: Dyed dark brown ringneck pheasant neck feather fibers*
>   *tied in at each side and extending to the center of the body.*

Rosborough uses lots of head cement on the shank of this fly before wrapping the body. He then flattens it with pliers. The result is a slightly widened body which lets the wingcase lie tight over the back instead of flaring. All of Rosborough's flies are works of art, this one perhaps the most delicate and beautiful of all. Schwiebert tentatively identifies the insect model of this pattern to be the species *Taeniopteryx pacifica.* It is an excellent pattern for any of the small dark stonefly nymphs.

Presentation

The presence of small brown stonefly nymphs in a stomach sample, or an obvious emergence, will dictate when to reach for a nymphal pattern.

At such times your imitation need not be weighted. It should be fished dead drift just under the surface. The naturals have little swimming ability; the imitation should be given no unnatural movement in the water.

Adults

The adults of the smaller stoneflies are not often available to trout in great numbers. Most species crawl out of the water in the nymph stage and emerge where trout cannot get at them. Egg laying flights are usually more sporadic than the concentrated spinner falls of mayflies. In cases where these stoneflies are important as adults the following patterns will imitate them.

> *BROWN BUCKTAIL CADDIS*
> *Hook: Mustad 94840 (1X fine), Nos. 12-16.*
> *Thread: Brown.*
> *Tails: None.*
> *Hackle: Brown, palmered.*
> *Body: Brown yarn.*
> *Wing: Brown bucktail.*

We list this variation of the Bucktail Caddis as a stonefly imitation for two reasons: it fishes well for the small stoneflies, and you are likely to have some Bucktail Caddis patterns in your fly boxes. If you find fish rising selectively to any of this complex it is likely that a Bucktail Caddis or a variation of it will imitate the natural closely enough to fool fish.

> *LITTLE BROWN STONE (Polly Rosborough)*
> *Hook: Mustad 38941 (3X long), Nos. 12-14.*
> *Thread: Brown.*
> *Tail: Dark brown ringneck pheasant body plummage fibers.*
> *Ribbing: Brown thread, six turns.*
> *Body: Seal brown synthetic yarn.*
> *Wing: One dark grizzly hackle tip tied flat over the body and*
>   *extending to the bend of the hook.*
> *Hackle: Dark grizzly, as collar.*

This pattern gives a better outline of the body and wings of the natural than given by the Bucktail Caddis. It should be used in situations where the fish are selective to adults of the small brown stoneflies, and will not accept a more suggestive pattern.

FAMILY: PERLODIDAE

GENUS: *ISOPERLA*

ISOGENUS

Common Name: Little Yellow Stones.

Emergence and Distribution

Isoperla

J   F   M   A   M   J   J   A   S   O   N   D
          1————————31

Isogenus

J   F   M   A   M   J   J   A   S   O   N   D
               1————15

There are approximately fourteen species of *Isoperla* and nine species of *Isogenus* in the West. While these two genera are of main importance to fly fishermen, there are other genera in the family Perlodidae. The genus *Arcynopteryx* is a large perlodid, up to one inch long, occasionally encountered in the far northern Rockies and Pacific Northwest.

Perlodids are late spring and early summer emergers. Species of *Isoperla* are very common in May and June. At higher elevations or colder localities emergence extends through July and into August. Species of *Isogenus* start emerging slightly earlier than *Isoperla,* but there is extensive overlap; it is not uncommon to find adults of both genera emerging in the same place at the same time.

There are populations of Little Yellow Stones in all clean, fast flowing western streams. They are often overshadowed by the presence of the larger Golden Stones and Giant Salmon Flies. Where large populations of these smaller genera occur their imitations can be very important.

Isoperla

Nymph Characteristics
   a. No external gills.
*b. Color: Body light yellow or brown with distinct longitudinal dark stripes on abdomen.
   c. Tails long, approximately body length.
   d. Size: Body length 7-16mm (1/4 - 5/8 in.).

Adult Characteristics
   a. Wings light tan to very pale yellow, lying flat on top of abdomen.
   b. Two well developed tails, sometimes extending past wing tips.
   c. Color: Body yellow to brown; lighter on underside of abdomen.
   d. Size: Body length 7-16mm (1/4 - 5/8 in.).

Isogenus

Nymph Characteristics
   a. External gills often absent; if present appear only as short, simple filaments.
 *b. Color: Body light yellow, tan, or dark brown; distinct transverse bands on abdomen.
   c. Tails long, approximately body length.
   d. Size: Body length 13-22mm (1/2 - 7/8 in.).

Adult Characteristics
   a. Wings light brown to pale tan, lying flat on top of abdomen.
   b. Two well developed tails, generally extending past wing tips.
   c. Color: Body light to dark brown dorsally, light tan to yellowish-orange ventrally.
   d. Size: Body length 13-22mm (1/2 - 7/8 in.).

Habitat

   Isoperla and *Isogenus* are widely distributed throughout the western region. They are abundant in small, swift mountain streams, but are also common in larger valley rivers. Clean, well oxygenated water is their main requirement.

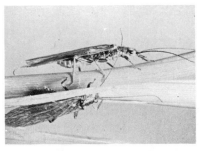

   The nymphs of these two genera are found in similar habitats. Medium to fast rocky runs harbor the best populations, although one perlodid, *Arcynopteryx compacta,* is often found in high lakes in the Rocky Mountains.

   As the nymphs near maturity they gradually migrate to side eddies, shallow pools or slicks near riffles. From these slow water areas they crawl up logs, rocks, or brush to emerge.

Habits

   Nymphs of these genera are predatory and quite active. Species of *Isogenus* are especially active, crawling quickly along the bottom. They are frequently dislodged from the bottom and drift in the current. When dislodged they swim with a side-to-side, snake-like wiggle. Their swimming is feeble, but unusual among the stoneflies. During their pre-emergence migrations from fast riffles to slow shallows more nymphs are dislodged. Emergence to adults normally occurs from afternoon to late evening.

   The adults of these genera are more active than other stoneflies. During the day they can be seen on the foliage or fluttering over the stream. In the evening large numbers of ovipositing females congregate over the flats and riffles. Hundreds of females dip to the water to release several hundred to a thousand eggs each. The best fishing often occurs during these swarms. The adults die several days after mating and oviposition. The entire life cycle requires roughly one year.

Imitation

   Patterns for these smaller Plecoptera can be important where they are not overshadowed by hatches of Golden Stones or Salmon Flies. Both nymph and adult stages are taken by trout.

Nymphs

   Little Yellow Stone nymphs are slender but have little taper from front to back. Their imitations should be dressed on 2X or 3X long hooks. The bodies should be narrow and only slightly tapered. Colors range from light yellow to dark brown.

PARTRIDGE AND YELLOW AND FUR THORAX
(Sylvester Nemes)
Hook: Mustad 9671 (2X long), Nos. 10-12.
Thread: Yellow.
Body: Yellow floss.
Thorax: Hare's mask fur.
Hackle: Gray or brown partridge.

This pattern makes a good rough resemblance to a Little Yellow Stone nymph which has lost its grip and is tumbling in the currents. It is not in keeping with Neme's way of fishing his soft-hackled flies, but we suggest that if the pattern is to be used specifically for these genera it should be tied with rough, tannish-yellow dubbing and weighted with a few turns of lead wire.

LITTLE YELLOW STONE (Polly Rosborough)
Hook: Mustad 38941 (3X long), No. 10.
Thread: Light yellow.
Tail: Small bunch of dyed chartreuse barred mallard fibers
*   tied short.*
Body: Dubbed dyed chartreuse rabbit fur.
Legs: Dyed chartreuse barred mallard fibers tied in at
*   throat.*
Wingcase: Bunch of dyed chartreuse barred mallard fibers
*   tied in at head and extending 1/3 over body.*

This dressing, like most of Polly's patterns, calls for dyed materials. Rabbit fur is available, dyed in a spectrum of colors, from most shops. If you do not want to do any dying yourself you might find a shop with chartreuse-dyed mallard flank feathers and rabbit fur. If not, you can try substituting natural feathers and fur. The results might be just as pleasing to the fish.

Presentation

Some *Isoperla* and *Isogenus* nymphs are able to swim. This calls for a brisk hand twist retrieve when fishing in slack currents or eddies. In riffles and runs the current can be allowed to tumble the nymphs freely or be used to give them a swimming movement. It should be remembered that the naturals do not swim fast. By either mending the line or feeding slack into the drift, the fly can be kept moving slowly with the current.

Adults

Little Yellow Stone adult imitations should be well hackled. Downwing styles represent the insect floating on the surface. Polly Rosborough's dressing represents the adult hovering over the surface.

Adults should be tried on standard dry fly hooks, or on 3X long shank hooks. Body colors are tan to yellowish-brown or yellowish-orange.

BUCKTAIL CADDIS
Hook: Mustad 94840 (1X fine), Nos. 10-12.
Thread: Tan.
Tails: None.
Hackle: Ginger, palmered.
Body: Yellow wool yarn or floss.
Wing: Natural brown bucktail.

This is the standard Bucktail Caddis dressing. It will imitate the adult Little Yellow Stones closely enough in many situations. It is especially good when fished in fast runs or riffles. Many western anglers carry this pattern as an imitation for caddis hatches; we recommend trying it as a suggestive pattern for Little Yellow Stones. Part of the well known effectiveness of the pattern is probably due to its resemblance of these genera.

LITTLE YELLOW STONE (Polly Rosborough)
Hook: Mustad 38941 (3X long), Nos. 10-12.
Thread: Yellow.
Egg Sac: Crimson hackle, clipped short under tail.
Tail: Dyed pale yellow grizzly hackle fibers.
Rear Hackle: Dyed pale yellow grizzly, short.
Ribbing: Yellow thread.
Body: Chartreuse synthetic yarn.
Front Hackle: Dyed pale yellow grizzly.

This dry pattern by Polly Rosborough offers the hovering effect of moving wings with its fore and aft hackles. Floatation is excellent, and the imitation of the fluttering wings may often be as valuable as an exact copy of the natural.

Because Little Yellow Stonefly females can be caught in the currents when depositing their eggs, Polly has tied a pattern to match the drowned adult.

LITTLE YELLOW STONE FEMALE (Polly Rosborough)
Hook: Mustad 38941 (3X long), Nos. 10-12.
Thread: Yellow.
Tail: Dyed pale yellow grizzly hackle fibers.
Egg Sac: Large bunch of crimson red hackle fibers tied in
  above the tail and clipped down to about 1/16 in.
Ribbing: Yellow thread.
Body: Chartreuse synthetic yarn.
Hackle: Dyed pale yellow grizzly.
Wings: Two dyed pale yellow grizzly hackle tips tied flat over
  the body and extending to the bend of the hook.

While the angler does not think of "spent" stoneflies as he does spent mayflies, they do often get into the water and from there into trout stomachs. As he has so often, Polly observed this and created a pattern to take advantage of it.

FAMILY: CHLOROPERLIDAE

GENUS: *ALLOPERLA*

Common Name: Little Green Stone.

Emergence and Distribution

J   F   M   A   M   J   J   A   S   O   N   D

          1————————————31

Twenty-three species of *Alloperla* are recognized from the West. While this is a large variety of species, their time of emergence is fairly well defined. A few species emerge in late March or early April; others as late as September. The majority, however, emerge in late spring and summer. The best hatches are often in June and July. Weather conditions and location can alter the time of a specific hatch by several weeks.

Good populations of *Alloperla* are scattered from the Rockies to the Pacific. Small coastal streams, such as those found in the Olympic Mountains of Washington and the Coast Range of Oregon, often have excellent populations of these Little Green Stones.

The name Little Green Stone refers to the adult stage. We have collected *Alloperla* nymphs which were bright green; predominantly, though, they are light to chocolate brown.

Nymph Characteristics
*a. Wingpads rounded, parallel to the body.
*b. Two tails half the length of the abdomen.
 c. No gills.
 d. Color: Usually uniform brown; a few species are green.
 e. Size: Body 7-13mm (1/4 - 1/2 in.).

Adult Characteristics
*a. Light pale-yellow or green wings; wings lie flat when at rest.
 b. Two well developed tails half the length of the abdomen.
*c. Color: Light green to yellow.
 d. Size: Length 10-13mm (3/8 - 1/2 in.).

Habitat
Species of *Alloperla* are most abundant in small to medium-sized streams, but a few species also occur in large rivers. The nymphs abound in moderate currents and protected areas in fast water. Along the Pacific Coast large packs of alder leaves commonly form at the heads and tails of riffles. These leaf packs provide the nymphs with excellent cover and their major source of food. Along streams with few trees, or under conifer forests, the nymphs are prevalent in swift, shallow runs, but stay well protected under rocks and gravel.

Habits
The nymphs of *Alloperla* are not very active. They crawl across the bottom and feed on leaves or other plant material. They are poor swimmers and prefer areas protected from the main current. If dislodged from the substrate they drift helplessly until they again catch the bottom. In one year or slightly less the nymphs are mature and ready to emerge.

Emergence occurs close to their nymphal habitat. Gravel bars and protruding rocks in shallow runs are common emergence sites. Emergence is sporadic, typically occurring in the afternoon or evening.

Like the nymphs, adults of *Alloperla* are relatively inactive. During the day they remain well hidden on the undersides of alder leaves or other streamside foliage, where mating occurs. In the evening, about the time shadows fall across the stream, they become active. Large swarms, sometimes thousands, of females cloud the air. Little red egg masses can be seen on the tips of their abdomens as they begin ovipositing. The females stop flying at a height of eight to fifteen feet and glide down to the water's surface. The eggs are released when the abdomen touches the water. The female then flies up again and repeats the process several times. Many females are trapped in the surface film, resulting in active feeding by trout during these large swarms. Adults die several days after mating, and the entire life cycle is completed in approximately a year.

Imitation

Fishing literature offers little in the way of imitations for the *Alloperla* stoneflies. A few traditional patterns, or slight variations of them, will usually be all that is needed when fish are feeding on them.

Nymphs

Such standard patterns as the Teeny Nymph and Gold Ribbed Hare's Ear in sizes 12 through 16 fish very well for the brown colored species of these nymphs. When they are actively migrating, soft-hackle dressings such as Neme's Pheasant Tail and Partridge and Green might be more effective.

> *PHEASANT TAIL (Sylvester Nemes)*
> *Hook: Mustad 94840 (1X fine), Nos. 12-16.*
> *Thread: Brown.*
> *Tails: 2-3 pheasant center tail fibers.*
> *Body: 3-5 pheasant center tail fibers wound on together with*
>   *fine copper wire.*
> *Hackle: Brown or gray partridge.*

If you carry a variety of soft-hackle patterns, this may be one of the best. The hackle should be rather sparse. It is an easy matter to snip out a few of the hackle fibers with scissors or clippers at streamside, to make it a better imitation of the *Alloperla* nymphs.

> *PARTRIDGE AND GREEN AND FUR THORAX*
> *(Sylvester Nemes)*
> *Hook: Mustad 94840 (1X fine), Nos. 12-16.*
> *Thread: Green.*
> *Body: Green floss.*
> *Thorax: Hare's mask fur.*
> *Hackle: Gray partridge.*

This fly is an excellent pattern for green *Alloperla* nymphs.

Presentation

Alloperla nymph patterns should be fished dead drift. The naturals have little swimming ability, so tumbling their imitations along the bottom is most effective. In small streams drift the nymphs into the heads of pools or by large rocks, where the largest fish often hide.

Adults

Patterns tied for Little Green Stone adults are color variations of those for the Little Yellow Stone.

> *GREEN BUCKTAIL CADDIS*
> *Hook: Mustad 94840 (1X fine), Nos. 12-16.*
> *Thread: Pale green.*
> *Tail: None.*
> *Hackle: Pale green, palmered.*
> *Body: Pale green yarn.*
> *Wings: Pale green hackle fibers.*

The Bucktail Caddis variation is almost always all that is needed to imitate these stoneflies. The standard Bucktail Caddis dressing, with yellow body and ginger hackle, is a good imitation of the pale yellow species of *Alloperla*. If a more exact imitation is desired, we recommend you tie one along the lines of Polly Rosborough's Little Yellow Stone dry pattern.

FAMILY: PERLIDAE

GENUS: *ACRONEURIA*

Species: *Acroneuria californica.*

Common Name: Golden Stone.

Species: *Acroneuria pacifica.*

Common Name: Brown Willow Fly.

Emergence and Distribution

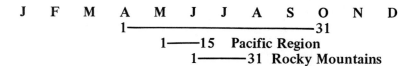

Acroneuria californica, the Golden Stone, is the most abundant species of the family Perlidae in the Pacific Northwest. Emergence normally begins in early to mid-May and ends before July. Water temperature is the major influence on the timing of emergence, with hatches earlier in warm coastal streams and later in cold mountain waters.

Acroneuria pacifica, the Brown Willow Fly, is the dominant species in the Rocky Mountains, although *A. californica* is also common. Colder water temperatures in the Rockies retard emergence until early June. It lasts until August or even September. Spring-fed streams with constant temperatures often have irregular emergence patterns.

Nymph Characteristics
  *a. Profusely branched gill tufts at the base of each leg. *A. pacifica* also has two gill tufts between tails.
  *b. Two tails as long as or longer than abdomen.
   c. Thoracic segments with distinct irregular dark markings.
   d. Color: Abdomen light to dark brown with distinct light banding.
   e. Size: Mature nymphs large; body length 25-38mm (1 - 1-1/2 in.).

Adult Characteristics
  *a. Gill remnants appearing as fleshy knobs at base of each leg.
   b. Wings light brown; held flat over abdomen when at rest.
   c. Tails well developed, nearly length of abdomen.
   d. Color: Body golden yellow (*A. californica*) or brown with yellowish-orange underbody (*A. pacifica*).
   e. Size: Large stoneflies; body length 25-38mm (1 - 1-1/2 in.).

Habitat
Acroneuria nymphs are very abundant in large rivers. They prefer fast, heavy riffles broken by rocks and boulders. Swift, tumbling runs of

small mountain or coastal streams also produce good populations. The abundance of such water in the West explains their wide distribution, ranging from New Mexico north into Canada and west to the Pacific Ocean.

Before emergence the nymphs seek slower water along the bank. This often means long migrations from the riffles, exposing many nymphs to feeding fish. Adults are found crawling over streamside vegetation.

Habits

Acroneuria nymphs crawl actively over substrates studded with rocks and stones. They are voracious predators: their active crawling is mainly in search of prey. This activity, coupled with their fast-water habitat, results in many nymphs being dislodged and drifting in the currents. The drifting nymphs wiggle and bounce through the water trying to grasp the substrate. They are poor swimmers, and are fed upon heavily by opportunistic trout.

Complete nymphal development requires two to three years. As a result many nymphs are available to fish the entire year, not just in the period before emergence. Pre-emergence migrations often occur en masse in the late afternoon and evening; reckless feeding by large trout is the common result. Once on shore the nymphs head for streamside foliage, sometimes crawling fifty or more feet from the water. After an emergence site is selected, the nymphal exoskeleton splits and the adult crawls slowly out. During the peak of the hatch hundreds of nymphal shucks are scattered along the stream, giving testament to this final transformation.

The adults clamber and flutter along streamside vegetation, where they mate. Many are blown into the water on windy days. Their clumsy flight spells doom for others. Pocket water near the bank is a favorite place for fish to wait for such mishaps. Most adult activity occurs in the evening. Females, laden with dark masses of eggs protruding from their abdomens, flutter in swarms above the water. In seeming random fashion females drop to the water, releasing their burden. Those adults which don't end their lives in trout stomachs return to the foliage to die of old age five or six days later.

Imitation

Acroneuria hatches are among the most famous and most important in the year of the western angler. The nymphs have two to three year life cycles. This year-around availability, combined with their large size and active natures, makes them a prime food for fish and an excellent model for flies. The adults are busy on the streamside foliage, and often fall to the water. Trout wait along the undercut banks of waters like Oregon's Deschutes and Montana's Madison for these clumsy insects to fall in. During the long summer weeks when they are available a large dry fly will almost always drum up fish.

Nymphs

Acroneuria nymphs are long, flattened in cross-section, and only slightly tapered from front to back. Their imitations should be tied on 3X and 4X long hooks. Colors range from brown to golden yellow.

> *YELLOW STONE NYMPH (Charles Brooks)*
> *Hook: Barbless, (3X, 4X long), No. 8.*
> *Thread: Brown.*
> *Weight: 15-20 turns lead wire.*
> *Tails: Cinnamon turkey or light mottled pheasant, forked,*
>   *three fibers per side.*
> *Rib: Antique gold yarn, one strand.*
> *Reinforcing*
> *Rib: Fine gold wire.*
> *Body: Brown yarn of a yellowish shade.*
> *Gills: Light gray or white ostrich herl.*
> *Hackle: One natural and one brown-dyed grizzly, large and*
>   *webby.*

Note: *Gills and hackles are wound on together.*

This pattern follows Charles Brooks' tied-in-the-round theory. No matter what angle the trout sees the fly from, it sees exactly the same thing. Brooks ties this way because the natural insect, while it does not swim well, is able to stabilize itself in the current, thus presenting a constant color to the trout. But an artificial fly, when fished dead-drift, tumbles in the water. A fly tied with contrasting belly and back colors, while a more exact copy of the insect, will constantly flash its light underside as it rolls over. Brooks used diving gear to watch trout while friends fished to them. He concluded fish were put off by flies with contrasting colors. Therefore, his patterns are tied so they present a stable color pattern to interested trout.

> *GOLDEN STONE (Polly Rosborough)*
> *Hook: Eagle Claw 1206 (3X long), Nos. 4-6.*
> *Thread: Antique gold.*
> *Tail: Dyed dark gold barred teal feather tied over the back with*
>   *ribbing thread.*
> *Body: Gold synthetic yarn.*
> *Legs: Dyed gold barred teal fibers tied in at throat.*
> *Wingcase: Dyed dark gold barred teal fibers tied in at head*
>   *and extending over 1/3 of the body.*

Polly Rosborough recommends this pattern never be weighted. It is a more exact copy of the natural golden stonefly nymph than Brooks' suggestive Yellow Stone.

Presentation

Brooks' weighted dressing is designed to fish on the bottom. He recommends a Hi-D wet tip or wet head line and short leader, four to six feet long. Short casts should be made upstream; the fly should be tumbled back down by the current, with no drag and no imparted action.

The Rosborough tie is designed to be fished the opposite of Brooks' pattern. It should be cast up and across stream, given a few feet of drift to sink just under the surface, then worked with a pulsing of the rod tip as it makes its swing in the currents. This action represents the struggles of the natural. It is interesting to note that Rosborough's pattern and method of fishing it answer nicely the problem of a fly with a light belly and darker back; the tension of the line as the fly passes through its drift keeps it from rolling over and over, flashing its different colors.

Brooks' and Rosborough's patterns are suited perfectly to the waters they fish. Brooks fishes the heavier, rougher stretches of Yellowstone area rivers, while Rosborough has developed his tying technique to fit the gentle waters of southern Oregon streams. The patterns used by each of these gentlemn, and the methods of presenting them, are compatible with the waters they fish. The angler choosing between the two would be wise to study the nature of his own rivers and choose the pattern which has evolved on waters of the same type.

When trout are not feeding on a particular emergence they are usually holding in sheltered areas where boulders break up the current. This is perfect habitat for *Acroneuria* nymphs, making their imitations excellent for searching out sullen, non-working trout. Although the angler is more likely to see the adult Golden Stone on streamside vegetation, the trout is more likely to see the nymph. This stage is very important.

Adults

Acroneuria adults are large. Their imitations are usually tied with lots of hackle for good floatation. Hooks used are typically 3X and 4X long. Golden yellow bodies and natural bucktail wings reflect the colors of the natural.

BUCKTAIL CADDIS
Hook: Mustad 94840 (1X fine), Nos. 4-8.
Thread: Tan.
Hackle: Ginger, palmered.
Body: Gold wool yarn.
Wing: Natural golden-brown bucktail.

This caddis pattern, tied with the traditional dressing given, is probably the most popular Golden Stone dry fly in the Northwest, where it originated. It is used in late May, June, and early July on waters like Oregon's Deschutes to match heavy hatches of *Acroneuria californica* occurring there.

SOFA PILLOW (Pat Barnes)
Hook: Mustad 9672 (3X long), Nos. 4-10.
Thread: Brown.
Tail: Dyed crimson red goose quill section.
Body: Red floss, thin.
Wing: Red fox squirrel tail tied over body and extending to the end of the tail.
Hackle: Brown.

This pattern is the standard imitation of the Golden Stone outside of the Northwest. It is not a closer copy of the natural than the Bucktail Caddis, but its success cannot be argued over the many years since its creation in the forties by Pat Barnes, of West Yellowstone, Montana. The heavy hackles suggest the whirring wings of the natural. Perhaps this impression of the natural, and its action, looks more realistic to fish than imitations which are more exact.

GOLDEN STONE (Polly Rosborough)
Hook: Mustad 38941 (3X long), No. 8.
Thread: Antique gold.
Ribbing: Dyed gold hackle tied Palmer over the body.
Body: Antique gold synthetic yarn.
Wing: Natural light brown bucktail dyed gold.
Hackle: Dyed gold tied on as a collar in front of wing.

This pattern combines the palmered hackle of the Bucktail Caddis, the bushy hackle collar of the Sofa Pillow, and the golden coloration of the natural.

Presentation

All of the dry patterns can use a little creativity in their presentation. As with the Big Yellow Mayfly imitations discussed earlier, dry Golden Stone patterns should first be presented dead-drift over rising or visible fish. If that fails they should be twitched a little as they near the fish. Even skittering them across the surface of a riffle or run can sometimes excite trout into striking.

Adult *Acroneuria* spend their time in streamside grasses and willows. They are often blown into the water by high winds. We have seen them bunch up on a blade of grass, suspended over the water, until there were so many it collapsed under their weight, precipitating them into the feeding lanes below. Because of their heavy bodies they often sink. Polly Rosborough has developed a wet fly pattern to meet this situation, and to fish when ovipositing females are being swept under the water.

GOLDEN STONE WET FLY (Polly Rosborough)
Hook: Eagle Claw 1206 (3X long), Nos. 4-6.
Thread: Antique gold.
Tail: None.
Rib: Antique gold thread.
Body: Gold synthetic yarn.
Hackle: Dyed gold.
Wing: Dyed gold bucktail.

This pattern calls for some dying of materials. If you cannot talk your supplier into doing it for you, and do not want to do it yourself, we suggest dressing a sparse Bucktail Caddis with swept-back, wet style hackle, and fishing it below the surface.

Golden Stones and Brown Willow Flies are widely distributed throughout the West. Because of their satisfying size they are a favorite of feeding fish. Their movement in search of prey as nymphs, and their clumsy streamside clamboring and flying as adults, often get then in trouble with trout. A likely imitation is unlikely to be passed up during the period of their activity.

FAMILY: PTERONARCIDAE

GENUS: *PTERONARCYS*

Species: *Pteronarcys californica.*

Common Names: Giant Salmon Fly, Dark Stonefly.

Emergence and Distribution

J   F   M   A   M   J   J   A   S   O   N   D
              15————————31

The emergence of *Pteronarcys californica* generally begins earlier than that of *Acroneuria californica* or *A. pacifica,* but considerable overlap of the three is common. The Salmon Fly begins to make its appearance in mid-April; heaviest emergence is usually in May and June. Water temperature is again the major factor influencing the time of emergence. It usually begins when water temperatures reach 50°F or more. Populations in cold mountain streams emerge a month or two later than those in warmer coastal streams.

Large populations of *Pteronarcys californica* occur in New Mexico, through Montana and Wyoming, north to Alberta and British Columbia, and west to Washington, Oregon, and California. There are three other species in the family Pteronarcidae spread over the same area: *Pteronarcella badia* in the Rockies, and *Pteronarcella regularis* and *Pteronarcys princeps* in the Pacific Northwest. These species may be more abundant than *P. californica* locally, but overall *P. californica* predominates.

Nymph Characteristics

*a. Heavily branched gill tufts on ventral thoracic segments and on the first two abdominal segments.

*b. Lateral corners of prothorax directed outward into long, slender spines.
c. Tips of wingpads pointed.
d. Two stout tails shorter than abdomen.
e. Color: Body dark brown to black.
f. Size: Body length of mature nymphs 25-50mm (1 - 2 in.).

Adult Characteristics

*a. Gill remnants on first two abdominal segments.
b. Two well developed tails.
c. Wings dark gray, heavily veined; held flat on top of abdomen when at rest.
d. Color: Body dark brown dorsally with yellow to salmon-red underbody.
e. Size: Adults large; body length 25-50mm (1 - 2 in.).

Habitat

The giant nymphs of *P. californica* abound in large western streams like Oregon's Deschutes and Montana's Big Hole and Madison. They extend into small streams as well, but their dominance diminishes as streams become smaller and the water colder.

The nymphs are riffle dwellers. Fast riffles well broken by rocks and boulders often harbor unbelievable numbers of these large nymphs. They cluster around the bases of rocks where debris accumulates. Strong currents running through aquatic plants are also favored habitat of *P. californica* nymphs. Pteronarcid and *Acroneuria* nymphs commonly occur together.

Habits

P. californica nymphs are docile grazers and detritivores in contrast to the predaceous *Acroneuria*. The major food supply of *P. californica* is plant and animal debris that accumulates around rocks in the riffles they inhabit. The tremendous populations of these nymphs on many streams attest to the richness of this food source.

While not as active as *Acroneuria* nymphs, their fast water habitat and large numbers make pteronarcids common components of stream drift. The nymphs cannot swim; they drift helplessly until their grip on the bottom is regained. Large fish snatch these juicy morsels eagerly off the bottom.

Two to four years, depending on the food supply and water temperature, are required for the nymphs to mature. They are a staple in the diet of fish throughout the year. Emergence begins each spring or early summer when mature nymphs begin migrating from the riffles to shallows and eddies along the shore. Hundreds of thousands of nymphs migrate each day in the late afternoon or evening. During this time fish feed ravenously in the riffles and shallows. In the fading rays of evening light the nymphs crawl the final distance to shore and out of the water. Here their nymphal shucks split and the adults emerge.

During the early stages of emergence fish concentrate on nymphs, but their tastes switch to the new delicacy as adults attain prominence.

The adults are clumsy fliers, often running when disturbed, or remaining motionless to avoid detection, rather than flying. They congregate and mate on streamside foliage. Many fall, or are blown, into the water. It is primarily during egg laying, however, that adults are vulnerable.

Oviposition begins in late afternoon and continues through the evening. Gravid females form swarms over the water and flutter clumsily, with their heavy bodies hanging awkwardly below their wings. They drop to the water randomly to release clusters of eggs. Each female releases several clusters, if they are lucky enough to escape the jaws of overstuffed trout. This is when dry flies disappear in ferocious splashes, like herring thrown into the seal tank at the zoo.

Imitation

Each year anglers juggle vacations in order to be in the right place at the right time for the Giant Salmon Fly hatch. The Deschutes, Henry's Fork, Madison, Yellowstone, and many other famous western waters produce salmon flies in such numbers that even the largest trout work shorelines greedily.

Nymphs

Those who limit themselves to fishing dry patterns of these stoneflies miss half the hatch. The underwater migration of the nymphs from their rough-water habitat to the quieter water along the banks exposes them to trout for days prior to their emergence. Some of the finest fishing of the season takes place in these pre-hatch days; we would rather be on a stretch of stonefly water just before an emergence than during it.

The rise of a trout to a dry fly is a thrill, but it is one that can be experienced during most mayfly or caddisfly hatches. The special way a trout slams a stonefly nymph imitation can only be enjoyed for a short span of time, and then only if the right pattern is presented in the right way.

BOX CANYON STONE (Mims Barker)
Hook: Eagle Claw 1197B or Mustad 3906B, Nos. 2-8.
Thread: Black.
Tails: Dark brown goose quill fibers taken from the back of
   a flight quill and tied in a "V."
Body: Black yarn, twisted to give segmented effect.
Wingcase: Brown mottled turkey section tied in over the
   thorax.
Legs: Brown mottled turkey section tied in over the thorax.
Legs: Furnace hackle wrapped through the thorax.
Note: *Bend the hook shank 30° just behind thorax.*

In the few years since its creation in 1973, by Mims Barker of Utah, this nymph has worked its way to the top of the list of salmon fly imitations. It is easily tied from materials available at any fly shop. It catches the size, form, and color of the natural in a realistic manner. It can be weighted to present it on the bottom in heavy water, or left unweighted to present it on the bottom in shallow waters, just before the hatch. The Box Canyon Stone is a pattern which fits the needs of those who like to tie a simple fly, without searching for special materials or dying special colors.

MONTANA STONE (Charles Brooks)
Hook: 3X long, Nos. 4-8.
Thread: Black.
Weight: 20-25 turns lead wire diameter of hook shank.
Tail: Six fibers raven or crow primary.
Rib: Brown dyed flat monofilament.
Body: Black fuzzy yarn.
Hackle: One grizzly saddle and one grizzly dyed dark brown;
*   strip hackles off lower side of each hackle before tying it in.*
Gills: Light gray or white ostrich herl, tied in with the hackles.

Once the materials are at hand this is an easy pattern to tie. Based on Brooks' tying-in-the-round theory, it presents the same view to a fish no matter how it is tumbled or turned by the currents. As with his Yellow Stone pattern, it is designed for fishing on the bottom in the heaviest currents.

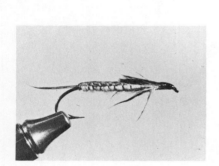

DARK STONE (Polly Rosborough)
Hook: Eagle Claw 1206 (3X long), Nos. 2-6.
Thread: Tan.
Tail: Two fibers of dyed dark brown ringneck pheasant quill.
Body: Dubbed cream badger fur; paint the back of body with
*   a dark brown enamel; apply color down to the middle of*
*   the sides; work the enamel well into the fur so the fuzzy*
*   effect is not destroyed.*
Legs: Dyed dark brown ringneck pheasant quill fibers tied
*   in at throat.*
Wingcase: Pheasant church window feather dyed dark
*   brown.*

This pattern is very similar in style to Rosborough's Golden Stone. It is shaped by the same rivers. Polly mentions adding weight to the fly only to keep it from breaking the surface at the end of a drift, not to sink it to the bottom. Like the Golden Stone pattern, he fishes it on a cross-stream swing after letting it sink a few inches.

Presentation

When the emergence of salmon flies begins the nymphs quay up along the shorelines. Lifting a softball-size rock in a quiet backwater may reveal as many as ten of these huge nymphs. Trout hold in the breaks between the fast water and the slow to pick off migrating nymphs. The edges of current tongues below long, broken riffles are favorite lies. At this time of year the angler should take a few preliminary casts into the shallows he would normally wade through to reach fishable water. We have taken Deschutes River redsides up to three pounds from knee deep water when the salmon fly nymph migration is on.

Everybody who fishes over this hatch creates his own patterns. There are probably more *Pteronarcys* nymph imitations than any other fly. Our theory is that if it is big, black, and on the bottom it will catch fish.

Adults

When the hatch is in full swing, and more adult salmon flies are faltering along the banks than nymphs are migrating to them, trout become anxious to accept floating patterns.

Salmon fly adult imitations are usually tied on 3X long hooks, in sizes 2 through 6. Orange bodies, reflecting the underbellies of the naturals, are almost universal in these dressings. Fox squirrel tail and natural bucktail are the most common wing materials.

> *DARK STONE BI-VISIBLE (Pat Trotter)*
> *Hook: Mustad 9672 (3X long), Nos. 2-6.*
> *Thread: Orange.*
> *Tail: Clump of brown bucktail, forked.*
> *Body: Wrap with orange thread, then tightly palmer as*
> *   many multi-color variant hackles as the shank will hold;*
> *   wrap them one after the other.*
> *Head: Orange.*

This pattern was brought to our attention by Dr. Pat Trotter, well known Washington fly fisherman and writer. The idea came from the late Preston Jennings, an eastern writer (*A Book of Trout Flies*) and the late Letcher Lambuth, a pioneer in the study of Northwest insects. Lambuth and Jennings corresponded about the appearance of the stonefly on the surface of the water. They agreed the insect's wings were aflutter more than still, and that an imitation should reflect this motion rather than copy the folded wings of a resting stonefly. Jennings sent Lambuth a bi-visible pattern as an example. Dr. Trotter tied some up, based on their notes, years later and found them more effective than traditional imitations. He summed up their appeal in a letter to us: "Kind of strange for a stonefly, perhaps, but not if you look at those real insects buzzing across the surface. Their wings are a whir of motion."

> *BIRD'S STONE FLY (Cal Bird)*
> *Hook: Mustad 9672 (3X long), Nos. 4-6.*
> *Thread: Black or orange.*
> *Tails: Two strands of heavy moose hair, laquered, or two*
> *   stripped hackle veins.*
> *Body: Orange wool or floss.*
> *Ribbing: Furnace or reddish brown trimmed saddle hackle.*
> *Wings: Dark bucktail or fox squirrel tail.*
> *Hackle: Furnace saddle hackles.*
> *Antennae: Lacquered moose hair; two strands, or two lacquered*
> *   hackle veins, stripped.*

This is the standard dry pattern used for imitating the *Pteronarcys* hatch. It offers an excellent silhouette of the natural. The heavy saddle hackles at the front may also represent some of the whirring-wings effect discussed for Trotter's Dark Stone Bi-Visible. Bird's Stone is harder to tie, but you might find the traditional pattern more appealing.

Presentation

With dry patterns it should be kept in mind that a short skittering movement of the fly might entice a fish which has refused a drag free float. This motion ties in closely with the theory of fluttering wings.

Polly Rosborough has developed a wet pattern to imitate drowned adults.

> *DARK STONE WET (Polly Rosborough)*
> *Hook: Eagle Claw 1206 (3X long), Nos. 4-6.*
> *Thread: Black.*
> *Tail: Dark brown mottled turkey tail feather fibers tied*
> *   short.*
> *Ribbing: Gray buttonhole twist thread.*
> *Body: Tangerine orange synthetic yarn.*
> *Hackle: Soft dark furnace.*
> *Wing: Coffee brown bucktail tied rather sparse.*
> *Head: Fluorescent orange lacquer band is applied across the*
> *   top at the base of the wing (optional).*

This pattern should be fished when the females return to the river to deposit their eggs. It may also be effective after typical desert-country thunderstorms, which often blow stoneflies into the water.

The Giant Salmon Fly hatch is considered by many to be the most important hatch of the year. It is without question among the most exciting; a time of madness when the biggest cannibal fish follow the insects and are even taken on the surface. It is a show that should not be missed.

Old Classification System *Adapted from* *The Stoneflies (Plecoptera)* *the Pacific Northwest by* *Stanley Jewett, Jr.*	*New Classification System* *Adapted from* *The Stoneflies (Plecoptera) of* *the Rocky Mountains by* *R. W. Bauman, et. al.*

Suborder FILIPALPIA

Suborder ARCTOPERLARIA

I.   Family PELTOPERLIDAE

       Genus *Peltoperla* Needham 1905   Family **Peltoperlidae**
       Subgenus *Soliperla* Ricker 1952
       Subgenus *Yoraperla* Ricker 1952   Genus *Yoraperla*

II.   Family NEMOURIDAE   Family **Nemouridae**
      Subfamily NEMOURINAE   Subfamily Amphinemurinae
       Genus *Nemoura* Pictet 1841
       Subgenus *Malenka* Ricker 1952   Genus *Amphinemura*
       Subgenus *Ostrocerca* Ricker 1952   Genus *Lednia*
       Subgenus *Podmosta* Ricker 1952   Genus *Malenka*
       Subgenus *Prostoia* Ricker 1952
       Subgenus *Soyedina* Ricker 1952   Subfamily Nemourinae
       Subgenus *Visoka* Ricker 1952   Genus *Nemoura*
       Subgenus *Zapada* Ricker 1952   Genus *Podmosta*
      Subfamily LEUCTRINAE   Genus *Prostoia*
       Genus *Leuctra* Stephens 1835   Genus *Soyedina*
       Subgenus *Despaxia* Ricker 1943   Genus *Visoka*
       Subgenus *Moselia* Ricker 1923   Genus *Zapada*
       Subgenus *Paraleuctra* Hanson 1941
       Genus *Megaleuctra* Neave 1934
       Genus *Perlomyia* Banks 1906   Family **Leuctridae**
      Subfamily CAPNINAE   Subfamily Leuctrinae
       Genus *Capnia* Pictet 1841   Genus *Despaxia*
       Genus *Eucapnopsis* Okamoto 1922   Genus *Paraleuctra*
       Genus *Isocapnia* Banks 1938   Genus *Perlomyia*
      Subfamily TAENIOPTERYGINAE   Subfamily Megaleuctrinae
       Genus *Brachyptera* Newport 1851   Genus *Megaleuctra*
       Subgenus *Doddsia* Needham and
          Claassen 1925   Family **Capniidae**
       Subgenus *Taenionema* Banks 1905   Genus *Bolshecapnia*
       Genus *Taeniopteryx* Pictet 1841   Genus *Capnia*

III.   Family PTERONARCIDAE   Genus *Eucapnopsis*
       Genus *Pteronarcella* Banks 1900   Genus *Isocapnia*
       Genus *Pteronarcys* Newman 1838   Genus *Mesocapnia*
      Genus *Paracapnia*
      Genus *Utacapnia*
      Family **Taeniopterygidae**
      Subfamily Brachypterinae
      Genus *Doddsia*
      Genus *Oemopteryx*
      Genus *Taenionema*
      Subfamily Taeniopteryginae
      Genus *Taeniopteryx*
      Family **Pteronarcidae**
      Genus *Pteronarcella*
      Genus *Pteronarcys*

Suborder SETIPALPIA

IV. Family PERLODIDAE
    Subfamily ISOGENINAE
        Genus *Arcynopteryx* Klapalek 1904
        Subgenus *Frisonia* Ricker 1943
        Subgenus *Megarcys* Klapalek 1912
        Subgenus *Setvena* Ricker 1952
        Subgenus *Skwala* Ricker 1943
        Subgenus *Perlinodes* Neeham and
          Claassen 1925
        Genus *Isogenus* Newman 1833
        Subgenus *Chernokrilus* Ricker 1952
        Subgenus *Cultus* Ricker 1952
        Subgenus *Isogenoides* Klapalek 1912
        Subgenus *Kogotus* Ricker 1952
        Subgenus *Osobenus* Ricker 1952
    Subfamily ISOPERLINAE
        Genus *Calliperla* Banks 1947
        Genus *Isoperla* Banks 1906
        Genus *Rickera* Jewett 1954
    Subfamily PERLODINAE
        Genus *Diura* Billberg 1820
        Subgenus *Dolkrila* Ricker 1952

V. Family CHLOROPERLIDAE
    Subfamily PARAPERLINAE
        Genus *Kathroperla* Banks 1920
        Genus *Paraperla* Banks 1906
        Genus *Utaperla* Ricker 1952

    Subfamily CHLOROPERLINAE
        Genus *Alloperla* Banks 1906
        Subgenus *Alloperla* Banks 1906
        Subgenus *Neaviperla* Ricker 1943
        Subgenus *Suwallia* Ricker 1943
        Subgenus *Sweltsa* Ricker 1943
        Subgenus *Triznaka* Ricker 1952
        Genus *Hastaperla* Ricker 1935

VI. Family PERLIDAE
    Subfamily ACRONEURINAE
        Genus *Acroneuria* Pictet 1841
        Subgenus *Acroneuria* Pictet 1841
        Subgenus *Callineuria* Ricker 1954
        Subgenus *Hesperoperla* Banks 1938

        Genus *Claassenia* Wu 1934

Family **Perlodidae**
Subfamily Isoperlinae

  Genus *Isoperla*

Subfamily Perolidnae
  Genus *Arcynopteryx*
  Genus *Cultus*
  Genus *Diura*
  Genus *Isogenoides*
  Genus *Kogutus*
  Genus *Megarcys*
  Genus *Perlinodes*
  Genus *Pictetiella*
  Genus *Setvena*
  Genus *Skwala*

Family **Chloroperlidae**
Subfamily Chloroperlinae

  Genus *Alloperla*
  Genus *Hastaperla*
  Genus *Neaviperla*
  Genus *Suwallia*
  Genus *Sweltsa*
  Genus *Triznaka*
Subfamily Paraperlinae

  Genus *Kathroperla*
  Genus *Paraperla*
  Genus *Utaperla*

Family **Perlidae**
Subfamily Acroneuriinae
  Genus *Acroneuria*
  Genus *Calineuria*
  Genus *Doroneuria*
  Genus *Hesperoperla*
  Genus *Perlesta*
Subfamily Perlinae
  Genus *Claassenia*
  Genus *Neoperla*

Chapter Four
Dragonflies/Damselflies
Order: Odonata

Dragonflies and damselflies are prominent inhabitants of lakes and ponds. The nymphs are large and often occur in great numbers. This makes them readily available to fish and interesting to even the largest fish. A few Odonata also live in streams. These species, however, are of marginal importance in the West.

Odonata are among the most primitive winged insects. Fossil records indicate the earliest dragonflies lived almost 300 million years ago. Their survival to the present day, with only minor changes from their primitive ancestors, reflects the success of their unique adaptations. The oldest fossils come from North America and Russia, and reveal that some species had wing spans almost two feet across. One can only guess at the size of their immature stages.

The order Odonata is divided into three distinct suborders: Anisoptera, the dragonflies; Zygoptera, the damselflies; and Anisozygoptera, an unusual intermediate group now found only in Japan and the Himalayas.

Labium

Figure 25. Dragonfly nymph with extended labium.

Odonata have incomplete metamorphosis, with egg, nymph, and adult stages. Nymphs have well developed compound eyes and distinct but short antennae. The gills of dragonfly nymphs are internal, located in a rectal chamber within the abdomen. Damselflies have three flat, tail-like gill lamellae at the end of the abdomen. One character unique to Odonata nymphs is an extensible labium (lower lip) for capturing prey. Normally this arm-like labium is held over the mouth. When prey comes close the labium is shot forward to grasp it.

Adult Odonata have large compound eyes and short antennae. Adults have no tails, but some females have long ovipositors that can be mistaken for tails. The most noticeable features are the four large wings, which are attached to a stout thorax. Dragonflies hold their wings horizontally, at right angles to their bodies, when at rest. Damselflies at rest hold their wings together and vertically over the abdomen. A unique set of direct flight muscles powers the wings and give the Odonata their exceptional aerial abilities.

After hatching from the eggs, nymphs immediately begin to feed on small invertebrates or crustaceans. They are voracious predators throughout their development, which can require from one to five years. They molt ten to fifteen times before maturity and the transformation to adults.

Mature nymphs crawl out of the water on cattails, logs, and grasses; emergence occurs on land. Adults may require an hour or more to emerge from the shuck and be ready to fly. Newly emerged adults are easy prey for birds, frogs, and other Odonata.

Dragonfly adults are exceptional fliers. They fly fifteen to twenty miles per hour, and have been timed at a maximum speed near thirty-five miles per hour. Damselflies fly much slower. Adults of both groups feed by catching prey in the air, using their legs as a spiny, basket-like trap. They usually feed for one to two weeks before mating begins.

Most male Odonata patrol well defined mating territories, chasing out all intruders except receptive females. When a female approaches, various courtship behavior often precedes mating. The male may fly side to side with the female, or in circles about her, to induce copulation. Male Odonata possess a unique accessory organ, for the transfer of sperm during mating, located on the underside of the second and third abdominal segments. Prior to mating the male transfers spermataphores from his genitals on the last abdominal segment to the accessory organ. The male then holds the female behind the head with special claspers on the tip of his abdomen. The female bends her abdomen under the male to contact the accessory organ and receive the sperm.

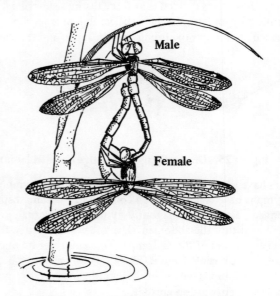

Figure 26. Dragonflies in mating position.

After copulation the male may continue to hold the female while she lays the eggs. Some adults die soon after mating, others survive for several weeks. Most adult Odonata live twenty to sixty days.

DRAGONFLIES (SUBORDER: ANISOPTERA)

Dragonfly nymphs can be recognized by their stout bodies and the way they swim. They have internal gills surrounding a rectal chamber. By bringing water inside the rectal chamber and quickly squirting it out the nymphs dart through the water in jet-propelled bursts. Adult dragonflies are easily recognized by their large compound eyes—they surround nearly the entire head—and the horizontal position of their wings when at rest.

Callibaetis sp. (nymph)

Ephemerella grandis sp. (nymph)

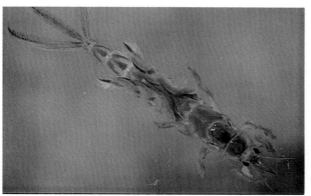

Hexagenia limbata (nymph)

Heptagenia sp. (nymph)

Baetis sp. (dun)

Ephemerella grandis sp. (dun)

Rhithrogena morrisoni (dun)

Hexagenia limbata (spinner)

Callineuria californica
(nymph)

N. H. Anderson
OSU Dept. of Entomology

Zapada sp. (nymph)

Pteronarcys californica (adult)

Chloroperlidae (adult)

Coenagrionidae (nymph)

Coenagrionidae (adult)   **Claire Kunkel**

Libellulidae (adult)   **Russ Davies**

Corixidae (adult)

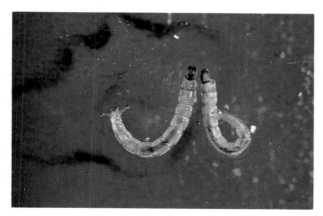

Chironomidae (larva)

Chironomidae (adult)   **N. H. Anderson**
OSU Dept. of Entomology

Rhyacophila sp. (larva)

Limnephilidae (larva)

Limnephilidae (pupa)

Limnephilidae (adult)

Limnephilidae (adult)

Sialis californica (adult)   Russ Davies

FAMILY: AESCHNIDAE

Common Names: Green Darner, Devil's Darning Needle, Horse Stinger.

Emergence and Distribution

```
J   F   M   A   M   J   J   A   S   O   N   D
                1————————————— 30
                  1—————————31
```

Peak actvity of the family Aeschnidae occurs in the warmest summer months. A few are seen in late spring and early fall, but most emerge in June, July, and August.

More diverse populations of these dragonflies occur in the east and south, but good numbers are found throughout the West.

Nymph Characteristics
*a. Antennae slender and bristle-like.
*b. Labium flat, not forming a scoop-shaped mask over front of face.
*c. Body hourglass shaped; abdomen comparatively long and streamlined.
d. Color: Body shades of brown or green.
e. Size: Mature nymphs large; 25-50mm (1- 2 in.).

Adult Characteristics
*a. Large compound eyes, meeting on top of head.
b. Color: Brightly colored body, usually of blue and green; wings clear.
c. Size: Body large, 50-100mm (2-4 in.).

Habitat
Dragonflies of the family Aeschnidae are common inhabitants of ponds, lakes, and quiet margins of streams or rivers. The nymphs crawl actively through shoreline vegetation. They are often referred to as "climbers." Submerged logs and branches also provide excellent habitat for them as they search for prey.

Adult aeschnids are usually seen close to the waters from which they emerged. They are strong fliers, however, and sometimes roam far from any lake or pond. We have seen them in prairie country, patrolling feeding territories miles from the nearest pond.

Habits
Aeschnids are extremely active dragonflies. Their nymphs are fierce predators, restlessly searching for prey. Water beetles, mayflies, aquatic bugs, leeches, tadpoles, small fish, and even smaller dragonflies all serve to make a meal.

Dragonfly nymphs have a unique jet-propelled swimming motion. By expanding their rectal gill chamber they take in water. A sudden contraction expels the water in a stream and propels the insect forward. A series of such movements thrusts it through the water in quick, three- to six-inch bursts. This active swimming motion makes twitched imitations very effective.

Nymphs feed for two to three years before reaching maturity. They

then select a suitable site for emergence. This is typically along shoreline grasses, cattails, or protruding logs where they crawl several inches—or as far as fifty to sixty feet—from the water. Prior to emergence great numbers of nymphs sometimes migrate to shallow areas. These mass migrations trigger feeding frenzies among fish cruising the shoreline.

Time of emergence is largely determined by temperature. Under suitable conditions (temperatures above 60°F) aeschnids emerge between sunset and midnight. They first crawl up a support and firmly attach their claws to it. The exoskeleton then splits open and the adult slowly emerges. When free of the shuck its wings stretch out and dry. The entire process takes from one to three hours; by first light the adults are ready to fly. At higher altitudes or latitudes, or during periods of cold weather, emergence is often depressed until early or mid-morning. If temperatures remain too cold emergence will be delayed until a warmer day, sometimes resulting in a mass emergence once favorable conditions arrive.

After emergence adults progress through several distinct phases. The first phase occurs immediately after emergence, before the adults can fly. At this stage they are called "teneral" adults. They are very susceptible to predation by birds, small mammals, and insects, including other dragonflies. Predation on the teneral adult stage is the main reason for nocturnal emergence.

When their wings are dry and the air is warm the adults take flight. This begins an active feeding phase that lasts for one or two weeks. Aeschnid adults are strong fliers, often roaming many miles from water in search of food. Using their legs as a basket-like trap, adults capture and consume their prey while flying. The adults are beneficial, feeding heavily on mosquitoes and other small insects. Despite tales that frighten children, they are absolutely harmless to man.

Mating, the next phase, occurs over or near a pond, lake, or slow moving stream. Males establish specific territories, defending them from other males. When a female enters his territory the male approaches her and copulation begins. Large species normally land on nearby vegetation to mate; smaller species mate in the air. Copulation generally lasts only five to twenty seconds. When it is complete the female may or may not be held by the male while she lays her eggs. After oviposition adults often live another week or more, again feeding heavily on small insects.

Imitation

We have seen trout go after low-flying adults, forming "V's" and cutting bold wakes across the calm surface of lakes. We have heard of, but not seen, successful takes. There is enough evidence, however, to indicate adult patterns would be useful in many situations. But the nymphal stage of the aeschnids is the most important to the angler.

Aeschnid nymphs are active in their search for prey. This activity often gets them in trouble with trout. When alarmed, or dislodged from cover, they use their jet-like swimming ability to regain safety. Patterns successfully mimicking this behavior will seldom be refused by feeding fish.

Nymphs

Aeschnid nymph imitations should be tied on 3X or 4X long hooks, in sizes 2 through 12. Colors range from green to dark olive and brown.

WOOLLY WORM
Hook: *Mustad 79580 (4X long), Nos. 8-12.*
Thread: *Match body color.*
Rib: *Narrow silver or gold tinsel (optional).*
Hackle: *Grizzly or ginger, palmered.*
Body: *Green, olive, or brown chenille.*

Woolly Worms tied on long shank hooks represent the slender nymphs of the Aeschnidae very well. They should be tied with soft palmered hackles, as in lakes there is no current to work the fibers.

CAREY SPECIAL (Col. Thomas Carey)
Hook: *Mustad 9672 (3X long), Nos. 4-12.*
Thread: *Black.*
Tail: *Ringneck pheasant rump fibers.*
Body: *Peacock herl.*
Hackle: *Ringneck pheasant rump feather.*

The Carey Special is a popular lake fly and an excellent pattern for dragonfly nymphs. Its soft pheasant hackles sweep back when the fly is retrieved, representing both the body and legs of the natural. Body colors of the Carey can be varied to suit the natural you are imitating. Peacock herl is excellent for many; we have also found dark brown and olive yarns effective.

RANDALL'S GREEN DRAGON (Randall Kaufmann)
Hook: *Eagle Claw 1206, Nos. 4-8.*
Thread: *Olive.*
Weight: *Lead wire, diameter of hook, wrapped over rear 1/2 of hook and flattened with pliers.*
Tail: *Olive stripped goose tied in short "V."*
Rib: *Clear flat monofilament.*
Body: *40% olive rabbit and 60% insect green seal (clip body after ribbing).*
Rear Legs: *Olive stripped goose extending back along body with tips curving in.*
Thorax: *Same as body.*
Wingcase: *Olive duck quill segment tied down at the rear and front of thorax, with 1/4 in. extending over body and clipped in "V."*
Front Legs: *As rear legs, but tied in front of thorax.*
Head: *2-3 turns of body dubbing mixture.*

Randall Kaufmann's Green Dragon is an excellent pattern for fishing deep lakes. The pattern is from his *American Nymph Fly Tying Manual*, the first codification of nymph patterns, traditionally an unstandardized and unruly lot.

The Green Dragon is an excellent design and should serve as the basis for color variations to match the naturals on your favorite waters.

Presentation
Presentation of nymph imitations is based on the swimming behavior of the naturals. Short strips of the line will retrieve the fly in darts like a jetting dragonfly.

In shallow lakes a dry line used with a long leader serves to fish the fly just above weedbeds and shoreline debris. Wet tip lines or full sinkers can be used to probe deeper waters. Takes on these large patterns will seldom be subtle: because of the natural's ability to escape, fish take them boldly.

Adults

There are very few patterns given in fly fishing literature for the adult stage of the dragonflies. The scarcity of patterns is somewhat paralleled by the infrequency of need for them. The listed dressing is a good model on which to base experimental imitations.

> *DRAGON FLY (Dan Bailey)*
> *Hook: 9672 (3X long), Nos. 6-10.*
> *Thread: Blue.*
> *Tail: Natural bucktail (tips of body).*
> *Body: Natural bucktail.*
> *Rib: Blue thread.*
> *Wings: Four grizzly hackle feathers.*
> *Hackle: Brown or grizzly.*
> *Head: Blue or brown chenille.*

Presentation

This pattern is listed in Dan Bailey's catalog. We cannot give many hints on presentation. We have, however, observed that naturals, when caught in the water, cause quite a commotion with their wings. A quivering action imparted with the rod tip might be in order.

FAMILY: LIBELLULIDAE

Common Names: None.

Emergence and Distribution

J   F   M   A   M   J   J   A   S   O   N   D

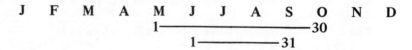

1————————————30

1————————31

The family Libellulidae contains some of the most beautiful dragonflies in the West. Adults with bright blue or red bodies and black patterned wings are common. These eye-catching adults can be seen around lakes and ponds from the Pacific Coast through the Rocky Mountains. Peak emergence of libellulids occurs during warm summer weather, primarily in June, July, and August.

Nymph Characteristics
*a. Labium spoon-shaped, covering face to base of the antennae.
*b. Body oval and squat, not streamlined; often covered with fine hairs.
 c. Color: Body similar to color of substrate; usually shades of brown and green.
 d. Size: Mature nymphs 18-30mm (3/4 - 1-1/4 in.).

Adult Characteristics
*a. Compound eyes large, but not meeting on top of head.
 b. Color: Showy body colors, in shades or red, blue, green, and black; wings of some species also colored.
 c. Size: Body length ranges from 25-75mm (1 - 3 in.).

Habitat

Libellulids are still-water dwellers, rarely found in streams or rivers. The nymphs are found on sandy or silty substrate among aquatic plants and debris. They camouflage themselves by nestling in the substrate and catching debris on their fine hairs. They then wait for any prey that passes within striking distance.

Adult libellulids are seen near the shorelines of lakes and ponds. They are excellent flyers, but do not stray far from water.

Habits

The nymphal behavior of libellulids contrasts sharply with that previously described for aeschnids, which actively hunt their prey, much like cats stalking mice. Libellulid nymphs, on the other hand, partially cover themselves with bottom silt and wait to ambush their prey, like frogs waiting for flies. Because of this behavior libellulids are commonly referred to as "sprawlers". This behavior is important to remember when imitating the nymphs; their patterns should be crawled slowly across the bottom, with none of the twitching action given aeschnid patterns.

Libellulid nymphs mature after feeding for two to three years. When ready to emerge they move to shallow water where aquatic plants or protruding logs provide suitable emergence sites. Then they crawl out of the water on the emergent vegetation, where the exoskeleton splits open and the adult emerges. This often requires an hour or more to complete.

The time of emergence is largely dependent on temperature. During warm weather, when nighttime temperatures remain above 50 or 60°F., emergence is generally nocturnal. If temperatures are lower, however, emergence will likely be retarded until morning, when temperatures rise to a suitable level.

After emergence, libellulid adults feed actively for one to three weeks before mating. They consume large quantities of small insects. After mating, females deposit their eggs on the surface by flying inches above the water and dipping their abdomen every couple of feet. Each time the abdomen touches the water a cluster of eggs is released. It is not unheard of for a large fish to bust clear of the water to intercept a female in mid-air. Once mating and oviposition are completed, adults live and feed for one to several weeks before dying.

Imitation

The sprawling nymphs of the family Libellulidae are also called "silters". They lay in wait for their prey, camouflaged by mud, silt and debris. They are capable of the same jet-propelled swimming as the aeschnids, but seldom rely on it. They are more content to crawl laboriously across the bottom.

Libellulids are shorter, wider and flatter than aeschnids. Patterns used to imitate them can be similar to aeschnid patterns but should be tied on shorter hooks. Fly fishing literature reveals very few patterns created as imitations of libellulids.

WOOLLY WORM
Hook: Mustad 3906B (1X long), Nos. 8-12.
Thread: To match body color.
Rib: Narrow silver or gold tinsel (optional).
Hackle: Ginger or grizzly, palmered.
Body: Olive, brown or gray chenille.

Libellulidae patterns are typified by a rotund, scruffy appearance. Woolly Worms, when used specifically to imitate them, should be tied on standard length or 1X long hooks. The bodies should be wrapped with heavy chenille.

> *ASSOM DRAGON (Charles Brooks)*
> *Hook: 3X long, Nos. 4-10.*
> *Thread: Brown 3/0 Nymo.*
> *Weight: Twelve wraps lead wire.*
> *Body: Natural brown seal fur on the skin; cut a strip 1/16 to*
> *   1/8 inch wide and 3/4 inch long; wrap this on the hook with*
> *   the fur side out.*
> *Hackle: Brown dyed grizzly hackle, long and soft.*

Libellulid adults can be adequately imitated by altering the size and color of the aeschnid adult pattern. Fishing adult patterns may prove an interesting experiment, but they are not necessary patterns.

FAMILY: GOMPHIDAE

Common Names: None.

Emergence and Distribution

J F M A M J J A S O N D

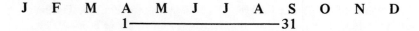

1————————————31

Members of the family Gomphidae are widely distributed throughout the West. One typical species, *Progomphus borealis,* has been recorded from Arizona, California, Colorado, New Mexico, Oklahoma, Oregon, Texas and Utah. Another species, *Octogomphus specularis,* has a known range along the Pacific Coast from Mexico to British Columbia.

The typical life cycle for this family lasts three years, with emergence occurring in the spring and summer months. Gomphids are more secretive than other dragonflies, and are not often observed and collected.

Nymph Characteristics
*a. Antennae four segmented; the fourth segment very small, located at the tip of a broad, flattened third segment.
 b. Labium flat, not spoon-shaped.
 c. Body oval and squat, but with fewer hairs on the body than libellulids.
 d. Color: Body shades of drab browns and greens.
 e. Size: Mature nymphs 18-30mm (3/4 to 1-1/4 inches).

Adult Characteristics
*a. Compound eyes large but not touching on top of head.
 b. Color: Body yellow and brown, or black; wings clear.
 c. Size: Body length ranges from 25-75mm (1 to 3 inches).

Habitat
Nymphs of the family Gomphidae are found in both flowing and still waters. In ponds and lakes they cover themselves with a thin layer of silt and debris on sandy bottoms. In streams we have collected nymphs from fast riffles, slow eddies and pools. They are always in areas with loose substrate, in which they can partially bury themselves.

Adult gomphids, like other dragonflies, are excellent fliers. They are, however, less visible, often perching secretively on sandbars or low vegetation near water.

Habits

Except for their occurrence in streams, gomphid habits closely resemble those of libellulids. They sprawl on the bottom and camouflage themselves with silt and debris. In streams they partially bury themselves in the bottom, then wait for passing prey. Fishing nymph patterns should be keyed to this sedentary behavior.

The nymphs are mature and ready to emerge in the spring or summer of their third year. They usually crawl out on the shore rather than emergent vegetation. Once they are out of the water the nymphal skin splits along the back and the adult struggles to free itself. After an hour or more the adult escapes the shuck and then must wait for its wings to dry. As with other dragonflies, emergence is temperature dependent, usually taking place three or four hours before sunrise.

Gomphid adults typically sit on gravel bars or low vegetation and dart out over the water to catch their prey. This feeding pattern continues for several weeks after emergence before mating begins.

After mating, females oviposit by lightly touching the water with the tip of their abdomen. A cluster of eggs is released each time the abdomen contacts water. Females occasionally precede egg laying with graceful aerial displays of figures "8" and "S". Like other dragonflies, adult gomphids may feed for several weeks after mating and oviposition are completed.

Imitation

Gomphid appearance and behavior are so strikingly similar to libellulids that the same patterns and presentations should be used to imitate them. Where they occur in streams their imitations should be dead-drifted through riffles or hand-twisted across the bottom of runs and pools.

DAMSELFLIES (SUBORDER: ZYGOPTERA)

Damselflies are easily recognized from dragonflies, both as nymphs and as adults. Their slender bodies contrast sharply from the robust bodies of dragonflies. Damselfly nymphs have three flattened, tail-like gill lamellae, and lack internal gill chambers. They do not swim with jet-propelled bursts. Instead, they swim slowly, with laborious back-and-forth undulations of the abdomen.

Damselfly adults have large eyes, but they are bead-like and widely separated on top of the head. The wings of resting damselflies are held together and above the abdomen rather than spread horizontally, like the wings of dragonflies. Damselflies can change directions quickly in flight, but they are not fast fliers.

The two important families of damselflies are so similar that their imitations will be discussed in one section.

FAMILY: LESTIDAE

Common Names: None.

Emergence and Distribution

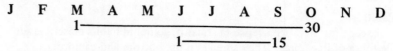

Lestids are common damselflies in the West. Members of the family are large; *Archilestes grandis,* one of the largest in the West, has a wing span of almost three inches. Lestids are widespread, with species found in all of North America. They are primarily summer and fall emergers, with adults appearing from June through September, depending on altitude and latitude. Most species have a one year life cycle.

Nymph Characteristics

*a. Extensible labium narrowed at the base; labium extending to middle or hind legs when retracted.
b. Antennal segments approximately equal in length.
c. Slender body ending in three tail-like caudal gill lamellae.
d. Color: Body shades of green or brown.
e. Size: Mature nymphs 18-35mm (3/4 to 1-1/2 inches).

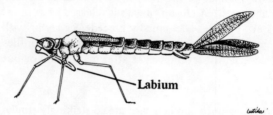

Figure 27. Lestid nymph.

Adult Characteristics

a. Wings clear, their bases narrow or strap-like.
b. Body slender; elongate.
c. Color: Shades of blue and/or green.
d. Size: Up to 60-75mm (2-1/2 to 3 inches).

Habitat

Lestids are stillwater insects. Ponds and lakes are normal environments, but some species also live in very slow streams and rivers. Underwater vegetation is the usual haunt of the nymphs, where they find both prey and shelter from other predators.

Adults lack the quickness and agility in flight of their dragonfly cousins. They are commonly seen hanging on leaves and stems, or in graceful flight very near such resting areas.

Habits

Lestid nymphs stalk their prey among underwater catacombs formed by mazes of plant stems. Once close enough to small nymphs or larvae their extensible labium is shot out like a frog's tongue, grasping the prey. They are active hunters, like the aeschnid dragonflies, but lack the ability to jet through the water. When traversing open water the nymphs wiggle from side-to-side, using their broad, tail-like gills as sculling oars. Despite a lot of movement the nymphs swim slowly, stopping every few inches.

Once mature, the nymphs move to shallows where plant stems or debris protrude from the water. At times large numbers of nymphs may move to the shallows together. If you are lucky enough to be standing at lakeside with fly rod in hand during such a migration, be ready for some fast fishing. At emergence the nymphs crawl out of the water on a plant stem or branch several inches to several feet high. They then latch onto the stem, the nymphal shuck splits open, and the adult emerges. This may take less than a minute or nearly an hour, depending on the species and the temperature. Temperature also influences the time of emergence. On warm days it occurs in late evening or early morning; cool temperatures may retard it well into the day, leaving the new adults vulnerable to predation.

Once in the air, adult damsels fly slowly. They normally feed by sitting on a perch, periodically flying out over the water to capture mosquitoes or other small insects in their basket-like legs. They return to the perch to feed. They are most active during the warmest part of the day.

Damselflies mate similar to dragonflies. The male grasps the female behind the head, while at the same time the female bends her abdomen under the male to contact his accessory organ. Damselflies usually mate while hanging from vegetation instead of in the air. Copulation may last from one to several minutes.

Lestids normally oviposit above the waterline by inserting the eggs inside plant stems, small twigs, or grasses. The male often holds the female while this is done. The eggs hatch in the fall or pass the winter inside stems and hatch the following spring.

FAMILY: COENAGRIONIDAE

Common Names: None.

Emergence and Distribution

J F M A M J J A S O N D
        1————————————— 30
             1————— 15

Members of the family Coenagrionidae are the most abundant damselflies in the West. In *Aquatic Insects of California* fifteen genera are listed, as opposed to two genera of lestids. Genera such as *Agria, Enallagma,* and *Ischnura* are found in every western state. They are a consistent food source for trout, bass and panfish.

The life cycle of coenagrionids closely follows that of lestids, taking approximately one year from egg to adult. Adult emergence is heaviest in spring and summer, commonly occurring from May through August.

Nymph Characteristics
*a. Extensible labium short and stout, reaching only to front legs when retracted.
 b. Antennal segments equal in length.
 c. Slender body with three tail-like caudal gill lamellae.
 d. Color: Body shades of green or brown.
 e. Size: Mature nymphs 12-25mm (1/2 to 1 inch).

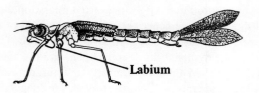

Figure 28. Coenagrionid nymph.

Adult Characteristics
  a. Body slender and elongate.
  b. Wings clear; wing bases narrow or strap-like.
  c. Color: Body bright shades of blue, brown, red, yellow or green.
  d. Size: Up to 50mm (2 inches).

Habitat
Coenagrionids are more widely distributed than lestids. Nymphs may be found in most still waters, even temporary ponds, but they also occur in large rivers and slower side water areas of streams. They prefer the same type of underwater vegetation as lestids. Adult coenagrionids are seen along pond and stream margins on warm summer days.

Habits
The habits of both nymphs and adults are similar to those described for the family Lestidae. The nymphs climb through submerged vegetation in search of prey and swim slowly with exaggerated undulations of the abdomen. Emergence occurs along pond or stream banks, where the nymphs crawl up logs, grasses or other vegetation. Temperature is again the major factor controlling time and duration of emergence. When conditions are favorable—temperatures 60°F. or more—emergence is most common in the late evening or early morning. The flight of adults is typically slow. They feed over the water or adjacent fields, catching prey in their basket-like legs and resting on grasses to eat it. Rather than ovipositing above the water like lestids, coenagrionids normally oviposit on the water's surface or beneath it. The females of many species crawl down submerged plants several feet, inserting eggs inside the stem as she goes. During this process the female may stay submerged an hour or more. Other species lay eggs on floating mats of moss, algae or wood debris.

Imitation
Lestids and coenagrionids are so similar their imitations can be considered together. Most of the one year life cycle of damselflies is spent in the underwater stage; nymph patterns are much more important than adult patterns. Fish key on the nymphs during their on-shore migrations, as they crawl and swim awkwardly toward the shallows in search of vegetation on which they can crawl from the water to emerge.

Nymphs
Slender damselfly nymphs present a special problem in imitation: They swim with clumsy, snake-like side-to-side movements that generate a lot of wiggle but little forward progress. Copying this peculiar motion demands a very slow retrieve, and necessitates the use of materials that work in the water with little stimulus.

Damselfly nymph imitations are usually tied on 3X or 4X long hooks, in sizes 8 through 16. Hook sizes 10 and 12 are most popular. Most dressings that have been devised for damselfly nymphs are green or olive. It should be kept in mind that many species are olive and some are brown.

> *HEATHER NYMPH (Fenton Roskelley)*
> *Hook: 2X or 3X long, No. 10.*
> *Thread: Black.*
> *Tail: Scarlet hackle fibers.*
> *Body: Rear 1/2, chartreuse spun fur; front 1/2, peacock herl.*
> *Rib: Fine oval gold tinsel over rear half.*
> *Hackle: Grizzly hen, short.*

Fenton Roskelley, a Spokane, Washington, outdoor writer, designed this pattern for the lakes in his area. He also recommends a sparsely-tied Dragon Fly Nymph, a simple pattern with an insect-green chenille body and pheasant rump hackle. This is similar to the Carey Special mentioned as a dragonfly nymph pattern; a sparse Carey also works well when damselflies are migrating.

> *DAMSELFLY NYMPH (Marshall Escola)*
> *Hook: Mustad 9672 (3X long), Nos. 8-16.*
> *Thread: Brown.*
> *Tail: Green-dyed grizzly hackle tip.*
> *Body: Variegated green yarn.*
> *Hackle: Green-dyed hen grizzly, sparse.*
> *Wingcase: Knot of variegated green yarn tied on top.*

The Damselfly Nymph, tied by Marshall "Seaweed" Escola and detailed in Don Roberts' *Flyfishing Stillwaters,* is designed to be fished shallow, at times in the surface film. It has a hackle tip tail to represent the gill lamellae of the natural and a soft hen-hackle collar to give the pattern life-like action in the water.

> *GREEN DAMSEL (Polly Rosborough)*
> *Hook: Mustad 38941 (3X long), No. 10.*
> *Thread: Olive.*
> *Tail: Olive marabou fibers pinched off so they are short.*
> *Body: Dubbed pale olive rabbit fur.*
> *Legs: Dyed pale olive barred teal.*
> *Wingcase: Olive marabou, one shade darker than tail, extending*
> *   1/3 over body.*

Polly Rosborough's Green Damsel uses soft marabou fluff to give the wiggle action of the natural nymph. Both this pattern and Escola's Damselfly Nymph are green. Damselfly nymphs tend to adopt the color of the predominant vegetation in their habitat. If this is tan or brown, the nymphs will usually also be tan or brown. The concept of choosing a fly pattern based on the color of the lake bottom and its vegetation is not without basis in entomology.

Presentation

Presentation of these patterns should be based on the slow, forward movement of natural damselfly nymphs. A slow hand-twist retrieve is best; any but the slowest stripping retrieves will move the artificial too fast.

Don Roberts, in *Flyfishing Stillwaters,* makes note of the nymph's habit of diving for the substrate when alarmed. He recommends that damselfly nymph imitations be weighted at the thorax. With this weight distribution the artificial dives as soon as the retrieve is stopped.

Experimental ties given to us by Harry Hendrickson of Beaverton, Oregon, incorporate bead chain eyes for weight and marabou fibers for action. The painted bead chain eyes catch the wide head and eyes of the natural perfectly; they also cause it to dive when the retrieve is stopped. The long tail of marabou compresses and waves in the water, giving the fly the wobbling effect of the natural insect.

Adults

Damselfly adults rest on grass stems, cattails, bulrushes and other vegetation perilously close to the water from which they emerged. On windy days it is not unusual for them to be blown onto the water. Trout and other fish are aware of this possibility and capitalize on it eagerly when it happens.

Two color phases of adult damselflies predominate: Blue and ginger. Imitations of them should be tied on long shank, standard weight hooks, usually in sizes 14 and 16.

> *BLUE DAMSEL*
> *Hook: Mustad 79580 (4X long), Nos. 14-16.*
> *Thread: Gray.*
> *Tail: Light blue elk hair.*
> *Rear Hackle: Light blue, undersized.*
> *Ribbing: Fine silver wire.*
> *Body: Light blue floss tied thin.*
> *Wings: Two light grizzly hackle tips tied together on edge over the body.*
> *Front hackle: Light blue.*

> *GINGER DAMSEL*
> *Hook: Mustad 79580 (4X long), Nos. 14-16.*
> *Thread: Tan.*
> *Tail: Light tan elk hair.*
> *Rear Hackle: Light ginger variant, undersized.*
> *Ribbing: Fine gold wire.*
> *Body: Tan floss tied thin.*
> *Wings: Light ginger variant hackle tips tied together on edge over body.*
> *Front Hackle: Light ginger variant.*

The Blue and Ginger Damsels are listed in Terry Hellekson's *Popular Fly Patterns.* They represent the two colors most likely to be effective on western waters.

Presentation

Damselfly adult imitations should be fished in and around shoreline vegetation. On windy days they will skitter and roll across the surface enticingly. Hellekson also recommends using them on still, hot days when nothing is moving. It will be necessary to cast them out and let them sit, waiting for a cruising fish. A wary eye should be kept on the fly, however, as Kellekson says it can disappear, be rejected and reappear before you know what is happening.

Nymphs of the damselflies, with their inimitable undulating movements, are the greatest challenge to the fly fisherman. The dressings we have offered will solve the problem in some situations; at other times selective trout will turn away from them disdainfully. We have yet to use, or hear of, a damselfly nymph pattern that works all of the time.

Chapter Five

Waterboatmen and Backswimmers
Order: Hemiptera

Not all members of the order Hemiptera are aquatic. Many families are terrestrial, seldom approaching water; others are shore bugs, of little interest to fish. Water striders, those familiar surface skaters of mud puddles, ponds, and lakes, have powerful scent glands to discourage fish. Stomach samples have turned up trout with a taste for them, though this event is so rare that imitation cannot be recommended.

Two aquatic families of Hemiptera are important to fishermen: Waterboatmen (Family: Corixidae) and backswimmers (Family: Notonectidae). Both inhabit good trout water and both are favorites of hungry fish.

Hemiptera have incomplete metamorphosis. Their life cycle is unique among aquatic insects, however, as they do not have the marked metamorphosis of other groups, which change abruptly from underwater nymphs to terrestrial adults. Hemiptera nymphs are similar in appearance and habits to adults. They differ in size, degree of wing development, and maturity of sexual organs. The wings grow through each of five instars until they are fully formed and the insect is capable of flying.

Flight is an adaptation that allows aquatic Hemiptera to escape drying environments and colonize new habitats. Adults continue the underwater ways of the nymphs.

Aquatic Hemiptera typically over-winter as adults, which lay their eggs in the spring on submerged debris or the undersides of floating plants. Shortly after egg laying the adults die. The eggs hatch and the nymphs grow to maturity through the spring and summer months. This annual cycle places them in favor from the trout's point of view: They approach full size, in good numbers, at the same time other insects have emerged or are in their earliest, smallest instars. Waterboatmen and backswimmers become very important in lakes and slow flowing streams that are open to fishing in late fall, winter and early spring. We have seen these insects active along the shoreline when it was necessary to crack a quarter inch layer of ice to collect them.

With rare exceptions, aquatic Hemiptera utilize atmospheric oxygen. They pierce the surface film with their abdomen or antennae and entrain a bubble of air under their wings and along the underside of their abdomen. Oxygen is taken from the bubble through spiracles (openings in the exoskeleton) and a complex trachial system delivers it directly to individual cells. As oxygen is used it is replaced by oxygen diffused into the bubble from the water, allowing some Hemiptera to stay submerged for long periods.

Hemiptera have sucking, beak-like mouthparts. Many species are predators which inject enzymes into their prey, breaking down the tissues, and then sucking up the resulting liquid. Others, notably Corixidae, probe aquatic plants, sucking up nutrients from individual cells.

FAMILY: CORIXIDAE

Common Name: Waterboatmen.

Emergence and Distribution

Waterboatmen are the most abundant, therefore the most important, of aquatic Hemiptera families. They do not "emerge" in the same sense as mayflies or stoneflies; both nymphs and adults live in the same aquatic habitat. They do, however, reach maturity in late summer and fall. Waterboatmen are most important when other aquatic insects are least important, and after the last windfalls of terrestrials have been harvested by the trout.

Corixids are ubiquitous in the West; few lakes and ponds at any elevation are without them. Densities depend primarily on vegetation. In alkaline lakes with lots of plants they are almost always important to fish. A collecting net swept through weed choked waters, especially in the fall, may fairly squirm with them. In less productive waters populations are thin and of questionable value.

Corixidae Characteristics

*a. Sucking mouthparts short and rounded.
*b. Front tarsi scoop- or shovel-shaped.
 c. Antennae shorter than head, not visible from above.
 d. Forewings tough and leathery; held carapace-like over back.
 e. Color: Body green, tan or brown; lighter on belly than back.
 f. Size: 6-12mm (1/4 to 1/2 inch).

Habitat

In lakes waterboatmen thrive in shallow weedbeds, along vegetated shorelines, and on the ooze of the bottom. They can also be found in the slack marginal waters of most streams and rivers. Waterboatmen can be important in slow currents, especially where they flow through trailing beds of attached aquatic plants or over carpets of algae and moss.

Atlantic salmon in Oregon's Hosmer Lake cruise the borders of grass mats in the fall, probing for waterboatmen in the suspended root systems of the plants. The fish are visible, approaching along the banks in glass-clear water, turning now and then to take a natural. A small imitation cast several feet in front of them, on a long leader and a tiny tippet, will often be taken almost casually. The same is true in most lakes where fish can be seen working for waterboatmen along shorelines and weedbeds.

Habits

Waterboatmen typically spend the winter as adults. In spring they mate and lay their eggs, attaching them to underwater objects. The nymphs emerge and begin feeding immediately. They have a one year life cycle.

Corixids feed on the bacterial and algal growth on plants, or from the layer of ooze along the lake and pond bottoms. They accept such small organisms as come their way; midge larvae and other tiny animals make up an important part of their diet. Research has shown that they depend on some nutrients from animal origins, just as we must have certain vitamins. Waterboatmen use their beak-like mouth parts to probe plants, sucking nutrients from individual cells within the stems.

Waterboatmen have adapted each of their three pairs of legs to a

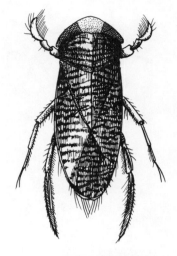

Figure 29. Corixidae adult.

specific task. The front legs are short and end in broad scoops. These are used to winnow a salad of acceptable ingredients from the growth on which they feed. The middle legs are for grasping a perch when the insect is at rest or feeding. The hind legs are like long oars fringed with hairs. These are used to propel the insect, just as a waterman rows his boat. Waterboatmen use them to move under water in one to three inch darts. It is important to remember this when fishing their imitations.

Waterboatmen rely on surface air for their oxygen. They break the surface tension with their antennae, located on the side of the head, and a bubble of air is drawn under the wings and around the abdomen. They do not penetrate deep water, favoring shallow weedbeds and shoreline vegetation where they can easily return to the surface.

The front wings of waterboatmen are leather-like and lay flat over the back. The hind wings are used for flying, and are folded between the protective forewings and the body of the insect. In flight the tough forewings are held forward, out of the way. In the spring some waterboatmen may leave their present habitat in search of new waters to colonize. Others remain in the same lake or pond as long as conditions are favorable.

Imitation

Corixids, in the proper place and season, are excellently suited for imitation. Due to predation by fish they tend to adopt the coloration of the bottom or predominant vegetation. The old method of choosing a fly to match the color of the lake bottom has more merit than meets the eye. Shades of tan, green, or brown are most common.

The roundness of the natural calls for stout patterns tied on standard length or 1X hooks. In smaller sizes—nos. 16 through 20—a ball of fur dubbing, approximating the size and color of collected specimens, has taken many fish.

> **CORIXID**
> **Hook: Mustad 3906B (1X long), Nos. 16-20.**
> **Thread: Dark olive or tan.**
> **Weight: None, or 3-4 turns.**
> **Body: Loose olive or tan fur.**

A few turns of lead wire help the fly penetrate the surface tension, sinking it quickly to the level of cruising fish. This is important in situations where casts are made to visible fish.

In larger sizes—12 and 14—waterboatmen can be approximated with herl patterns like the Zug Bug or Herl Nymph. Green, olive and natural-brown Teeny Nymphs have often fooled fish for us; they have a fair outline of the natural and the density necessary for quick sinking.

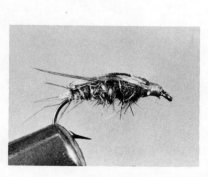

> **CORIXA BUG (Ernest Schwiebert)**
> **Hook: Mustad 3906B (1X long), Nos. 14-16.**
> **Thread: Dark brown.**
> **Tails: Two short pheasant fibers.**
> **Body: Dark brownish-gray hare's mask.**
> **Rib: Fine oval silver tinsel.**
> **Thorax: Dark hare's mask.**
> **Wingcase: Brown turkey.**
> **Swimmer legs: Two pheasant tail fibers.**
> **Legs: None.**

This more exact pattern copies both the darker backside and lighter belly of waterboatmen. The pheasant fiber legs work in the water when the fly is retrieved, mimicking the swimming motion of the natural. This dark brown dressing should be used as a model for imitations based on the color of the naturals you collect.

Presentation

Patterns should be presented to copy the waterboatmen's oar-like swimming. After the cast a few seconds should be allowed for the fly to sink. A pulsing retrieve, arrived at by twitching the rod tip while bringing in the line very slowly, will cause the fly to move through the water in short darts. On long casts this action will be difficult to achieve due to dampening by the line. Short casts, if possible to visibly cruising fish, are better. Dry lines and long, fine leaders will keep the flies in the upper waters inhabited by the corixids.

When casting to cruising fish it is best to let the fly sink without any action. If your timing is right it will reach the level of the fish as the fish passes it. This is close and exciting work. Often only a slight tilt and the flash of white jaws tell of a take. If the fly, presented with no action, fails to catch the attention of the passing fish, a few twitches of the rod tip should flag it down.

FAMILY: NOTONECTIDAE

Common Name: Backswimmers.

Emergence and Distribution

Like other Hemiptera, backswimmers have no real "emergence". They overwinter as adults, approaching adult size in late fall. They may hibernate, or remain active through the coldest months, depending on climatic conditions. They are most important to fishermen in fall, winter and spring. Like waterboatmen, they pick up the slack in the diet of fish after other insects have emerged.

Notonectids are found throughout the western region. They live in ponds and lakes at all elevations and have adapted to all of our western climates.

Notonectidae Characteristics
 *a. Sucking mouthparts form a short, 4-segmented beak.
 *b. Front legs with claws; not scoop-like; hind legs oar-like.
 *c. Swim on backs, with ventral side up.
 d. Antennae shorter than head; not visible from above.
 e. Forewings form carapace-like covering over back.
 f. Color: Pale tan to dark green, or white.
 g. Size: 6-12mm (1/4 - 1/2 inch.)

Habitat

Backswimmers are found in similar habitat to waterboatmen. Ponds and lakes, especially those with weedy shallows and vegetated shorelines, are favored. Because notonectids are predacious and their favorite prey is often their corixid cousins; populations of the two Hemiptera families often overlap.

We have not read accounts of backswimmers collected from river environments, nor have we collected them from flowing waters. Although they might occur in the backwaters and marginal areas of streams, it is doubtful they will be found important except in lakes and ponds.

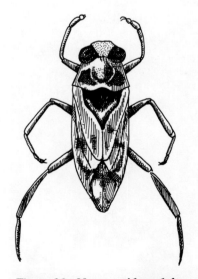

Figure 30. Notonectidae adult.

Habits

The backswimmer habit of swimming upside down gives the group its name and makes specimens easy to identify. The hind legs are used with the oar-like movement of waterboatmen; the resulting darts are the same.

Backswimmers are fierce predators. Their prey consists of anything they can subdue. Midge and mosquito larvae are prevalent in their diet. Mayfly nymphs, often found in heavy populations in the same shoreline habitat, are a favorite. Fish fry and waterboatmen are also common foods.

The fore and middle legs of backswimmers have evolved for grasping and holding prey. They are long, slender, and tipped with two sharp claws, not unlike those of raptorial birds. Their piercing mouthparts inject enzymes into their prey that break down the tissues. Then the resulting liquid is sucked out. Nothing of the prey remains but an empty shell.

Oxygen is obtained from surface air. The surface film is broken by hairs at the tip of the abdomen. A bubble is entrained along the ventral surface and under the wings. Oxygen enters the body through special pores called spiracles, and is delivered to cells by a tube-like trachial system. Backswimmers often hang at the surface, with their heads down and oar-legs outstretched, waiting for an unlucky organism to swim by. If there is prey in open water, notonectids will sometimes venture far from shore.

The forewings are hardened and held protectively over the hindwings and back of the insect. Flight serves the same purposes it serves for waterboatmen: Escape from drying habitat and colonization of new areas. Night-flying backswimmers are attracted to lights; they are sometimes seen in clusters at the bases of city lamp posts after a fatal flight.

Notonectid eggs are laid in the spring. They are inserted in plant stems, or glued to rocks, logs and vegetation. There can be one or more overlapping broods during a season, depending on climatic conditions. Winter is spent in the adult phase, either actively or hibernating in the substrate.

Imitation

Backswimmers do not as often occur in concentrated populations, common among waterboatmen. Their prime attraction to anglers is their willingness to move freely and boldly in cold weather. We fished a tiny irrigation pond one mid-January day, when an east wind iced our guides after every few casts. Fish rose sporadically, taking something near the surface with heavy swirls. The few stomach samples we finally managed to obtain were crammed with dark-olive backswimmers.

Simple dubbed patterns work well for the smaller sizes—16 through 20—of backswimmers, just as for waterboatmen.

> *NOTONECTID*
> *Hook: Mustad 3906B (1X long), Nos. 16-20.*
> *Thread: Dark olive or white.*
> *Weight: None or 3-4 turns.*
> *Body: Tan, dark olive, or dirty white fur.*

These simple dressings are usually adequate to match small backswimmers. The larger sizes are more likely to be important to fishermen in fall, winter and spring.

BACKSWIMMER (Al Troth)
Hook: Mustad 7957BX (1X long), Nos. 10-14.
Thread: Olive.
Shellback: Brown turkey.
Legs: Olive turkey fibers.
Body: Olive chenille.

This excellent dressing should be considered the basis for color variations to match naturals collected on your own waters. It is, however,
representative of many specimens we have collected throughout the West,
and matches them without any modifications.

Presentation

The backswimmers' habit and habitat are similar to those of waterboatmen. Presentation of patterns to imitate them has many parallels.
The patterns should be fished shallow, on dry lines. When the naturals
are being plucked from the surface film the imitation should be unweighted and fished as shallow as possible. If fish are cruising, probing
weedbeds and undercut banks, the fly should be slightly weighted to
penetrate the surface film quickly. If the fly is not taken as it sinks, a
twitching retrieve should be used to entice reluctant fish.

Chapter Six
Caddisflies Order: Trichoptera

Primitive ancestors of the caddisflies made their appearance, along with the stoneflies, about 260 million years ago. The oldest fossil specimens have been found in North America and Russia; later, more advanced forms are recorded from Australia, England and Germany. The earliest prototypes did not look like modern Trichoptera. It was not until the late Mesozoic period—70 to 140 million years ago—that forms easily recognized as caddisflies appeared.

Caddisflies evolved into an extremely diverse order. At present the world fauna is estimated at 10,000 species. In the United States and Canada about 1,200 species are known. In the western United States over 300 species occur: There are more species of caddisflies in the West than the western species of mayflies and stoneflies put together.

Caddisflies have adapted to a wide range of habitats. The greatest diversity occurs in cool, flowing waters. Unlike the stoneflies, however, caddisflies have also adapted to warm, still waters. Even temporary pools have been colonized. Some writers note that caddisflies become more important as stream quality deteriorates. This happens because many caddisflies can tolerate warmer water and lower oxygen levels than mayflies or stoneflies. However, the cool water forms disappear and the population diversity decreases, both indications of an unhealthy stream.

Caddisflies, unlike mayflies and stoneflies, have complete metamorphosis. Complete metamorphosis consists of four distinct stages: Egg, larva, pupa and adult. The development of each stage is described in detail in Chapter 1 under Metamorphosis.

The most intriguing characteristic of caddisflies is the case building behavior of many larvae. Caddis cases are constructed from a wide variety of material: Fine sand, small gravel, pebbles, sticks, pine needles, leaves (cut in various shapes), and plant stems. The case is held together by fine, sticky, silken threads lining the inside of the case.

Shapes of caddis cases are as diverse as the materials from which they are made. Some are finely tapered or rectangular, architecturally perfect; others look like something the cat drug in. The case material and design are often useful for identification to genera, but is too variable to distinguish specific species. Some larvae change the case material during development. *Making A Case for the Caddis,* by Margrett and Norm Anderson, is a delightful book describing case building behavior in detail.

Not all caddis larvae build cases. Free-living forms are more easily taken by trout. They are therefore more important for imitation.

Case building caddis pupate inside the larval case, while free-living forms build a rough shelter of sand and gravel for pupation. The length of the pupal stage varies with the species and with water conditions. Two to four weeks is typical, but it can last as long as four months.

Fully developed pupae cut out of the pupal case and swim to the surface or are buoyed up by gases produced under the pupal skin. Rising pupae are very attractive prey. Fish often feed on them selectively, making pupal imitations extremely important patterns.

Emergence from pupa to adult occurs in the surface film. The pupal cuticle splits open along the back of the thorax and the pre-formed adult emerges through the opening. Emergence is usually brief, taking only a few seconds. Strong, swirling rises are common during a caddis hatch as the fish race for ascending pupae and quick-emerging adults. There are exceptions, however. The pupae of some species, especially lake forms, float or buzz about in the surface film for what seems like a minute or more. They are lucky to escape the feeding sprees they trigger.

The adults, once free of the surface film, fly for streamside cover. Mating occurs on the foliage. Fertilized females then fly back to the water and oviposit by releasing clusters of eggs in the surface film or by crawling under water and placing gelatinous masses of eggs directly on the substrate. The submerged females then swim back to the surface. A few species lay egg masses above the water line, where the larvae can crawl into the water after they hatch. Most adult caddisflies live one to three weeks; a few live as long as four months.

Caddisflies are easily recognized. The larvae, because of complete metamorphosis, show no development of wingpads. They have minute antennae, normally visible only under magnification. Their legs are not long, but are well developed, ending with a single claw. Gill structures vary, but are normally found on the abdominal segments and appear as fine, fingerlike projections. Caddis larvae have no tails. Instead, a pair of anal hooks protrude from the last abdominal segment.

Adult features develop during the pupal transformation. Wingpads become obvious, reaching half the body length. Compound eyes develop. Antennae grow into long, slender filaments. Legs lengthen and become delicate. The anal hooks are lost, replaced by the reproductive structure of the adult.

The most obvious features of the adult caddis are their long, body-length antennae, four well developed wings held in an inverted "V", tent-like, over the abdomen, and the lack of tails. The wings of adult caddisflies are covered with hundreds of fine hairs, hence the order name Trichoptera, derived from the Greek *tricos* (hair) and *pteron* (wing).

Identifying the families and genera of caddisflies is easiest with larvae. They have a variety of visible characteristics such as gills, anal hooks, and sclerites. The characters on pupae and adults, however, are often difficult to discriminate; magnification and good comparative diagrams are usually necessary. For this reason, larval characteristics will be stressed in this section. Pupal and adult descriptions will be limited to general characteristics such as size and color. To identify most pupae and adults it is necessary to consult one of the scientific books listed in the bibliography (e.g., *Introduction to the Aquatic Insects of North America* by Cummins and Merritt).

FAMILY: RHYACOPHILIDAE

GENUS: *RHYACOPHILA*

Common Names: Rock Worm, Green Rock Worm.

Emergence and Distribution

J   F   M   A   M   J   J   A   S   O   N   D

1————————————————————————15
1——————————31

There are at least forty-five species of this genus in the West. They emerge anytime from April through November. Pinning down specific emergence dates is possible only on a stream by stream basis. Their wide emergence period, however, means they can be important many times throughout the season.

Rhyacophila are found in every western state and province. Mountainous regions, with lots of rough, free-stone streams, generally have the best populations.

Larval Characteristics
 *a. Pronotum (upper surface of the first thoracic segment) has a sclerotized shield. Other thoracic segments are not hardened.
 *b. Large, well developed anal hooks.
 *c. Larvae free-living; do not build cases.
  d. Gills are fine finger-like, or hair-like, filaments on abdominal segments, or they are absent.
  e. Color: Body ranges from light tan to bright green.
  f. Size: Body length 12-18mm (1/2 - 3/4 inch).

Pupal Characteristics
  a. Pupae enclosed in rough shelters of sand and gravel on bottom of stream.
  b. Color: Body light cream to green with dark brown wingpads.
  c. Size: Length 10-14mm (3/8 - 5/8 inch).

Adult Characteristics
  a. Three ocelli present.
  b. Antennae slightly shorter than body.
  c. Color: Body dark tan to green; wings mottled with brown or gray.
  d. Size: Length from head to tip of wings 10-14mm (3/8 - 5/8 inch).

Habitat
Rhyacophila inhabit only cool, flowing waters. Mountain streams, which are considered the ancestral habitat of Trichoptera, contain the richest fauna of this primitive genus. Rhyacophilids are more abundant in the West than other areas of the country because the numerous mountain ranges in the West have so many suitable streams.

Rocky, tumbling riffles are the dominant habitat of the larvae. They thrive in cold, highly oxygenated waters and do not survive where pollution warms the water or lowers oxygen levels. Pupation occurs in the same fast-water habitat, inside rough gravel shelters built and attached to the substrate by the free-living larvae.

Habit

Rhyacophilids are the best known of the free-living caddisfly larvae. They crawl along riffle bottoms, using their legs and large anal hooks to keep a firm grip. Many lose their hold, however, and where they are abundant they are constantly found in trout diets. Drifting larvae lack any swimming ability; they are easily taken by fish and easily imitated by fishermen.

These active riffle dwellers feed mostly on other insects. In nine to ten months the larvae are fully grown and ready to pupate. The pupal case, made from bits of sand and gravel, is attached securely to the substrate. Inside the case a parchment-like cocoon covers the developing pupa. The pupa is fully developed and ready to emerge in three to four weeks. It cuts free of the sand and gravel shelter and swims quickly to the surface. Helpless emerging pupae are fed upon eagerly by the largest fish, often just under the surface. At this time pupal imitations are deadly.

At the surface the adult emerges from the pupal shuck within seconds, and quickly flies to nearby vegetation. Most adults fly erratically. They cause showy, splashy rises as feeding fish try to catch them. Mating takes place on shoreline vegetation shortly after emergence. Fertilized females then return to the water, in the afternoon or evening, to oviposit. *Rhyacophila* lay their eggs on the surface, releasing a cluster of eggs each time the abdomen touches the water. The entire life cycle takes approximately one year.

Imitation

All three stages—larva, pupa and adult—of the genus *Rhyacophila* are valuable to the angler.

Larvae are easily collected for imitation. Shuffling through the rocks in a choppy riffle will send at least a few specimens cascading into your net.

Pupae are more mysterious. This is such a fleeting stage that a sample is hard to get. When a rise comes on but you can't quite make out what is happening, these are likely suspects. Hold a screen net below a riffle for a few minutes, then examine it to see if any pupae are caught in the meshes, or turn over rocks and look for the sand and pebble cocoons. If you find one pick it apart carefully and observe the maturity and color of the insect inside. If these methods fail, catch a fish and examine its stomach contents. That is always easy advice to give, but hard advice to follow.

The adult is also often hard to observe, especially if egg laying flights start at dusk. But an observant angler will notice them dancing erratically and dipping to the surface, usually over or upstream from brisk riffle areas.

If adults are not seen, shake some streamside vegetation. This will often scare out hundreds of hiding specimens.

Larvae

Imitations of the free-living caddis larvae may be the most valuable nymph patterns to the western angler. Rhyacophilids roam freely through riffles, searching for prey. They are often cast loose and taken by feeding trout. Their imitations should be tied on 1X or 2X long hooks. English bait hooks are also excellent; they reflect the curved body of the natural. Weighted patterns are often used because the larvae do not swim and remain close to the bottom. Colors range from tan to bright green.

ZUG BUG (Cliff Zug)
Hook: Mustad 3906B (1X long), Nos. 8-16.
Thread: Black.
Tail: Three peacock berl fibers; clip so tail is equal to two-
thirds the length of the body.
Ribbing: Oval silver tinsel.
Body: Peacock berl.
Throat: Brown partridge.
Wingcase: Gray partridge.

The suggestive Zug Bug is an excellent pattern for the larvae of *Rhya-cophila*. It is an excellent searching pattern; like the Gold Ribbed Hare's Ear, it will imitate many different insects. We carry it in a range of sizes, some unweighted and some with a few turns of lead wire under the body. Whenever we are fishing a riffle, especially if it is a shallow, chattery riffle of the kind loved by these larvae, we try tumbling Zug Bugs along the bottom. If there are fish working in the riffle we will usually turn at least a few.

GREEN ROCK WORM (Polly Rosborough)
Hook: Eagle Claw 1197B, No. 8.
Thread: Black.
Body: Caddis green synthetic yarn.
Legs: Dyed green speckled guinea fibers tied in as throat.
Head: Black ostrich berl.

Polly Rosborough's Green Rock Worm is a closer copy of the rhya-cophilid than the Zug Bug is. It is a very simple fly to tie. Used as the basis for a few color variations, it can imitate all of the free-living caddis-fly larvae. The many western species vary from light tan through bright green.

LATEX CADDIS LARVA (Raleigh Boaze)
Hook: Mustad 37160, Nos. 10-16.
Thread: Black.
Underbody: Olive green floss.
Body: Cream latex.
Head: Peacock berl.

This Latex Caddis Larva, on its curved hook, imitates the body of the rhyacophilid perfectly. It also catches the translucence of the natural, with the green core of floss "glowing" through the latex. When tying this pattern be careful not to stretch the latex so far that it no longer feels soft.

Presentation

Rhyacophilid patterns should be presented on the bottom, without any action. Upstream, or up and across, casts will allow the imitation to sink and let it drift naturally, without influence from line or leader.

The amount of weight needed varies with the strength and depth of the riffle fished. Additional weight can be put on the leader above the fly if necessary. For heavy riffles over two feet deep a sink tip line improves the drift of the fly. It also makes it more difficult to detect a strike. We prefer to fish with dry lines wherever possible. A longer leader and weighted fly make casting harder, but we find such a combination more pleasant to fish and more productive than a wet tip line and short leader.

Rhyacophilid larvae are so prevalent, and their imitations so effective, that we almost always reach for a Zug Bug or other rock worm pattern when we are fishing a riffle and no insects are hatching.

Pupae

Some of our most frustrating experiences have been over sporadic emergences of rhyacophilid caddis. The adults appear on the water in the midst of rising fish. It almost always seems to be a perfect situation for dry fly fishing, yet artificials are refused consistently. It usually happens as last light fades, compounding the problem. When we tried experimenting with a few soft-hackled flies during these evening hatches our success rate improved remarkably.

Selective fish nearly always concentrate on the ascending pupae when caddisflies are emerging, and ignore the adults entirely. Pupae are vulnerable throughout their rise to the surface; the adults ride the current briefly and are safe in the air before trout have much chance at them. Pupae range in size from 10 through 16. Colors vary from light cream to green, with dark brown wingpads.

PARTRIDGE AND GREEN (Sylvester Nemes)
Hook: Mustad 94840 (1X fine), Nos. 10-16.
Thread: Green.
Body: Green floss.
Hackle: Gray partridge.

The simplest pupal patterns are the soft-hackled flies originated in the last century by fishermen on the British border rivers between England and Scotland. While mentioned in earlier works, they were not given popular notice until Sylvester Neme's work, *The Soft-Hackled Fly,* was published in 1975. His patterns consist of simple floss bodies with hackles of partridge, grouse, snipe, or other soft feathered bird. Some patterns include a fur thorax. The hackles work with the currents, representing the trailing wings and antennae of ascending caddis pupae. These simple patterns can be excellent imitations during a specific hatch. They also are great searching patterns when it is hard to tell what is going on.

SOLOMON'S CADDIS PUPA (Larry Solomon)
Hook: Mustad 3906B or 9671, Nos. 12-18.
Thread: Dark olive.
Body: Olive green fur or sparkle wool.
Rib: Dark olive monocord.
Wing: Mallard wing quill sections tied along sides.
Legs and Antennae: Brown partridge.
Head: Peacock or ostrich herl.

Solomon's Caddis pupa is from *The Caddis and the Angler,* by Larry Solomon and Eric Leiser. This is the first angling book devoted entirely to caddisflies. It covers caddis entomology, angling techniques, and lists dressings for dozens of imitations. Solomon's Caddis Pupa incorporates the working qualities of fur or wool with the imitative quality of duck quill segment wings.

BLUE DUN HACKLE (James Leisenring)
Hook: Partridge Long May, Nos. 12-14 (sub 94840).
Thread: Primrose yellow silk.
Hackle: Light-blue-dun ben.
Tail: 2-3 blue-dun fibers (optional).
Rib: Very narrow flat gold tinsel.
Body: Mole fur spun on primrose-yellow silk.

The Blue Dun Hackle is from *The Art of Tying the Wet Fly and Fishing the Flymph* by James E. Leisenring and Vernon S. "Pete" Hidy. The concepts outlined in their book have immediate application to the problem of imitating caddis pupae. Mr. Hidy, and the late Mr. Leisenring, wrote that the body is the most important part of a fly. This is an interesting concept, opposing the hard floss bodies used on Neme's soft-hackles, and the latex or monofilament bodies wrapped around many of today's imitations.

The bodies of these patterns—properly called "flymphs"— are prepared separately from the rest of the fly. They are made on a special spinning block. Various furs are spun on Piersall's gossamer silk. Both fur and silk colors are selected to match the natural. When the body is wound and the fly is placed under water the silk shows translucently through the surrounding dubbed fur, reflecting the undercolors of the imitated insect.

An additional advantage of flymphs is their ability to entrain a few tiny bubbles of air in the fibers of body and hackle. These sparkle under water, just as the gases trapped under the cuticle of a rising pupa gleam with reflected light.

The concepts outlined in Leisenring and Hidy's book have proven themselves time and again over the years since it was first published in 1941. The tying methods they prescribe take patience, but have a special charm that rings of the old ways, the traditional ways of tying flies and catching trout.

Presentation

Presentation of rhyacophilid pupal patterns must be based on their rapid ascent to the surface. The "rising-to-the-surface"method, described by Charles Brooks in *Nymph Fishing for Larger Trout,* presents the pupae perfectly. The fly is cast across or across and down stream, on a short leader and Hi Density or wet tip line. It is then fished with a series of lifts which alternately bring it to the surface and let it sink again. This method may require a weighted fly and is enhanced by weight on the leader above the fly.

Flymphs are dressed to fish in the top few inches of water. Mr. Hidy tells us they are most effective if cast just above and beyond a rising trout, popped under the surface with a slight tug on the line, then drifted in front of the fish. When no fish are rising they can be fished to holding water with a "Leisenring lift". This method calls for placing the fly well above the suspected lie of a fish, allowing it to sink, then raising it through the water, by stopping the rod, when the fly reaches the position of the fish.

Adults

Dry patterns should be used when the adults are dancing over the surface and fish are actively feeding on them. They are also effective searching patterns in the late evening when fish are rising but it is difficult to determine what they are taking.

Adult *Rhyacophila* range in size from 10 to 18. Body colors are usually dark tan to green; wing colors mottled brown or gray.

> **DARK BUCKTAIL CADDIS**
> *Hook: Mustad 94840 (1X fine), Nos. 10-14.*
> *Thread: Brown.*
> *Tail: None.*
> *Hackle: Brown, palmered.*
> *Body: Muskrat fur.*
> *Wing: Natural dark brown bucktail.*

The Bucktail Caddis is a western dressing designed to meet western fishing conditions. It will float well in rough water, yet gives a good silhouette of the caddisfly adult. The Dark Bucktail Caddis listed is a variation to match the predominant color phases of the rhyacophilids. You should not hesitate to vary the materials to suit the requirements of local hatches.

> **GRAYISH-OLIVE/DUN CADDIS (Dave McNeese)**
> *Hook: Mustad 94840 (1X fine), Nos. 12-18.*
> *Thread: Gray.*
> *Body: Grayish olive fur.*
> *Wing: Dark bronze hackle fibers or deer hair equivalent.*
> *Hackle: Bronze dun.*

Dave McNeese's Grayish-Olive/Dun Caddis is a refinement of the Bucktail Caddis pattern. Dave uses blends of gray and olive fur to get the desired body color. The use of hackle fibers for the wing gives a realistic silhouette: Bucktail tends to flair, while hackle lies flat over the body.

> **SKITTERING CADDIS (Leonard M. Wright, Jr.)**
> *Hook: 94833 (3X fine), Nos. 14-18.*
> *Thread: Black.*
> *Tail: None.*
> *Body: Peacock herl.*
> *Rib: Fine gold wire.*
> *Wing: Brown spade or shoulder hackle fibers.*
> *Hackle: Brown.*

The Skittering Caddis is designed to be fished with the action as well as the appearance of the natural. In *Fishing the Dry Fly as a Living Insect*, Leonard M. Wright, Jr. calls for dressing the fly with the finest, highest floating hackles. He recommends it be fished with a "sudden inch" movement; a short hop just after it lands on the water. This represents the fluttering motion of the ovipositing female.

Presentation

Adult rhyacophilids are available to trout during their evening ovipositing flights. They do not form mating swarms, as the mayflies do, and are more sporadic in their return to the river. Their imitations should be fished in late afternoon and evening. A traditional drag-free float is usually best, however a slight twitch will sometimes enhance the appeal of the pattern, and a skittering retrieve across the water's surface may even stir up lethargic trout.

Rhyacophilids often dive under water, or crawl under it on rocks, to deposit their eggs. The Blue Dun wet fly imitates the female as she returns to the surface. The Leadwing Coachman is a similar wet pattern with a dark olive body.

The success of many wet fly patterns may be due to their resemblance to caddis females. Wet fly patterns might also be mistaken for ascending pupae. If you are not sure what stage trout are taking, soft-hackles, flymphs, or wet fly patterns are good ways to hedge your bets.

FAMILY: HYDROPSYCHIDAE

GENUS: *HYDROPSYCHE*

Common Name: Spotted Sedge.

Emergence and Distribution

```
J  F  M  A  M  J  J  A  S  O  N  D
         1——————————————— 30
            1——————————— 31
```

Hydropsyche is a diverse genus, represented by twenty-five or more species in the West. They have adapted to flowing waters from small headwater streams to large valley rivers, and therefore occur over a wide range of elevations. This, coupled with the large number of species, makes for complicated and varied emergence dates. Emergence is most common from early spring through the warm summer months.

Larval Characteristics
  *a. Each of the three thoracic segments with a dorsal sclerotized shield.
  *b. Thickly branched gill filaments along ventral abdominal segments.
  c. Large anal hooks, usually with a tuft of long hairs at their base.
  d. Larvae build crude shelters on the substrate, not true cases.
  e. Color: Similar to *Rhyacophila,* ranging from light tan and brown to bright green.
  f. Size: Body length 12-18mm (1/2 - 3/4 inch).

Pupal Characteristics
  a. Pupae encased inside crude larval shelter on stream bottom.
  b. Color: Tan to green.
  c. Size: 10-14mm (3/8 - 5/8 inch).

Adult Characteristics
  *a. Ocelli absent.
  *b. Antennae as long as body.
  c. Color: Body grayish-tan to olive green; wings brown, often marked with gray.
  d. Size: Body length from head to wing tips 10-18mm (3/8 - 3/4 inch).

Habitat

Rhyacophila and *Hydropsyche* are commonly found in the same habitat, but the latter is often more abundant. The larvae of hydropsychids feed on material strained from the current through capture nets. They are found only in running water with sufficient flow to bring food into the nets. Slow moving glides or runs are adequate for some species. Others occur only in fast riffles. They are generally found on rock and gravel substrates, although logs and mosses are also common habitat.

The amount of particulate material—small plant and animal life—in the stream has a direct influence on the number of hydropsychids present. Streams below dams and lakes are often high in particulate matter; these areas typically have tremendous populations of hydropsychids. This is part of the reason for the richness of many streams below irrigation reservoirs.

Habits

The most interesting and distinctive habit of the hydropsychids is the net-spinning behavior of the larvae. The larva builds a rough shelter, on a rock or log, from bits of sand, gravel, twigs and any other handy material. It is held together by a fine lining of silk. To the front of this shelter a silk web is spun, positioned so the current flows through it. This underwater spider web strains food from the current like a stationary plankton net. Periodically the larva comes out to graze on the particles trapped in it.

The larvae reach full size, and are ready to pupate, after feeding for almost a year. They close off the end of the larval shelter, spin a silken cocoon, and pupate inside. In approximately three weeks the pupae have fully developed wingpads, antennae, legs, and other adult features. All is ready for the final ascent to the surface. They emerge from fairly fast water; their rise to the surface carries them downstream, often to waiting trout. Emergence generally occurs in the late afternoon.

Adults pop quickly from those pupae lucky enough to make it past feeding fish. Surface swirls may change to jumping rises as fish switch their feeding from pupae to the winged stage. The adults fly to shoreline cover, where mating occurs within one to several days.

Fertilized females fly back to the riffles and glides to oviposit as evening approaches. It is common for female hydropsychids to crawl under water, where they lay their eggs in gelatinous masses on the substrate. They then attempt to swim back to the surface, with their wings arched back over the abdomen. This egg laying behavior can stimulate selective feeding on the swimming females. At such times traditional wet fly patterns come into their own.

Imitation

All three stages of the hydropsychid caddisflies are important to fishermen. The larvae are not as active as rhyacophilids, but where conditions are right they are much more abundant. Rivers tapped for irrigation, such as Oregon's famous Deschutes, return from the fields with a wealth of particulate matter and foster millions of these net-spinners.

The pupae usually make their run for the surface early in the afternoon, when anglers are apt to be out. The adults also tend to return to the river in the afternoon or early evening, making them more available as a fishable hatch than rhyacophilids, which usually return at dusk.

Larvae

Larvae of the net-spinning hydropsychids are similar in shape to the rock worms. Many are also the same color and can be fished with the same patterns. Although their life styles are different, they are found in riffles, just as the rhyacophilids, and tumble in the currents in the same manner when dislodged.

Sizes run from 10 to 16; colors are usually shades of tan and green. There are many tannish-brown species of *Hydropsyche*. We often find a Gold Ribbed Hare's Ear to be the best imitation.

> *DUBBED CADDIS LARVA*
> *Hook: 3906B (1X long), Nos. 10-16.*
> *Thread: Tan.*
> *Weight: 5-10 turns lead wire.*
> *Body: Dubbing fur to match natural.*
> *Thorax: Dubbing fur to match thorax of natural.*
> *Legs: Picked out thorax fur.*

The simple dubbed caddis larva usually uses a cream, tan or olive fur for the body and a darker fur, usually hare's ear or hare's mask fur, for the thorax. By tying them at streamside the natural can be matched closely, using a specimen from the river as a model. They take but a minute to tie, and the amount of weighting wire can be varied to suit the situation. A few colors of dubbing fur kept in stack paks or plastic slide-film sleeves provide a match for most naturals.

> *LATEX CADDIS LARVA (Poul Jorgensen)*
> *Hook: Mustad 3906, Nos. 10-16.*
> *Thread: Brown 6/0 nylon.*
> *Underbody: Tying thread and lead wire.*
> *Abdomen: Natural latex strip, 3/32 inch wide, tinted the color*
> *   of the natural.*
> *Thorax: Darkest-brown-dyed rabbit fur with guard hair, mixed*
> *   and spun in a loop.*
> *Legs: Underside of thorax left long and picked out.*
> *Head: Brown tying thread.*

Imitative latex larvae are tinted to the color of the natural with waterproof Pantone marking pens. This is an alternative to the method described for the rhyacophilids, where floss was wrapped under the transparent latex to give the correct body color.

Presentation

Larvae of the net-spinners cannot swim. When dislodged from their nets or retreats they tumble helplessly in the current until they are either eaten or regain a stable position. This behavior suggests their imitations should be fished dead-drift, just as the rock worm patterns.

Pupae

Pupal imitations solve some of those mysterious rises when there are lots of adults over the water and fish seem to be taking them, yet refuse all of the best dry fly offerings. Experimenting with sub-surface patterns approximating the size and color of the adults might supply the reason for refused dries. Pupae range in size from 10 through 16. They are usually shades of tan and green.

GOLD RIBBED HARE'S EAR

Hook: Mustad 3906 B (1X long), Nos. 10-16.
Thread: Tan.
Tail: Tan hair from the base of a hare's ear, tied short.
Rib: Fine gold wire.
Body: Mixed fur from an English hare's mask.
Thorax: Slightly darker hare's mask fur, with guard hairs.

We recommend the Gold Ribbed Hare's Ear as a suggestive pattern for both larval and pupal hydropsychids. It is an excellent imitation of both. As a larva it should be tumbled along the bottom. As a pupa it should be fished in the mid-depths or upper layer of current, either without pull from the leader or with a rising, swimming motion in imitation of the ascending natural. The same amount of weight can be used for both applications, in one case to put the fly on the bottom, in the other to sink it a foot or two between lifts toward the surface. It can also be fished with soft-hackle tactics, using a free float and mended casts to present the fly naturally to feeding trout. One warm June day we used this method to take over fifteen trout in the last hour of light from Oregon's Deschutes. The largest was over three pounds.

MARCH BROWN SPIDER SOFT-HACKLE (Sylvester Nemes)

Hook: Mustad 94840 (1X fine), Nos. 10-16.
Thread: Orange.
Rib: Narrow gold tinsel.
Body: Mixed hair from hare's face.
Hackle: Brown partridge.

This pattern, one of Sylvester Neme's soft-hackled flies, is similar to the Hare's Ear. It incorporates the hare's fur body and gold ribbing with hackle fibers to represent the trailing legs, antennae, and developing wings of the natural. Other soft-hackles, such as the Partridge and Orange or Partridge and Green, should be kept in mind to match the emerging pupae of the many hydropsychid species.

LITTLE WESTERN SEDGE PUPA (Ernest Schwiebert)

Hook: Mustad 3906, Nos. 14-16.
Thread: Dark-brown 6/0 nylon.
Body: Bleached peacock quill over brown nylon underbody.
Thorax: Dark-brown dubbing.
Wingcases: Medium-gray duck quill sections tied at sides.
Legs: Dark mottled partridge hackle.
Antennae: Lemon woodduck fibers.
Head: Dark-brown nylon.

Schwiebert's Little Western Sedge Pupa, from *Nymphs*, is a perfect example of the more imitative patterns. Using the abdomen color, thorax fur, and mallard-quill wingpads as the basis for imitation, an innovative tier can alter them to suit other emerging naturals.

Presentation

Pupal patterns are usually most effective when fished in the top few inches of the currents. If fish are working visibly, casts should be made slightly above their positions so the fly swings across them, or floats to them naturally. When used as a searching pattern the pupa can be fished dead in the surface layer, with a mended line drift. It can also be alternately sunk and raised toward the surface. Dry lines and fairly long leaders—nine to twelve feet—help both types of presentation.

Adults

Hydropsychid adult patterns are precious in June and July, especially in the afternoon after a summer thunder shower. Naturals oviposit in runs and glides above and below riffles. They often dance under brush and willows along the banks; fish respond by feeding heavily, with clumsy rushed rises.

Patterns in sizes 10 through 16, with tan or olive bodies and tan wings, are usually best.

> **BUCKTAIL CADDIS**
> *Hook: Mustad 94840 (1X fine), Nos. 10-16.*
> *Thread: Tan.*
> *Hackle: Ginger.*
> *Body: Tan fur or wool.*
> *Wing: Natural brown bucktail.*

The Bucktail Caddis is a Northwest pattern designed for good floatation. The given version is used on the Deschutes River in mid-summer to match a hydropsychid hatch which clouds along the river and oviposits every afternoon for over a month. We have seen similar species on many other western rivers.

> **ELK HAIR CADDIS (Al Troth)**
> *Hook: Mustad 94840 (1X fine), Nos. 10-16.*
> *Thread: Tan.*
> *Ribbing: Gold wire.*
> *Body: Dubbed hare's ear fur.*
> *Hackle: Furnace, tied at end of body, wrapped to back,*
> *   tied down with gold ribbing wire.*
> *Wing: Tannish-cream elk hair.*
> *Head: Elk hair butts, clipped.*

The Elk Hair Caddis is well known in the Rocky Mountain area; however its popularity is beginning to rival that of the Bucktail Caddis in all regions of the West. In the dressing given, from *Popular Fly Patterns*, it is a perfect match for many hydropsychid species. Like the Bucktail Caddis, the hackle, body, and wing colors can be altered to imitate other caddis species.

QUILL-WING CADDIS (Solomon and Leiser)
Hook: Mustad 94833 (3X fine), Nos. 10-16.
Thread: Gray.
Body: Light olive fur dubbing or match natural.
Wing: Two sections from paired turkey flight feathers.
Hackle: Dark ginger.

The Quill-Wing Caddis captures the tent-wing shape of the natural perfectly. It rests in the surface film rather than riding above it on palmered hackles. To make the wing fibers stick together the sections should be sprayed with Tuffilm or painted with vinyl cement before they are tied on. This will make them easier to tie, and more durable.

Presentation

All of the caddis dry fly patterns should be fished with traditional, upstream drag-free floats. If this does not produce, a slight motion might be given to the fly as it nears the lie of a trout. The Bucktail Caddis is often cast up and across stream. At the end of its drag-free drift it is pulled under water and fished out throught he rest of its swing as a wet fly. It can be either dead-drifted or given a swimming action with the rod tip. It imitates the dry adult on the upstream swing, an emerging pupa or drowned adult on the lower half of its drift, allowing the angler to imitate two stages with one cast.

Many Hydropsychidae species oviposit under water. When they are finished they swim back toward the surface. Traditional wet fly patterns, such as the March Brown or Hare's Ear, fished with traditional wet fly methods, imitate this behavior perfectly.

MARCH BROWN
Hook: Mustad 3906, Nos. 10-16.
Thread: Tan.
Tails: Three pheasant center tail fibers.
Body: Hare's ear fur.
Hackle: Brown hen, sparse.
Wing: Mallard quill primary sections.

HARE'S EAR
Hook: Mustad 3906, Nos. 10-16.
Thread: Brown.
Tail: Bronze mallard fibers.
Body: Dubbed hare's ear fur; pick out the body and make shaggy.
Wings: Hen ringneck pheasant quill sections tied over the body.

FAMILY: GLOSSOSOMATIDAE

GENERA: *GLOSSOSOMA*

AGAPETUS

ANAGAPETUS

Common Name: Turtle-case makers.

Emergence and Distribution

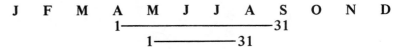

Three genera, including over twenty species, of glossosomatids are common in the West. The genus *Glossosoma* is the most diverse, with fourteen known species. This diversity makes pinning down specific emergence dates impossible except on specific waters.

Glossosomatids have adapted to most stream and river conditions found in the West. They occur over a wide range of elevations, and are common in both spring creeks and free-stone streams. They survive well in steep, rapid streams, or slower valley rivers. Adaptation to such a wide range of habitats further complicates emergence patterns. One must be on the lookout for these small and abundant caddisflies throughout the entire season.

Larval Characteristics
*a. Only pronotum with complete sclerotized shield; other thoracic segments membranous or with small sclerites.
*b. Larvae construct domed, tortoise-shell-like cases.
*c. Gill filaments absent.
 d. The three pairs of legs are equal in size.
 e. Anal hooks small and broadly joined to last abdominal segment.
 f. Color: Body light cream to brown with dark brown or black head and thorax.
 g. Size: Small, 3-10mm (1/8-3/8 inch).

Pupal Characteristics
 a. Color: Cream to brown body, darker thorax, and brownish-gray wingpads.
 b. Size: Small, 3-10mm (1/8 - 3/8 inch).

Adult Characteristics
*a. Three ocelli present.
 b. Antennae not quite body length.
 c. Color: Body light tan or brown; wings grayish-tan.
 d. Size: Length from head to wing tips 3-10mm (1/8 - 3/8 inch).

Habitat
Glossosomatid larvae prefer shallow runs in moderate to fast currents. More important than current is the substrate: cobble and large gravel, covered with a thin, slippery layer of diatoms and algae, hold the largest populations. They build their moveable igloo-like cases on the exposed upper surfaces of the substrate.

Prior to pupation the larvae often congregate in slower eddies, where they fasten their cases firmly to the rocky bottom. In certain areas the small domed cases completely encrust large rocks. They look like barnacles along rocky ocean beaches. These colonies of cases remain in place after the pupae have emerged.

Habits

Each group of caddisflies has some unique behavior; the glossomatids are no exception. They are adapted to feed specifically on the same rich, nutritious and slippery layer of periphyton—diatoms and algae— that often provides the angler with an unexpected soaking. Glossosomatid larvae, protected under their turtle-cases, graze across these periphyton fields, like cattle on Montana hillsides. They are well protected from predators under their domed cases, but the larvae are occasionally an element in stream drift, providing a snack for gourmet trout.

Glossosomatid larvae grow quickly, maturing in a year or less. When mature they attach their cases to the substrate with strands of silk, then spin a brown, parchment-like cocoon inside. The larvae molt into pupae, which develop over a period of two to four weeks.

At emergence the pupae cut out of the larval cases and swim, or are buoyed by trapped gases, to the surface. Because of their small size they often go unnoticed by fishermen, but not by fish. Drifting small soft-hackles and flymphs through glides and runs during a hatch of glossosomatids is a joy not to be missed.

Adults fly quickly off the surface to nearby vegetation, where mating occurs shortly after emergence. It is not uncommon to see these small caddis adults fluttering over the water's surface sporadically throughout the day. Afternoon and evening, however, provide the most activity as females begin to oviposit. Like hydropsychids, glossosomatid females commonly crawl under water to lay their eggs. Female adults have special hind legs adapted for swimming back to the surface. When such oviposition occurs fish may feed selectively on these swimming adults.

Imitation

The turtle-cased caddis are too heavily armored and too tightly bound to the substrate in the larval stage to interest fishermen. When the pupae leave their cocoons, however, they are vulnerable to trout and worthy of our notice.

> *CREAM SOFT-HACKLE*
> *Hook: Mustad 94840 (1X fine), Nos. 16-20.*
> *Thread: White.*
> *Body: Cream badger underfur.*
> *Hackle: Gray partridge.*
>
> *HARE'S EAR SOFT-HACKLE*
> *Hook: Mustad 94840 (1X fine), Nos. 16-20.*
> *Thread: Tan.*
> *Body: Tan hare's mask fur.*
> *Hackle: Brown partridge.*

The Cream and Hare's Ear soft-hackles in sizes 16 through 20 are selected to represent the range of glossosomatid colors. They emphasize the versatility of a small selection of these simple patterns.

Presentation

These tiny pupal patterns should be fished with free-drift, mended line tactics.

Adults

It is difficult, if not impossible, for anybody but a professional taxonomist to sort out the various small caddis adults during a mixed hatch. We have found no patterns specifically for the adults listed in the literature. Variations of the Elk Hair Caddis or Bucktail Caddis, in sizes 16 and 18, will provide effective imitation when adults are abundant.

FAMILY: HYDROPTILIDAE

Common Name: Microcaddis.

Emergence and Distribution

J F M A M J J A S O N D

1————————— 30
1———15

Little is known about the life histories of the tiny microcaddis. At least seventeen species in seven genera occur in the West, but because of their small size they are seldom collected. From the data available, it appears that adults emerge mostly in the summer. July, August and early September produce the greatest activity. Because of the insect's minute size it is not unusual for even large hatches to go unnoticed.

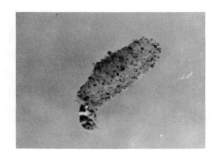

Larval Characteristics
  *a. Each thoracic segment with a sclerotized dorsal shield.
  *b. Gills absent from abdominal segments.
  c. Free-living during first four instars; fifth instar larvae build purse-shaped case of fine sand grains.
  d. Color: Body light cream; darker head and thorax.
  e. Size: Very small; mature larvae range from 2 to 6mm (1/16 - 1/4 inch.)

Pupal Characteristics
  a. Pupation occurs inside sand case of the larva.
  b. Color: Cream, tan or brown.
  c. Size: Minute; from 2 to 6mm (1/16 - 1/4 inch).

Adult Characteristics
  *a. Wings narrow; fringed with long fine hairs.
  b. Antennae shorter than forewings.
  c. Wings lie almost flat over abdomen; moth-like in appearance.
  d. Color: Light brown to tan.
  e. Size: Very small, 2-6mm (1/16 - 1/4 inch).

Habitat

Hydroptilids are adapted to a great variety of habitats: lakes, large warm rivers, cool spring creeks and high mountain streams. Larvae may be found on fine gravel or sand bottoms or in areas with a heavy growth of moss. They prefer slow to moderate currents rather than fast riffles. Because of their small size the larvae are hard to find even if one looks carefully for them. The fine sand case of the last instar larva blends in well with the substrate, appearing as little more than a large speck of sand.

Habits

The first four instars of the microcaddis are spent as free-living larvae. They build no case. During this stage they crawl discretely along the bottom of lakes or moderately flowing streams. These initial growth periods may be short; some species require only twelve to twenty-one days to reach the fifth and final instar. Fifth instar larvae build small purse-like cases of fine sand. This is the longest and most active stage. They eat small filamentous algae and diatoms. These small caddis larvae are sometimes found in the drift in large numbers. It is impossible to say how many are eaten by fish, but an effective imitation is a worthy challenge.

Pupae develop inside the larval case. When mature they cut out of the case and rise to the surface film for emergence. These midge-sized caddis pupae are fed upon eagerly when they emerge in large numbers. The deliberate head-to-tail rises of a midge hatch characterize the feeding behavior during a microcaddis emergence. At such times delicately tied, soft-hackles can produce well.

Newly emerged adults escape quickly from the surface film. These erratic fliers are as difficult to see as the small larvae. They may be confused with a hatch of midges or other small Diptera, but the four hairy wings of the caddis should serve to distinguish them.

Adult microcaddis are generally active throughout the day and evening. Like other caddis, they mate on shoreline foliage. Females return to the water after mating, with oviposition often occurring under water. Fish may feed on adults at the surface, or on submerged females returning to it. The extent of feeding on adults is not known. It probably depends on concentrations and vulnerability of the microcaddis, and the lack of overshadowing hatches of larger insects.

Imitation

Microcaddis are so small they are of little account on most western streams. On many smooth spring rivers, however, they become important. There are times when the angler who overlooks them will interest few trout.

The common name "microcaddis" applies to the family Hydroptilidae. However, other caddis families are also represented by diminutive species. The Philopotamidae, for instance, are often small. Patterns for the microcaddis are useful for the whole spectrum of tiny caddisflies. The wise angler should be aware of their presence and know how to imitate them when necessary.

Larvae

Larval imitations of the microcaddis should be simple. A few turns of dubbing to represent the abdomen and one or two wraps of narrow peacock herl for the head and thorax work well. A few turns of fine lead wire might be needed to sink the fly. Hooks sizes 16 through 24 represent most species.

> *BROWN CADDIS MIDGE NYMPH (Ed Koch)*
> *Hook: Mustad 7948A (1X stout), Nos. 16-24.*
> *Thread: Brown nymph thread.*
> *Body: Bobcat fur.*
> *Head: Peacock herl.*

CREAM CADDIS MIDGE NYMPH (Ed Koch)
Hook: Mustad 7948A (1X stout), Nos. 16-24.
Thread: Brown nymph thread.
Body: Cream fox fur.
Head: Peacock herl.

GRAY CADDIS MIDGE NYMPH (Ed Koch)
Hook: Mustad 7948A (1X stout), Nos. 16-24.
Thread: Gray nymph thread.
Body: Muskrat fur.
Head: Peacock herl.

OLIVE CADDIS MIDGE NYMPH (Ed Koch)
Hook: Mustad 7948A (1X stout), Nos. 16-24.
Thread: Black nymph thread.
Body: Olive spun fur.
Head: Peacock herl.

Presentation

These patterns may represent either cased or uncased larvae. Micro-caddis larval imitations should be fished dead-drift, usually on or near the bottom. They are especially effective for fish seen working in shallow, clear water.

Pupae

Microcaddis pupae call for simple imitations dressed on tiny size 18 to 22 hooks. The soft-hackle patterns outlined by Schwiebert in *Nymphs* cover an array of colors and imitate the pupae perfectly. We have selected five of his twelve patterns as representative.

OLIVE MICROCADDIS PUPA:
PARTRIDGE AND OLIVE (Ernest Schwiebert)
Hook: Mustad 7948A (1X stout), Nos. 18-22.
Thread: Dark brown 6/0 nylon.
Body: Medium olive rayon floss.
Legs: Dark partridge hackle fibers.

PALE MICROCADDIS PUPA:
SNIPE AND YELLOW (Ernest Schwiebert)
Hook: Mustad 7948A (1X stout), Nos. 18-22.
Thread: Medium brown 6/0 nylon.
Body: Dirty yellowish-gray dubbing.
Legs: Light mottled gray snipe hackle fibers.

BROWN MICROCADDIS PUPA:
PARTRIDGE AND BROWN (Ernest Schwiebert)
Hook: Mustad 7948A (1X stout), Nos. 18-22.
Thread: Dark brown 6/0 nylon.
Body: Dark brown dubbing.
Legs: Dark mottled partridge fibers.

ORANGE MICROCADDIS PUPA:
PARTRIDGE AND ORANGE (Ernest Schwiebert)
Hook: Mustad 7948A (1X stout), Nos. 18-22.
Thread: Dark brown 6/0 nylon.
Body: Dirty orange rayon floss.
Legs: Light mottled partridge backle fibers.

DUN MICROCADDIS PUPA:
DARK SNIPE AND HARE'S EAR (Ernest Schwiebert)
Hook: Mustad 7948A (1X stout), Nos. 18-22.
Thread: Dark brown 6/0 nylon.
Body: Dark brownish-gray hare's mask dubbing.
Legs: Dark mottled snipe backle fibers.

Presentation

These small soft-hackles should be dressed sparsely to increase the movement of the individual hackle fibers. Microcaddis pupal patterns should be fished just under the surface film. They are most effective when presented to rising fish, with dry fly tactics, using upstream casts. The soft-hackle tactics outlined by Sylvester Nemes in *The Soft-Hackled Fly,* using across stream casts and a series of mends to keep the fly drifting drag-free, are also effective.

Adults

We have not encountered situations in which microcaddis adults were important. If your fishing presents such a problem, we recommend the use of standard midge patterns. If these fail, Bucktail Caddis, Elk Hair Caddis, or Quill-Wing Caddis dressings may prove worth the trouble it takes to tie them in such small sizes.

Hydroptilids crawl under the water to deposit their eggs on underwater rocks and logs. Tiny soft-hackles or size 18 to 22 wet fly patterns such as the March Brown, Hare's Ear, or Blue Dun may prove effective if fish are feeding on returning females.

FAMILIES: BRACHYCENTRIDAE

LEPIDOSTOMATIDAE

Common Name: Grannom.

Emergence and Distribution (Brachycentridae)

J	F	M	A	M	J	J	A	S	O	N	D
1										15	
				1				31			

Emergence and Distribution (Lepidostomatidae)

J	F	M	A	M	J	J	A	S	O	N	D
		1						30			
		1					31				

These two families represent some of the most important case making caddis found in western streams. The Grannom pattern, imitating several species of the genus *Brachycentrus,* originated in England and is important across the United States as well.

In the West the family Lepidostomatidae is represented by a single genus, *Lepidostoma,* which contains approximately eighteen species. The family Brachycentridae is represented by at least four genera and eight species. This diversity is typical of western caddisflies.

Emergence of the different species often overlaps (see emergence chart). Emergence also extends over a long period of time, with the heaviest hatch periods dependent upon the dominant species in an area, stream conditions and yearly climatic factors. The array of species and habitats present in the West makes the determination of definitive emergence dates impossible. Familiarity with the insects in your home streams is necessary to successfully time your fishing over these case making caddis.

Larval Characteristics (Brachycentridae)
*a. No humps on first abdominal segment.
*b. Antennae minute; situated closer to mandibles than to eyes.
c. Top of first two thoracic segments completely sclerotized, third segment with several small sclerotized plates.
d. Larval case constructed of fine plant fragments or sand grains, forming a rectangular or round tapered case.
e. Size: Length 6-12mm (1/4 - 1/2 inch).

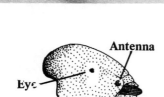

Figure 31. Brachycentrid larvae.

Eye   Antenna

Figure 32. Head of Brachycentrid

Pupal Characteristics

a. Pupation occurs inside larval case.
b. Color: Tan, or light to dark brown.
c. Size: 6 to 12mm (1/4 - 1/2 inch).

*Adult Characteristics

a. Ocelli absent.
b. Antennae equal to or slightly shorter than body length.
c. Color: Body light tan or brown; wings gray with brown markings.
d. Size: From 6 to 12mm (1/4 - 1/2 inch).

Larval Characteristics (Lepidostomatidae)

*a. Lateral humps present but dorsal hump absent on first abdominal segment.
*b. Antennae minute, situated closer to eye than to mandible.
c. Top of first two thoracic segments completely sclerotized, third segment with several small sclerotized plates.
d. Mature larvae may have one of three case types: Log cabin, tubular sand grain, or rectangular chimney-shaped cases.
e. Size: 6 to 10 mm (1/4 - 1/2 inch).

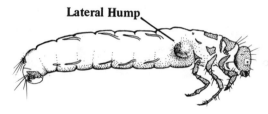

Figure 33. Lepidostomatid larvae.

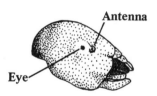

Figure 34. Head of Lepidostomatid

Pupal Characteristics

a. Pupation occurs inside larval case.
b. Color: Tan, cream, or light to dark brown.
c. Size: 6 to 12mm (1/4 - 1/2 inch).

*Adult Characteristics

a. Ocelli absent.
b. Antennae equal to or slightly shorter than body length.
c. Color: Body light tan or brown; wings gray with brown markings.
d. Size: 6 to 12mm (1/4 - 1/2 inch).

*The descriptions for brachycentrid and lepidostomatid adults are identical. They cannot be separated without a microscope and scientific key.

Habitat

Both families prefer running water. Lepidostomatids are generally found in backwaters, pools or quiet areas near shore. Occasionally they are found in ponds or lakes. Brachycentrids like faster water. Their finely constructed cases are often attached to the upper surfaces of rocks in riffles and runs. They are also found in large numbers in moss, filamentous algae or rooted plants growing in medium to fast currents.

These two families inhabit a wide range of stream sizes and types. Small mountain streams are the preference of several species; others prefer larger, slower streams where algae and detritus are abundant.

Habits

Lepidostomatids are primarily detritivores. Decaying leaves and pine needles are their dominant foods. Some species shred away the soft parts of leaves until only a skeleton of veins remains. Brachycentrids feed more on in-stream plant growth, rather than detritus of terrestrial origin. Diatoms, either scraped off rocks or filtered from the water, from the dominant food for several species. Others feed on filamentous algae, mosses or rooted plants.

During their development the larvae of both families are relatively slow moving and inactive. They are unable to swim. If washed off the bottom they drift with the current until the bottom can be regrasped. Brachycentrids live in faster water than lepidostomatids: Insect drift studies have shown that large numbers of brachycentrids are common in the drift. When in the drift the larvae are readily available to feeding trout.

Just prior to pupation the larvae attach their cases to the substrate and close off the front opening. Lepidostomatids often move to slower water to pupate; brachycentrids pupate in moderate to fast water. Pupal development is completed in approximately four weeks, at which time the pupae cut free of the cases and swim to the surface. The pupal skin splits open quickly, allowing the adults to escape. Emergence is heaviest in the evening.

Adults of both families mate on the foliage shortly after emergence. Eggs are laid in clusters under water, usually in slow to moderate currents near shore. Oviposition may occur throughout the day. Both families have one year life cycles.

Imitation

It is difficult to sort out and identify the various caddis groups during a rise. There are frequently two, three, or even more species from different families emerging at the same time. Brachycentrids and lepidostomatids, with a basketful of western species, and long hatching periods, are often involved in these mixed emergences. Until you encounter a selective rise to a specific species we recommend the use of a few suggestive patterns tied to match a variety of insects.

Larvae

Trout take the larvae of these two families readily, case and all. Twigs, pine needles, and other bits of organic debris in stomach samples often are a hint that trout have been feeding on cased caddis. When the water is not clear we have had excellent luck using Gold Ribbed Hare's Ears and Zug Bugs, two of our favorite searching patterns. Tied on 1X long hooks in sizes 10 through 16, they resemble the dark colors and stick-like shape of the naturals.

HERL NYMPH
Hook: Mustad 9671 (2X long), Nos. 10-16.
Thread: Black.
Body: Peacock herl.
Collar: Black ostrich herl.
Legs: Black hackle fibers.

We have found the simple Herl Nymph to be a taker even in glass-clear water when fish are taking caddis larvae in their cases.

Presentation

Typical of caddis, the larvae of brachycentrids and lepidostomatids have no ability to swim, and crawl laboriously across the bottom. Their imitations should be fished in the same way. Hand-twist retrieves and slightly weighted flies are the best combination.

We once lucked onto a desert stream below a reservoir just after the water had been shut down to a trickle flow. The fish were fat and sassy, but they were also confined to small pools, sheltered by overhanding willows and separated by miniature riffles. We fished for some time before we caught a fish on a large Zug Bug. Its stomach contained several Brachycentridae larvae. The Zug Bug was a good match in color and shape, but it was several sizes bigger than the natural. We switched to smaller sizes and began casting them into the deep water of the almost-still pools. After a few patient seconds to let them sink we began slow retrieves. The only hint of a take was usually a twitch at the end of the floating line. The fish were rainbows. They charged up and down the little pools and careened all over the surface. The amount of disturbance was startling: Fish fight wildly when confined in a small space. The largest weighed just over three pounds.

Pupae

Simple soft-hackled flies with fur bodies of hare's mask and hackles of brown partridge may be the most effective imitations for these pupae. They should be tied on standard hooks, in sizes 10 through 14.

AMERICAN GRANNOM (Ernest Schwiebert)
Hook: Mustad 3906, Nos. 10-14.
Thread: Dark brown 6/0 nylon.
Body: Dark brown dubbing ribbed with fine oval tinsel.
Thorax: Deep-chocolate-colored dubbing.
Wingcases: Slate-colored duck quill sections tied at the sides.
Legs: Darkly mottled partridge body hackle.
Antennae: Brown mallard fibers.
Head: Dark brown nylon.

This exact imitation copies some western species of Brachycentridae and Lepidostomatidae. It also will serve as a model on which to base variations for hatches you might encounter that are lighter or darker in color.

Presentation

Pupal patterns should be presented dead-drift on a mended line, or with a Leisenring lift to bring the fly up through the water in the suspected lie of a fish.

Adults

Dry patterns for these families have not been worked out. You must be prepared to create your own if you find them taken selectively. We suggest you base your fly selection on the water to be fished. If it is rough water the suggestive Bucktail Caddis style will be needed for its excellent flotation. If the water is gentle a delicate Quill-Wing Caddis will present a better outline of the natural and still float well. The patterns may be fished dead-drift or skittered over the surface under shoreline vegetation.

FAMILY: LIMNEPHILIDAE

Common Names: Cinnamon Sedge, Fall Caddis, Dark Sedge, Orange Sedge, Periwinkle.

Emergence and Distribution

J   F   M   A   M   J   J   A   S   O   N   D

1————————————————15

1——————————30

The family Limnephilidae contains the greatest number of species of any North American caddisfly family. Over three hundred species in fifty-two genera are now listed. This number will likely increase as more are discovered and classified.

The western states, with their wide variety of climates and habitats, contain a wealth of limnephilids. Dr. N. H. Anderson, in his *Distribution and Biology of Oregon Trichoptera,* states that there are thirty-five genera and about ninety species of limnephilids in Oregon alone. The number of species occurring in all the western states and provinces is not known, but it is likely well over 100 species.

The emergence periods of such a large and diverse family are obviously impossible to define precisely. Some limnephilids will be emerging through each of the spring, summer, and fall months, as shown by the emergence chart. Examination of various emergence records shows the period of greatest activity to be in the summer and fall.

Larval Characteristics

*a. Small antennae, located midway between eye and front edge of the mandibles.

*b. Lateral and dorsal humps present on first abdominal segment.

c. Cases constructed from a wide variety of materials: Rocks, sand, twigs, grass, leaves, pine needles, and even snail shells.

d. Size: Mature larvae 6-30mm (1/4 to 1-1/4 inches). Most species are moderate to large.

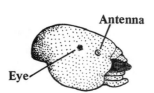

Figure 36. Head of Limnephilid

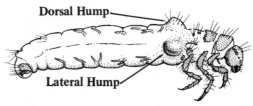

Figure 35. Limnephilid larvae.

Pupal Characteristics

a. Pupation occurs inside case of larva.

b. Color: Varies widely; includes browns, tans, greens and yellows.

c. Size: Similar to larvae; 6-30mm (1/4 to 1-1/4 inches).

*Adult Characteristics

*a. Ocelli present.

b. Antennae approximately body length for most species.

c. Color: Patterns on wings and abdomen highly variable.

d. Size: Range similar to larvae; 6-30mm (1/4 to 1-1/4 inches).

*Color and size cannot be used as diagnostic characteristics for this family because of the large number of species, and the wide variations between them.

Habitat

The array of habitats occupied by the family Limnephilidae is proportionate to the number of species. Lakes, ponds, sloughs, small mountain streams, fast and slow rivers, even ditches and temporary ponds and streams can harbor large numbers of these ubiquitous caddisflies. The larvae may be found on sand or silty bottoms, gravel and rocky substrates, and areas where wood sticks, leaves and other detritus accumulate.

The successful adaptation of many species of Limnephilidae to still waters makes this family particularly important in lakes. The Canadian Sedge (*Limnephilus* sp.) for example, is relished by large trout in lakes throughout Canada and the northern states. In some streams limnephilids are overshadowed by *Rhyacophila* and *Hydropsyche* species, but the limnephilids' tolerance of warmer and slower water makes them more important in many localities.

Habits

All limnephilids are true case makers. The designs and materials used for case making are seemingly endless. Sand grains, small gravel, twigs, pieces of leaves, grass stems, pine needles, and small snail shells are all grist for the mill. Some species change their case material during larval development. For example *Clistoronia magnifica*, a lake species, build cases of pine needles or leaf fragments as young larvae, but final instar larvae switch to a case of fine sand grains. Generally, stream species build cases of mineral material, which acts as ballast, keeping the larvae on the bottom. Lake species use plant material that is of neutral buoyancy.

Limnephilid larvae, whether from streams or lakes, do not swim. The larvae tend to stay on the bottom, where they feed heavily on detritus. Lake forms often climb among rooted vegetation, feeding on the leaves and attached algae. Stream specimens, because of their heavy cases, do not drift far if washed off the bottom. As a result, limnephilid larvae are not readily available to feeding fish. However, fish do feed on them, attested to by the amount of sand, gravel, and twigs found in fish stomach samples.

Most limnephilids mature within a year, although some take longer. Mature larvae select protected areas around rocks or other bottom cover for pupation. The final act of the mature larva is to attach the case firmly to the bottom and close off its opening. Pupation occurs inside this

safely sealed larval case. Complete pupal development requires from three to eight weeks, depending on the species and conditions. The famous Fall Caddis begins pupation as early as August and does not emerge until October.

Fully formed pupae cut through the larval case and swim quickly to the surface. Some swim to nearby shallows, where the adult emerges. As with other caddis, the pupae are particularly vulnerable to feeding fish. The large size of many limnephilids—up to one and one half inches long—makes the pupae attractive even to lunkers. Many species emerge in the late evening or at night and avoid heavy predation.

When free of the pupal shuck the adults fly to shoreline vegetation. Mating follows and the gravid females return to the stream or lake to oviposit. Most limnephilid adults oviposit at or near the water's surface, but several unique species lay their eggs above the water. When these hatch the larvae drop into the water to follow a typical aquatic life cycle.

Swarms of ovipositing adults often produce heavy feeding by fish late in the evening. As coming night inks out the stream, the last few females dance over its surface: A heavy splash, heard but not seen, fills the darkness and there is one less caddis. But enough survive to continue their underwater masonry, enriching our lives with the knowledge of their presence.

Imitation

Limnephilids are so diverse there is no hope for giving patterns to match all of them. They are a perfect example of the need to be aware of an insect family's behavior and life cycle, and being prepared to create patterns of your own to match it. The pupal and adult stages are always important. Even the larvae, armored as they are, can be important in certain situations.

Larvae

Larval limnephilids are all case-dwellers. Patterns for them should represent the insect as well as its house. Typical dressings are weighted. They depict the case with clipped palmer hackle or hair, the legs with black hackle, and have heads of dark herl. Sizes range from 6 through 16. Patterns like the Gold Ribbed Hare's Ear and Zug Bug, mentioned for the cased Brachycentridae and Lepodostomatidae, are also excellent for some limnephilidae.

> *CASED CADDIS (George Bodmer)*
> *Hook: Mustad 9671 (2X long), Nos. 10-16.*
> *Thread: Black.*
> *Ribbing: Copper wire.*
> *Underbody: Tapered dark brown floss or yarn.*
> *Overbody: Brown and black saddle hackle, palmered over underbody, then clipped short.*
> *Head: Black ostrich.*

This dressing is designed to represent species which build their cases of dark materials. Most river dwellers and some lake species are imitated well by it.

> *STRAWMAN (Paul Young)*
> *Hook: Mustad 9671 (2X long), Nos. 10-14.*
> *Thread: Brown.*
> *Tail: Mallard flank fibers.*
> *Body: Spun deer hair, clipped with a taper.*
> *Hackle: Light partridge or grizzly (optional).*

The Strawman represents those species which build their cases of light colored materials. Many lake species construct cases with grass and other vegetation. They are well represented by the Strawman.

> **CASED CADDIS**
> *Hook: Mustad 36890, Nos. 6-12.*
> *Thread: Black.*
> *Body: Natural case, glued to hook.*
> *Head: Black ostrich herl.*
> *Legs: Black hackle fibers, as throat.*

The heavier pebble-cased caddis are stream dwellers. It is unethical to scour the stream for live larvae, discarding the caddis worm and using the case for an imitation. The water ouzel, our entertaining dipper-bird, makes its living by fishing for periwinkles on the stream bottom. They eat the larvae and discard the case. During days on small, boulder-studded streams, look for the cases on top of rocks. They will be clean, dry and ready to slip over a hook shank to be glued with five minute epoxy.

Presentation

All of the larval patterns should be fished either dead-drift in fast water or with a very slow hand-twist retrieve in still water. Enough weight should be wound under the body to keep the fly on the bottom. In clear water lake situations it is often effective to cast the fly out, let it sink to the bottom, then watch for a cruising trout. As the fish approaches, give the fly a small movement to attract its attention. This works especially well with the Strawman.

Pupae

Many of the previously mentioned soft-hackled flies and flymphs serve as excellent imitations for limnephilid pupae. These pattern types also serve as perfect models for the creation of any pupal dressings you find necessary. The following patterns were designed for members of this family. They will give ideas for imitations in both a simple style and an exact copy of the natural.

> **DARK CADDIS EMERGENT (Polly Rosborough)**
> *Hook: Mustad 3906B (1X long), No. 8.*
> *Thread: Black.*
> *Ribbing: Orange thread.*
> *Body: Light orange synthetic yarn.*
> *Hackle: Furnace, clip top and bottom.*
> *Head: Black ostrich.*

Polly's excellent pupal pattern is a nice compromise between soft-hackle simplicity and exact imitation. It matches an emergence on his southern Oregon waters from the first of August until the end of the season in October. He recommends fishing it with short casts to rising fish, retrieving it with fast, two-inch jerks. Polly also ties a similar Light Caddis Emergent. *Tying and Fishing the Fuzzy Nymphs* lists valuable dressings for adult dry and wet flies in the dark and light colors.

MEDIUM CINNAMON SEDGE PUPA (Ernest Schwiebert)
Hook: Mustad 3906, Nos. 8-10.
Thread: Dark brown 6/0 nylon.
Body: Dark orangish fur dubbing.
Thorax: Dark brown fur.
Wingcases: Dark-brownish-gray duck quill sections tied at sides.
Legs: Darkly mottled grouse hackle.
Antennae: Lemon woodduck fibers.
Head: Dark brown nylon.

This imitative pattern is tied for a western limnephilid and will serve as the basis for size and color variations to imitate others.

Presentation

Many limnephilid pupae emerge by moving across the bottom to shallow water next to shore. There they emerge in the surface film or crawl out on streamside vegetation. This behavior is common among stream species and suggests that imitations should be presented on or near the bottom. If standard wet fly drifts, the mending tactics of Nemes, or a Leisenring lift prove fruitless, a tumbling dead-drift with a weighted pattern might produce during pupal migrations.

Many lake species emerge in open water. The pupae often must swim ten or twelve feet to the surface. A June hatch of a large limnephilid on Oregon's Hosmer Lake drives the Atlantic salmon into a feeding frenzy. They ignore dozens of adults gyrating across the surface, but swim fifteen feet to take a nymph of the wrong size and color — *if* it is swept up from the bottom in the manner of a caddis pupa dashing to the surface. This method calls for a floating line, long leader, weighted fly, and a cast well ahead of the cruising fish. As they approach the fly it should be brought to the surface with a steady lifting of the rod tip. Pupae do not stop on their way up; if you get nervous and stop your rod, or twitch it in a manner foreign to the natural, following fish will usually turn away. When fishing over heavily fished populations, such as Hosmer's educated salmon, it is helpful to cast to fish coming straight toward you. They will see the fly but not the line or leader.

Adults

Because limnephilids are larger than most caddis their adult imitations tend to be bushy and high floating rather than exact. Most are modeled after the famous Bucktail Caddis, itself an excellent dressing for many of these hatches.

BUCKTAIL CADDIS
Hook: Mustad 94840 (1X fine), Nos. 4-12.
Thread: Black.
Tail: Ginger hackle fibers.
Hackle: Ginger, palmered.
Body: Orange floss or yarn.
Wing: Natural brown bucktail.

This is the standard dressing for the Bucktail Caddis. It can be varied in many ways. The Elk Hair Caddis, created by Al Troth of Dillon, Montana, is a successful variation of this old pattern.

> *ORANGE CADDIS (Dave McNeese)*
> *Hook: Mustad 94840 (1X fine), Nos. 6-8.*
> *Thread: Gray.*
> *Hackle: Grizzly mixed with dyed orange.*
> *Body: Pale orange fur.*
> *Wing: Natural dun bucktail.*

This bucktail type was created by Dave McNeese for the Fall Caddis which emerges in late September and October. It is an important dressing on many western waters.

> *DARK CADDIS (Polly Rosborough)*
> *Hook: Mustad 94840 (1X fine), Nos. 2-8.*
> *Thread: Black.*
> *Rib: Very dark brown hackle, palmered.*
> *Body: Dirty orange wool or fur.*
> *Hackle: Very dark brown hackle collar.*
> *Wing: Dark brown deer hair or equivalent.*

Polly's Dark Caddis represents the adult stage of the pupa matched by his Dark Caddis Emergent.

Presentation

Exact imitations of such large insects are hard to float. In streams it is better to achieve a good float at the cost of imitation. On lakes we have found fish often concentrate on the pupae and ignore even natural adults. Where they do take them, large versions of the Quill-Wing Caddis might be more effective than less exact ties.

These large caddis adults often flop and skitter on the surface during emergence or oviposition. Imitating this behavior by skittering their patterns across the surface can produce smashing takes.

Chapter Seven
Alderflies and Dobsonflies
Order: Megaloptera

The order Megaloptera is made up of two families. Sialidae, or alderflies, are the dark, awkward, caddis-like insects seen in mid-summer along tree-shrouded streams and lakes. Corydalidae contains the large but infrequently seen dobsonflies, the larvae of which are called hellgrammites. An ancient order, the Megaloptera were evolving 270 million years ago. Primitive Megaloptera are believed to include the ancestral stock for several insect orders, including the caddisflies.

Megaloptera have complete metamorphosis, with larval, pupal and adult stages. The larvae are extremely predacious, using well developed mandibles for seizing and subduing prey.

Larvae leave the water and dig burrows in the soil for pupation. When development is complete the pupa digs back to the surface and sheds its shuck.

Megaloptera adults deposit their eggs in a unique manner. They do not return to the water, but lay their eggs in rows on the undersides of leaves, grass stems, or branches that overhang the water. When the larvae hatch they drop into the water and immediately begin searching for prey.

FAMILY: SIALIDAE

Common Name: Alderflies.

Emergence and Distribution

J F M A M J J A S O N D
1————————— 31

Alderflies begin to emerge with the first warmth of spring and are most active on the warmest days of late May, June and early July. Shallow ponds and lakes, which warm up fast, have the earliest emergences. Deep lakes, and streams cooled by snow melt or cold ground water, have later hatches.

Alderflies are distributed throughout the West. Populations are greatest in streams or lakes where trees form a heavy canopy over the water. The name alderfly stems from their prevalence in alder trees along British trout streams. Their greatest western importance is in the forested Pacific Northwest, from Oregon through Washington, and into British Columbia. They can be found, however, wherever habitat is suitable.

Larval Characteristics
  *a. A pair of lateral gill filaments on each abdominal segment 1 through 7.
  *b. Last abdominal segment ends in a long terminal process.
   c. Color: Light tan to brown.
   d. Size: 6-18mm (1/4 - 3/4 inch).

Adult Characteristics

*a. Pronotum thick, as wide or wider than head.

*b. Wings held tent-like over body; wings parchment-like, lacking hairs.

 c. Antennae one-half body length; tails absent.

 d. Color: Body and wings smoky-gray or black.

 e. Size: 6-18mm (1/4 - 3/4 inch).

Habitat

Alderfly larvae are found in both still waters and streams. Lake and pond dwellers hunt in the top layer of the substrate. They prowl through leaf packs, decaying vegetation and the muck and mud of the bottom.

In streams they prefer marginal areas and eddies; places where silt and debris are deposited. They are rarely found in riffles or fast running water. Still, dark pools, carpeted with decomposing debris built up over the years, are sure to have populations of alderfly larvae hunting through the layers of leaves.

Habit

Alderfly larvae are voracious predators. They live on midge larvae, small crustaceans, and if opportunity presents, each other. Their preference for prowling just under the substrate rather than over it reduces their exposure to fish. Stomach autopsies occasionally turn up sialid larvae. Seldom, however, are more than one or two found in a sample. We have seen no evidence that fish get chances to be selective for them.

When the larvae reach maturity in spring or early summer they crawl out on shore and burrow into the bank. The pupal stage is of no use to fishermen. Pupation takes one to two weeks.

Sialid adults congregate in willows and alders along streams and lakes. They are clumsy fliers, often preferring to run when disturbed. Their poor flight and habit of clambering about in trees overhanging water often gets them in trouble with trout. They are most active when the sun is warmest. They crawl along the edges of floating logs or fly hopefully from tree to tree. On the frequent occasions that bring them to water they sink almost immediately. Their surface struggles are brief and seldom succeed in anything but making a rent in the surface film. Trout often take them there; more often they take them after they have sunk. The most successful imitation is dressed and fished as a wet fly.

Alderflies mate on the foliage and deposit their eggs on objects overhanging the water. Eggs are laid in neat rows on the undersides of leaves or grasses. The larvae hatch at night in about one to two weeks, dropping to the water and beginning their search for prey. The typical alderfly life cycle lasts one year.

Imitation

The secretive habits of alderfly larvae reduce their importance as insects to be imitated. Pupation occurs in the soil; patterns for the pupae are pointless. Imitations of the adult stage can be valuable during emergences on tree-shrouded streams and lakes.

We offer larval patterns tentatively; the average angler will find few occasions to use them. The dressings for adults are patterns that we use every year, whenever alderflies are in season.

Larvae

Alderfly larvae are not often available to trout. At no time are they likely to be fed on selectively. We have, however, found them in occasional stomach samples, and their imitations may occasionally have value.

BROWN WOOLLY WORM
Hook: Mustad 9672 (3X long), Nos. 10-14.
Thread: Brown.
Hackle: Grizzly, palmered.
Body: Slender brown chenille

Alderfly larvae are among the many insects that can be suggested with Woolly Worms. A few of these dressings in various colors will take trout in many situations.

SMOKY ALDER LARVA (George L. Herter)
Hook: Mustad 9671 (2X long), Nos. 10-14.
Thread: Yellow.
Tail: Ginger hackle tip, clipped short.
Ribbing Hackle: White, short, clipped top and bottom.
Body: Back one-half brown or dark brown wool, front one-half yellow wool.
Hackle: Yellow, trimmed top and bottom.

This larval pattern is a closer copy of the natural. We suggest it as a dressing that will work for most western alderfly larvae if a situation is encountered in which a close copy is needed.

Presentation

In late spring and early summer, on days when trout are not working on the surface, we recommend crawling a brown Woolly Worm in sizes 10-14 across the bottom of a lake or pond. It might tap the trout's memory of a recent larva intercepted as it migrated toward shore for pupation.

Adults

The alderfly characteristic of sinking almost immediately on contact with water presents an interesting opportunity: They are usually matched with a wet fly. In lakes trout are generally more willing to accept a sunken alderfly imitation rather than a dry pattern. On streams, where fish are forced to make quicker decisions, a dry dressing is more effective.

ALDER (Wet Fly)
Hook: Mustad 3906, Nos. 8-12.
Thread: Black.
Rib: Narrow gold tinsel.
Body: Peacock herl.
Hackle: Black.
Wings: Dark brown turkey tail feather sections.

We have found this the most effective alderfly imitation in lakes and in streams of fair size. It copies the dark body and roof-like wings of the natural adult. It is fished wet; the hackle should be soft and the wings tied in wet fly fashion. We usually omit the rib on our own dressings, but include it here because it is standard for the pattern.

QUILL-WING ALDERFLY
Hook: Mustad 94833 (3X fine), Nos. 10-14.
Thread: Black.
Hackle: Coachman brown, palmered, clipped on top.
Body: Dark brown seal.
Wings: Dark gray mallard or goose quill sections.

This dressing is a takeoff on the dry Quill-Wing Caddis pattern. It is extremely effective in late June and early July on small, alder-canopied Pacific coastal streams. A dry fly is favored on these tiny waters because all casting must be done straight upstream, and the fish rise freely to dy flies.

Presentation

The wet Alder is presented with a standard wet fly stripping retrieve. The strips should be short: No more than four to six inches. It is usually fished in the shallows of lakes, or around fallen logs. A dry line and nine to twelve foot leader keep the fly near the surface, where trout cruise as they wait for a clumsy alderfly to land on the water.

The dry pattern is presented in streams with standard upstream casts. It is not a good floater; it fishes best in slick runs and still pools. It is not an easy fly with which to probe pocket water. Because it is dark it is difficult to see. Trout are accustomed to taking quickly in these waters, however, and while you may not see your fly you will often see a swirl or bold splash when it is taken.

FAMILY: CORYDALIDAE

Common Names: Dobsonflies (adults); Hellgrammites (larvae).

Emergence and Distribution

J F M A M J J A S O N D
1———30

Larvae of the family Corydalidae are called hellgrammites. Adults are called dobsonflies. We are fortunate this two-part naming system did not befall all aquatic insects; it would cause exactly twice the confusion.

Dobsonflies—the adults—appear in spring and early summer. They are large, with up to six-inch wingspans. They are short-lived—only two to three days—and feeble fliers. They are not often seen, nor are they important to fishermen.

Hellgrammites—the larval stage—are large and of interest to fish. They are distributed from Canada to California along the Pacific Coast. They are not common in the Rocky Mountains or the Great Basin area.

Larval Characteristics
  *a. Lateral gill filaments on abdominal segments 1 through 8.
  *b. Last abdominal segment with a pair of anal hooks.
  c. Large mandibles.
  d. Color: Black.
  e. Size: Up to 75mm (3 inches).

Adult Characteristics
  a. Long antennae.
  b. Some males with large sickle-shaped mandibles.
  c. No tails.
  d. Color: Dark gray or brown.
  e. Size: 50mm (2 inches) or longer.

Habitat
  Hellgrammites are found in fast, boulder-strewn currents. They crawl actively through the spaces between rocks, and beneath the actual bed of

the stream. They are primarily nocturnal, and are seldom collected unless the sample is taken deep in the gravel.

Some species have adapted to streams that dry up for part of the year. Hellgrammites are much more abundant in the Midwest and East than in the West.

Habits

Corydalids have a two to four year life cycle, most of which is spent as larvae. The larvae are fierce predators and feed heavily on any animal they can subdue. They are poor swimmers, preferring to crawl along the bottom. These large, strong larvae are rare in the drift.

When mature the larvae crawl from the water and burrow into rotten logs or dig under the soil for pupation. After about two weeks the adult emerges. Adults lack developed mouthparts or digestive tracts for feeding. Like mayflies they live only two or three days, just long enough to mate and deposit their eggs. The eggs are laid in rows on objects hanging over streambeds; wooden bridges are favorite sites. After five or six days the larvae emerge and fall to the water.

Imitation

Only the larval stage is important to fishermen. They are large, and a mouthful for any fish. Their secretive, nocturnal habits hinder their value, but in some localized situations their imitations are effective.

Our experience has been that hellgrammites live in the same type of habitat that Giant Salmon Fly nymphs, *Pteronarcys californica*, inhabit. These two are so parallel in size, form, color, and water type that we feel imitations for one will usually work for the other. Dressings for both make excellent searching patterns in rough water.

> *HELLGRAMMITE (Terry Hellekson)*
> *Hook: Mustad 79580 (4X long), Nos. 4-8.*
> *Thread: Black.*
> *Legs: One black and one brown saddle hackle tied palmer over the body; clip hackle on top and bottom, then trim in taper at sides, wide at front, narrow at back.*
> *Body: Black chenille.*

This is a simple dressing based on the Woolly Worm. The Black Woolly Worm can also be used as a hellgrammite imitation.

> *HELLGRAMMITE (Doug Prince)*
> *Hook: Mustad 9672 (3X long), Nos. 6-10.*
> *Thread: Black.*
> *Tail: Black goose quill fibers taken from the back of a flight quill and tied in a "V".*
> *Ribbing: Black ostrich herl, abdomen only; clip herl down to about 1/16 inch.*
> *Body: Black floss.*
> *Wingcase: Black goose quill section tied in over thorax.*
> *Thorax: Dubbed black rabbit fur with a strip of red wool yarn pulled across the bottom.*
> *Legs: Black hackle wrapped through thorax and one black goose quill fiber tied in at each side and tied so tips flare outward.*

Presentation

Hellgrammites are bottom dwellers. Their imitations should be weighted with enough turns of lead to get them down in fast water. The naturals seldom swim. Patterns for them should be tumbled along the bottom, fished exactly like the stonefly imitations which they resemble so closely.

Chapter Eight
Water Beetles
Order: Coleoptera

The worldwide species list of Coleoptera, both aquatic and terrestrial, is estimated at 300,000. Species which are semi-aquatic or truly aquatic number around 5,000. Probably between three and four hundred species of semi-aquatic beetles are found in the western region. This number will likely increase with increased collecting and taxonomic revision.

The earliest fossil records of aquatic beetles are from the Upper Permian era, approximately 200 million years ago. Fossils clearly related to present day aquatic beetles have been found from the Jurassic period, 180 to 135 million years ago. Evidence indicates that aquatic forms evolved from more abundant terrestrial groups.

Aquatic Coleoptera, or water beetles, are fairly easily distinguished from other aquatic insects. Adults are quickly recognized by the hardened front wings, or elytra, which cover the hindwings and abdomen. These give adult beetles a hard, shiny appearance.

Larval stages of aquatic beetles are not so easy to pin down. They are typified by three pairs of thoracic legs, a distinctly segmented abdomen, and either filament-like gills on each abdominal segment, a breathing tube at the end of the abdomen, or no external gills at all. Larval stages are most easily confused with free-living caddisflies and hellgrammites. However, aquatic beetle larvae lack anal hooks, which are found on both of these groups.

Beetles are found in every aquatic habitat. They are not commonly observed because of the underwater habits of both larvae and adults. Numerous species are found in rapid streams, ponds, puddles, and even water caught in tree boles. Lakes, ponds, and slow sections of streams hold the largest number of beetles and provide the greatest fishing opportunities.

All beetles have complete metamorphosis, passing through egg, larval, pupal and adult stages. Some actively hunt prey; others lie in wait to ambush their food. Many species have chewing mouthparts. Others use a pair of hollow mandibles to pierce the prey's skin, injecting a digestive enzyme. The tissue of the prey is liquefied and sucked up through the mandibles. Larval respiration is from the surface through a breathing tube, under water by using various types of gills, or by simple diffusion of oxygen through the cuticle. Larvae usually pass through three instars, maturing in less than a year.

The larvae of most families leave the water to pupate, but some remain under water as pupae. The pupae are not important as fish food, and are not worth imitating.

Adult water beetles, like the larvae, are aquatic. The majority of species are active swimmers with oar-like hind legs. Adults feed on other insects, or on plant and decaying organic material. Adults rely on atmospheric air and must periodically come to the surface for more. They carry a bubble of air under water and can remain submerged for several minutes.

Mating and egg laying also occur under water for most species. After mating, the female lays her eggs inside submerged wood or plant stems, or buries them in the substrate. Adults live longer than many aquatic insects, remaining active for two or more months. They often live through the winter and lay their eggs in the spring.

There are approximately thirty families of semi-aquatic or aquatic beetles. Only two, the Dytiscidae and Hydrophilidae, are of major importance to fishermen.

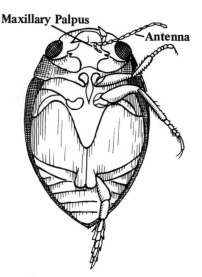

Figure 37. Ventral view of Dytiscid adult.

FAMILY: DYTISCIDAE

Common Names: Predaceous Water Beetles, Water Tigers, Diving Water Beetles.

Emergence and Distribution

Both larval and adult stages are aquatic; there is no emergence as it has been used for most other orders. Adults are present from late summer through the winter. Eggs are laid in spring and hatch in approximately one week. The larvae grow through the spring and summer months. When mature, they crawl from the water and form a pupal cell several inches under soil, logs or rocks. The adult emerges from the pupal cell in a month to six weeks and returns to the water.

Dytiscidae is the largest family of aquatic beetles. They are abundant throughout the world and are the most common aquatic beetles seen by casual observers. There are approximately thirty-eight genera of dytiscids in the West.

Larval Characteristics
*a. Mandibles large and sickle-shaped; designed for piercing and sucking.
*b. Each leg with five segments ending in two movable claws.
*c. Last abdominal segment ending in a hollow breathing tube.
 d. Color: Body brown, tan or olive.
 e. Size: Up to 38mm (1-1/2 inches).

Adult Characteristics
*a. Antennae not club-like; longer than maxillary palpi.
 b. Hind legs oar-like; fringed with long lateral hairs.
 c. Color: Body shiny; black or brown.
 d. Size: Length ranging from 6 to 38mm (1/4 to 1-1/2 inches).

Habitat

Dytiscids are found mainly in ponds and lakes, but also inhabit fast flowing streams and rivers, and even hot springs up to 105°F. Lakes and slow areas of streams with plenty of weedy shallows harbor the largest populations. The larvae search for prey near the bottom in shallow water; adults swim actively near the surface. Dytiscids are well adapted to the varied stream and lake conditions found in the West. A dedicated fisherman will sooner or later find the situation where fishing a dytiscid pattern can save an otherwise fishless day.

Habits

Larval dytiscids are fierce predators, commonly called water tigers. They stalk the weedy areas of streams and lakes, or hide in the weeds, ready to ambush prey as it swims by. They breathe atmospheric air obtained through breathing tubes at the tips of their abdomens. This reliance on surface oxygen prevents them from entering deep water. Many species are large, up to one and one half inches long. Their prey includes most aquatic insects and occasionally tadpoles or small fish.

Once the prey is captured an enzyme that breaks down tissue is pumped through large hollow mandibles into the victim. The liquefied tissue is then sucked up through these mandibles. The larvae are often active, but they normally crawl rather than swim. Their imitations should be fished slowly across the bottom or in weedy areas.

When the larvae are mature, typically in late summer and fall, they crawl a short distance from the water to pupate. This may occur in damp soil or under logs, sticks or rocks. Once the adults emerge they head back to the water, where they return to the predaceous ways of the larvae. Using well developed, oar-like hind legs, they swim quickly through underwater vegetation in search of food. The sucktorial mouthparts of the larvae are replaced by chewing mouthparts.

The submerged adults carry a bubble of air under the front wings. Because they must return to the surface and replace the bubble, they remain in the top two to four feet of water.

Winter is passed in the adult stage. Many beetles remain active through the winter, even under ice. Others hibernate during cold weather. In the spring they mate and lay eggs. After mating, females lay their eggs in stems or leaves of submerged plants, or in soft bottom substrates.

Imitation

The larval stage of water beetles is the most important to fishermen. Even larvae are seldom found in stomach samples in sufficient numbers to convince us they are taken selectively. Adult beetles are found in autopsies on rare occasions, but not often enough to make imitation worthwhile.

> *WOOLLY WORM*
> *Hook: Mustad 9672 (3X long), Nos. 8-16.*
> *Thread: To match body color.*
> *Hackle: Olive, brown, or grizzly, palmered.*
> *Rib: Gold or silver narrow tinsel (optional).*
> *Body: Olive, brown, or tan chenille.*

Many beetle larvae have filament-like gills on their abdominal segments. These are represented perfectly by the palmered hackle of a Woolly Worm. Our experience indicates beetles are taken as opportunity presents. A rough suggestion of the natural, offered by the various color phases of these simple dressings, will usually take trout when stomach samples reveal dytiscids are in their diets.

> *OLIVE DIVING BEETLE LARVA (Ernest Schwiebert)*
> *Hook: Mustad 9672 (3X long), Nos. 12-14.*
> *Thread: Dark olive 6/0 nylon.*
> *Gills: Two dirty olive-gray hackle points.*
> *Body: Dirty olive-gray dubbing on olive silk, ribbed with a*
> *   roughly dubbed wrapping of hare's mask guard hairs.*
> *Thorax: Dubbed like body with a brown mottled turkey*
> *   quill section dyed olive tied over the thorax like a wingcase.*
> *Legs: Dirty olive-gray hen hackle palmer-tied along thorax.*
> *Head: Dark olive nylon.*

This pattern is from Schwiebert's *Nymphs.* He also gives dressings for Black and Brown Diving Beetle Larvae. We doubt western anglers will often find situations where exact imitations are needed. There are, however, certain small, weedy trout ponds and lakes where dytiscid populations are heavy, and where dressings more imitative than Woolly Worms are called for. In these places, one of the diving beetle larva patterns, or modifications of them, will increase the odds for taking fish.

Presentation

Dytiscid larvae often rest near the surface on plants, with their breathing tubes contacting the air. When prey approach, they dive to attack. Thus they usually hang out in and around weedbeds, especially in areas where aquatic vegetation grows to the surface of the water. This gives them cover and decreases their vulnerability to trout, making it unlikely that they will be fed on selectively.

Diving beetle larva patterns should be presented in or near weedbeds. They should be fished with dry lines, and kept near the surface. A very slow hand-twist retrieve will move the fly in the approximate manner of the natural. When trout are cruising, especially when no hatches are in sight and they are feeding opportunistically, a dytiscid imitation will usually take them.

FAMILY: HYDROPHILIDAE

Common Name: Water Scavenger Beetles.

Emergence and Distribution

The life cycle of hydrophilids follows closely that of dytiscids. Eggs are usually laid in spring, with the larvae active through the summer. Mature larvae leave the water to pupate, but the adults are again aquatic. Adults are active throughout the fall and winter. Large dispersal flights of adults regularly occur in early spring. Some species vary this pattern by laying eggs in fall and overwintering as larvae. Both larvae and adults occupy similar habitats, so there is no real emergence.

The range of hydrophilids extends across the western region. They are found at elevations ranging from sea level along the Pacific Coast to high mountain lakes in the Rockies. These underwater scavengers are often overlooked, but they provide a steady supplement to the trout's varied diet.

Larval Characteristics
   *a. Legs with four visible segments ending in a single claw.
   b. Large sickle-shaped mandibles.
   c. Color: Body brown, tan or olive.
   d. Size: Length of mature larvae 12-25mm (1/2 to 1 inch).

Adult Characteristics

*a. Antennae shorter than maxillary palpi, with the end segments club-shaped.
b. Underbody covered with very fine hairs.
c. Color: Uniform dark; shiny.
d. Size: 8-25mm (3/8 to 1 inch).

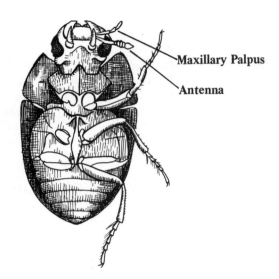

Figure 38. Ventral view of Hydrophilid adult.

Habitat

Hydrophilids and dytiscids live in similar habitats. Weedy shallows along the margins of ponds and lakes hold the largest numbers. A few species are also at home in slow-water areas of streams and rivers.

Habits

Hydrophilid larvae are active predators. Except for the genus *Berosus*, they must get their oxygen at the surface. They hunt in shallows or near the tops of aquatic vegetation. *Berosus* larvae breathe with gills, and remain under water, where they hunt along the bottom. The effectiveness of palmered patterns fished slowly along the bottom may be in part due to their resemblance to these underwater beetles.

When the larvae reach maturity they crawl a short distance from the water and form a pupal cell in damp soil. The pupae develop for several weeks. When the adults emerge from the pupal cuticles they dig out of the cell and crawl back to the water.

Hydrophilid adults do not return to the predaceous ways of the larvae. They become water scavengers, swimming along the bottom or through weedy margins feeding on algae or dead plant and animal material. They swim with alternate kicks of oar-like hind legs, unlike dytiscids, which swim with strong synchronous kicks. The adults swim to the surface and obtain a bubble of air, holding it under the elytra and against the underside of the abdomen. Dytiscids and hydrophilids can be distinguished when they renew their bubble: Dytiscids break the surface film with the tip of the abdomen; hydrophilids break the surface with the side of the head, using their clubbed antennae.

Adults are ready to lay eggs in spring. This is often preceded by extensive dispersal flights as they look for new or more suitable habitat. Most species lay their eggs in a transparent bag-like case or cover them with a loose blanket of silk. The egg cases are laid under water, attached to various objects. The adults die shortly after egg laying.

In the tropics dead adults are so numerous they often form windrows hundreds of miles long. They are collected by natives and used for food, decoration, aphrodisiacs, and even pillow stuffing.

Imitation

Like the dytiscids, only the larvae of hydrophilids have any importance to fishermen. Also like dytiscids, they are found sporadically in stomach samples, making their importance marginal. Suggestive patterns are probably all the average angler will need in his fly boxes to imitate them. Olive, brown, black and gray Woolly Worms in sizes 10 through 16 cover their size and color spectrums.

> *BROWN SCAVENGER BEETLE LARVA (Ernest Schwiebert)*
> *Hook: Mustad 79580 (4X long), Nos. 10-14.*
> *Thread: Dark brown 6/0 nylon.*
> *Body: Dark gray hare's mask dubbing mixed with guard
>   hairs.*
> *Gills: Dark brown hackle stripped on one side and trimmed
>   short to simulate gills, palmer-tied along body.*
> *Thorax: Dark gray hare's mask mixed with guard hairs.*
> *Legs: Dark brown hen hackle.*
> *Head: Dark brown nylon.*

This dressing, and Schwiebert's Black and Gray Scavenger Beetle Larvae, offer imitations of the surface breathing Hydrophilidae. We have also collected olive species; imitation should always be based on collected specimens.

> *BROWN ALGAE LARVA (Ernest Schwiebert)*
> *Hook: Mustad 9671 (2X long), Nos. 14-16.*
> *Thread: Dark brown 6/0 nylon.*
> *Body: Dark muskrat dubbing.*
> *Gills: Dark brown hackle palmered along body.*
> *Thorax: Dark muskrat dubbing.*
> *Legs: Small brown hackle palmered over thorax.*

The Brown Algae Larva is dressed to imitate the gill-breathing forms of Hydrophilidae. These species are not dependent on surface oxygen, and are able to feed along the bottom.

Presentation

Surface breathing species should be fished with the same presentation as dytiscid patterns: Retrieved slowly around shallow weedbeds. Gill-breathers should be fished along the bottom, hand-twisted to represent the laborious crawling of the naturals.

Chapter Nine

True Flies
Order: Diptera

The true flies are an extremely diverse group. They include a wide variety of insects, from crane flies to house flies to mosquitoes. They began evolving in the late Permian era, 250 million years ago. Modern forms appear in fossil records from the Jurrasic period, 180 million years ago.

The order evolved into species which live in all environments—terrrestrial, aquatic, and even parasitic. There are species in every known water habitat. They can be disease carriers (mosquitoes), fierce biters (blackflies), and nuisances (no-see-ums). They can also be beneficial, providing the bulk of food for rapidly growing salmon and trout fingerlings, and at times for adult fish.

Diptera larvae are difficult to distinguish from each other. Most appear as simple tubes, like small, segmented worms. Their heads may be well developed, or they may be greatly reduced. In some groups they are retracted into the thoracic segments, making it difficult to tell which end is which. There are no true jointed thoracic legs on Diptera larvae. Prolegs—fleshy, jointless, often stump-like appendages—may be present on one to several body segments.

Some aquatic Diptera pupate free in the water; others pupate in silken cases under water or on land. Many pupae appear to have the head and thorax lumped together, and have wingpads extending to the middle of the body. The pupae of others are enclosed in a smooth, cylindrical puparium; features such as head, legs and wings are not visible.

Adult Diptera have only one pair of wings. Except for several species of mayflies, other aquatic insects have two pairs. The second pair of Diptera wings have evolved into halteres, miniature knobbed gyroscopes which stabilize the insect in flight. Most aquatic Diptera adults have slender bodies and long, delicate legs.

Diptera have complete metamorphosis. Different species display all of the egg laying habits previously discussed for the other orders. Some dip their eggs to the surface, others deposit them on stems and leaves; many crawl under the water and attach them to plants, rocks and logs. Larval behavior is just as diverse, ranging from hungry predators to peaceful plankton feeders. The larval stage can be as short as a month, or as long as one year.

Pupation can occur in the water or in damp soil along the stream or lake shore. Pupal development generally takes from a few days to a few weeks. Adults mate on foliage or in the air before oviposition takes place. There are many families of aquatic Diptera. The most important—midges, mosquitoes and crane flies—are discussed in the following pages. Other groups, of less importance to fishermen, include blackflies (Simuliidae), net-winged midges (Blephariceridae), no-see-ums (Ceratopogonidae), soldier flies (Stratiomyidae), snipe flies (Rhagionidae), and dance flies (Empididae).

FAMILY: CHIRONOMIDAE

Common Name: Midges

Emergence and Distribution

J   F   M   A   M   J   J   A   S   O   N   D
1————————————————————31

    The family Chironomidae is an unruly group, with *Aquatic Insects of California* listing over forty-five genera. They emerge in all months; there is no time when they are not important to some fish. Late spring, summer and early fall hatches are often overshadowed by larger insects, but trout are always aware of them and almost always willing to take them. Fishermen will find chironomids most important at times when other hatches are light or non-existent. Late fall, early spring, and even the coldest winter days have midge hatches. These hatches provide surprising action in waters that are open year around.

    Midges occur throughout the West. It can be said with confidence that any water holding trout will also have chironomids.

Larval Characteristics
  *a. Well developed head capsule.
  *b. First thoracic segment and last abdominal segment each with a pair of prolegs.
  c. Color: Light cream, tan, brown, green, black, red and most shades in between.
  d. Size: 1-10mm (1/32 to 1/2 inch).

Pupal Characteristics
  a. Body segments visible, but head and thorax closely coupled.
  b. Last abdominal segment with a short, two-lobed swimming paddle without midrib.
  c. Numerous fine respiratory filaments on prothorax.
  d. Color: Light cream, tan, brown, green, black, red and most shades in between.
  d. Size: 1-10mm (1/32 to 1/2 inch).

Adult Characteristics
  *a. Males with hairy, plume-like antennae.
  b. Slender body and wings.
  c. Non-biting; mouthparts are reduced.
  d. Color: Light cream, tan, brown, green, black, red and most shades in between.
  e. Size: 1-10mm (1/32 to 1/2 inch).

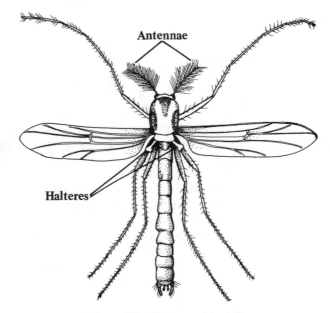

Figure 39. Chironomid adult.

Habitat

Species of Chironomidae are found in virtually every fresh-water environment, from sewage treatment plants to the fastest riffles in clear streams. They are most important in ponds, lakes and slow stretches of streams with lots of aquatic plants. Spring creeks are noted for heavy— and frustrating— midge hatches. Lakes with soft, mucky bottoms often produce larger hatches than those with sandy bottoms.

Habits

Most midge larvae are algae and detritus feeders. They live in weedbeds and on the bottom, where algae and decaying animal and plant material abound. Some species are predators, feeding primarily on smaller chironomid larvae. Several genera spin fine silk nets to capture plankton and detritus. At regular intervals they devour the net, along with its contents, before spinning a new net.

Some midge larvae are free-living, burrowing through silt, clambering over gravel, or moving about in aquatic vegetation. Others build cases of silk and fine sand, similar to those of some case-building caddisflies. These small silken cases are common on rocky substrates in flowing waters. Midge larvae are extremely abundant in stream drift, and provide a major component in the diet of small fingerlings and occasionally large fish.

Pupation occurs in the larval case or in a burrow in bottom silt. Mature pupae float to the surface and the adult emerges shortly after. There is usually a brief wait—a few seconds to a minute or more—when the pupa hangs from the surface film. This is the most vulnerable stage of the insect.

Once the adult is free of the pupal shuck it flies away quickly. This is the most visible stage; it is not the easiest to fish. Most adults crawl under water to deposit their eggs in gelatinous strings or masses. They die soon thereafter. The mouthparts of adults are reduced. Adults occasionally make a nuisance of themselves by swarming around your face, but they do not bite.

In warm water a midge species can go through several generations in one year. In colder climates the same species may have a single emergence during the year. The length of the life cycle varies widely in the West.

Imitation

The term midge has come to refer to any tiny fly pattern, but when it is used as a common name for the Chironomidae family of aquatic Diptera the term can refer to some rather large organisms. In some lakes we have fished over midges as large as size 10. At the other end of the scale there are midges too small to imitate.

Dave Whitlock created a series of midge imitations, covering the larval, pupal and adult stages. He adds an emerging pupal pattern and a still-born adult imitation. This series approach is perhaps the best way to look at midge imitations.

> MIDGE LARVA (Dave Whitlock)
> Hook: Mustad 94842 (1X fine, up eye), Nos. 18-28.
> Thread: To match body color.
> Rib: Thread or fine gold wire.
> *Body: 50/50 blend of beaver belly and Flyrite.
> Head: Same as body.

*Common colors are tan, red, brown, green, black, olive and light olive.

> RISING MIDGE PUPA (Dave Whitlock)
> Hook: Mustad 94842 (1X fine, up eye), Nos. 16-28.
> Weight: Four to 6 turns of 1/2-amp fuse wire.
> Thread: To match body color.
> Tail: One or two ostrich herl tips, very sparse and short.
> Abdomen: 50/50 blend of beaver belly and Flyrite and Polly II.
> Thorax: Same dubbing blend but a bit darker, plus one or
>   two turns of natural gray ostrich herl.
> Head: Same color as thorax.

EMERGING PUPA (Dave Whitlock)
Hook: Mustad 94842 (1X fine, up eye), Nos. 16-28.
Thread: To match body color.
Rib: Very fine gold wire or tying thread.
Tail: Gray ostrich herl tips, tied short.
Abdomen: Deer hair laid along the shank and ribbed.
Thorax: Deer hair as above and overwrapped with two to three
turns of ostrich or peacock herl.
Head: Same color as body.
(Deer hair colors: black, natural dun-brown, green, brown, olive
or red.)

STILLBORN MIDGE (Dave Whitlock)
Hook: Mustad 94842 (1X fine, up eye), Nos. 18-28.
Thread: To match body color.
Pupal Shuck: Ostrich herl or hen-hackle tip equal to hook
shank length.
Body: 50/50 blend of beaver belly and either Flyrite or Polly II.
Wings: Two white or dun hen hackle tips.
Hackle: One or two turns of cock hackle trimmed off top and
bottom.

GRIFFITH'S GNAT (George Griffith)
Hook: Mustad 94842 (1X fine, up eye), Nos. 18-28.
Thread: Olive.
Body: Peacock herl.
Hackle: Grizzly, palmered.

HENRYVILLE SPECIAL
Hook: Mustad 94842, Nos. 18-28 (1X fine, up eye).
Thread: To match body color.
Body: Floss or Polly II, palmered with grizzly hackle.
Wing: Barred woodduck flank or mallard wing quill.
Hackle: Dun or dun-brown.

There are several things worth noting as we look at this progression of patterns matching the stages of midges. The first stage, the larva, is extremely difficult to fish effectively. While fish feed opportunistically on larvae, according to Whitlock, most midge feeding is on the pupal stage. When rises are visible in the surface, it still is likely that fish are taking pupae rather than adults. Stillborn patterns are more important than standard dry imitations. It is common for midges to get stuck in the pupal shuck; trout find them easy pickings.

Another important point is matching the various stages of a midge hatch: As the insect leaves each shuck behind, progressing to the next stage, it becomes one size smaller. Thus one might fish a No. 16 larva, No. 18 pupa and a No. 20 adult pattern, all for the same species.

Presentation

Presentation of the larval patterns, assuming one finds a situation where stomach samples or other evidence points to the need for them, should be deep in the water. A very slow hand twist retrieve is best. Weighted flies are often necessary.

Presentation of pupal patterns covers two phases. The first is that in which the pupa is rising to the surface of a lake or stream. They are buoyed up by trapped gases, with little swimming movement. A slightly weighted fly, allowed to sink close to the bottom on a long leader and dry line, can be risen smoothly to the surface to imitate this behavior. The ribbing reflects the sparkle of light inherent in a bubble of gas.

The second stage of the midge pupa, the emerger, is fished suspended from the surface film. This imitates the pause of the natural as it hangs from the surface. In this stage it is best to fish the fly with a partially greased leader. Whitlock also recommends dressing the built-up head and thorax region of the fly with line dressing to insure the fly will suspend in the surface film with the abdomen hanging straight down.

The stillborn stage represents the adult after it has penetrated the surface film but before it frees itself from the pupal skin. This skin trails from the back of the struggling adult; its entrapment of the emerging insect assures an easy mark for cruising trout.

The last stage, the adult midge, is less productive than pupal or stillborn adult stages. Adult patterns are most useful in situations where an easily seen fly is needed.

The traditional approach to midge imitation is somewhat simpler; the flies are also easier to tie.

TRADITIONAL MIDGE LARVA
Hook: Mustad 3906B (1X long), Nos. 12-24.
Thread: To match body.
Rib: Silver or gold wire or tying thread.
Body: Slender dubbing to match natural.

The natural larvae are simple segmented tubes. These dubbed patterns represent that simplicity.

TRADITIONAL MIDGE PUPA
Hook: Mustad 94833 (3X fine), Nos. 12-24.
Thread: To match body.
Rib: Fine wire or tying thread.
Body: Slender dubbing to match natural.
Thorax, Legs, Wingcases, Head: Slightly darker fur dubbed in a
* loose clump at the hook eye.*

Pupae are similar to the larvae. Their partially developed heads, thoracic segments, and wingpads are clumped together. The simple traditional midge pupa represents them very well.

TRADITIONAL MIDGE ADULT
Hook: Mustad 94833 (3X fine), Nos. 14-26.
Thread: To match body color.
Body: Fur or floss to match natural.
Hackle: Two to three turns dry fly hackle to match body color.

When fish are not selective these hackled ties will take them as readily as more exact imitations. A small box filled with an assortment of sizes and colors, representing the three stages, will cover many midge situations. We would suggest the following colors as most useful: black, blue dun, brown, ginger, olive, and cream.

FAMILY: CULICIDAE

Common Name: Mosquitoes.

Emergence and Distribution

J F M A M J J A S O N D
    1————31

Most fishermen are familiar with this family of insects. There are few who cannot identify it—by sight or sound.

Mosquitoes emerge in the warm spring and summer months. The "best" hatches are in June and July. Some trout waters in swampy or marshy areas fairly hum with the beating of their tiny, high-speed wings.

Mosquitoes are distributed throughout the West. One rarely has to go looking for them.

Larval Characteristics

  *a. Thoracic and abdominal segments with many small hairs.
  *b. Hang in surface film with heads down; breathe air from atmosphere.
  c. Well developed head capsule.
  d. Color: Cream, light tan or dark brown.
  e. Size: 5-10mm (1/4 to 1/2 inch).

Pupal Characteristics

  a. Body segments visible but head and thorax closely coupled.
  b. Hang in surface film with heads up.
  c. Wingpads not extending to middle of body.
  d. Last abdominal segment with two swimming paddles, each with a midrib.
  e. Color: Cream, light tan or dark brown.
  f. Size: 5-10mm (1/4 to 1/2 inch).

Adult Characteristics

  *a. Mouthparts shaped as a long piercing-sucking proboscis.
  *b. Slender wings, often with rows of fine hairs.
  c. Color: Light brown or black, often with distinct light banding.
  d. 5-10mm (1/4 to 1/2 inch).

Habitat

Mosquitoes are restricted to standing water. They are found in lakes, ponds, stock watering troughs and puddles. They thrive in marshes and swamps with broad reaches of shallow water.

There are mosquitoes at all elevations, from sea level to the highest alpine lakes. It is in the latter that they are most available to fish. They are not open-water inhabitants, preferring sheltered areas and shallow water.

Habit

Mosquito larvae hang from the surface film, feeding on tiny planktonic organisms floating in the water. A siphon tube on the last abdominal segment penetrates the surface film and oxygen is taken directly from the air. When disturbed, the larvae submerge with rapid contortions of the entire body. They cannot stay down indefinitely because of their need for air. It is this same need that kills them when oil is spread over the water in which they live: they can no longer reach the surface to breathe.

Mosquito pupae also hang from the surface. They break the film and breathe through the spiracles located on their thorax. The adult emerges out of the pupal shuck in the surface film. In alpine lakes this often takes place where fish can feed on them; in other waters they are rarely available to fish.

Female mosquitoes require a blood meal for their eggs to develop. They normally pester woodland inhabitants such as rodents and mammals, but man is a favored donor. Mating normally occurs in the air. Eggs are laid on the water's surface or on damp surfaces next to the water. Adult life is short, lasting only a few days.

Imitation

It is questionable whether mosquitoes are more important to fishermen than fishermen are to mosquitoes. Most water inhabited by mosquitoes is poor habitat for trout. There is little doubt that many mosquito imitations have been created for incorrectly identified midges (Chironomidae). But mosquitoes can be important in alpine lakes, especially just after ice-out in spring.

Larvae

The larval stage is perhaps the most important of the mosquito life cycle. Most of their life is spent in this stage, and during it they are exposed by the need to take oxygen from the surface film. They are never far from the surface, and spend much of their time suspended from it, making them easy marks for cruising trout.

> *PUBLIC ENEMY NO. 1 (Donald Roberts)*
> *Hook: 9672 (3X long), Nos. 12-16.*
> *Thread: Black.*
> *Tail: Grizzly hackle fibers, short and sparse.*
> *Body: Grizzly hackle stem.*
> *Wings: Two grizzly hackle tips, tied short.*
> *Thorax: Black ostrich herl or green peacock herl.*
> *Beard: Soft gray deer hair or squirrel tail.*

The name of this pattern leaves little doubt that the natural was correctly identified. Its creator, Don Roberts, author of *Flyfishing Still Waters*, suggests his pattern be fished ". . . around, over, and under the snags and debris along the edges of alpine lakes."

> *MOSQUITO LARVA*
> *Hook: Mustad 3906B (1X long), Nos. 14-18.*
> *Thread: Gray.*
> *Tail: Grizzly hackle fibers.*
> *Body: Grizzly saddle hackle stem.*
> *Feelers: Grizzly hackle fibers tied in over the eye of the hook.*
> *Thorax: Grizzly saddle hackle trimmed to shape.*

Presentation

Mosquito larvae are dependent on surface air for their oxygen supply. They are therefore restricted to the few inches of water near the top. Their habit of hanging head down from the film, and wriggling with great contortions to escape when disturbed, is difficult to duplicate. Don Roberts recommends a staccato twitching retrieve interspersed with pauses. We find this the best approach to fishing larval imitations.

Pupae

The shape, size and color of mosquito pupae is very similar to that of the larvae. They differ in the way they hang from the surface film—heads up instead of heads down. This is a minor distinction; few trout are so fussy they will pass up a larva when they are feeding on pupae. They are unlikely to refuse the given larval patterns when feeding on any stage of mosquitoes.

EMERGENT MOSQUITO (Randall Kaufmann)
Hook: Mustad 3906, Nos. 12-18.
Thread: Black.
Tail: Three short fibers of black moose body hair.
Body: Stripped peacock herl over slight taper of dark fur.
Thorax: Peacock herl.
Wings: Two grizzly hackle tips tied short over top of thorax.

Presentation

The emergent pattern, and larval patterns fished as pupae, should be fished dead-drift in the surface film. A dry line and partially dressed leader will help this presentation.

Adults

When the mosquito has emerged it assumes greater importance to the fisherman, less to the fish. It is no longer readily available as trout food; however, the trouter is readily available as its food. Adult patterns, and their usefulness, are limited.

ADAMS (Leonard Halladay)
Hook: Mustad 94840 (1X fine), Nos. 14-18.
Thread: Black.
Tails: Brown and grizzly fibers, mixed.
Body: Muskrat.
Wings: Grizzly hackle tips.
Hackle: Brown and grizzly, mixed.

This traditional pattern does an acceptable job of imitating mosquitoes. In the pristine alpine lakes where mosquitoes are most important trout are generally not so selective that they will refuse it.

MOSQUITO
Hook: Mustad 94840 (1X fine), Nos. 12-18.
Thread: Black.
Wings: Grizzly hackle tips.
Tail: Grizzly hackle fibers.
Body: Dark and light moose mane wrapped together.
Hackle: Grizzly.

This pattern catches the dark and light segmentation of the natural mosquito body perfectly. It is an excellent pattern to carry on any alpine fishing trip.

The preference of mosquitoes for very shallow water makes them a marginal insect in terms of trout food. Their heavy presence around a favorite lake, pond or stream is often misleading. They usually emerge from nearby seeps and standing water; they are less likely to emerge from larger bodies of water.

FAMILY: TIPULIDAE

Common Name: Crane flies.

Emergence and Distribution

J F M A M J J A S O N D
1 ———————————————— 31

Crane flies, some of which are mistaken for monstrous mosquitoes, begin emerging in April and continue through the summer and fall months. Because they pupate on land the moment of emergence is not important. The larvae are available to fish after a spate, when they are washed out of the silt and gravel of the bottom. Adults are most active during and after warm summer rain showers.

Crane flies are distributed throughout the western region. Heaviest populations occur in streams with bottoms of fine gravel, silt or sand.

Larval Characteristics
*a. Head well developed but normally retracted inside the first thoracic segment and not visible.
*b. Body cylindrical; some species with six or seven pairs of abdominal prolegs.
*c. Last abdominal segment usually with two large spiracles for breathing.
d. Color: Light cream, tan, brown, gray or olive.
e. Size: 12-50mm (1/2 to 2 inches).

Adult Characteristics
*a. Very long legs in relation to body size.
*b. Mouthparts reduced; non-biting.
c. Color: Light to dark brown.
d. Size: 12-50mm (1/2 to 2 inches).

Habitat
Many crane fly species are terrestrial, living in damp soil. Other groups are semi-aquatic, burrowing along stream margins and in swampy areas. The larvae of most truly aquatic groups live under gravel and silt in the beds of streams. They prefer loose substrates for their burrowing. Fine gravel mixed with silt, or silt and debris, are excellent habitats.

Tipulid larvae can be collected from the swiftest riffles or the slowest backwater areas. The collector must agitate the bottom to a depth of several inches before they will show in any sample.

Habits
Crane fly larvae are worm-like in appearance and behavior. They are not readily available to trout under ordinary circumstances. During and after a spate, however, when flood waters disturb the bottom, many tipulid larvae are washed into the current and exposed to fish. Because of their size—often one to two inches long—they are taken greedily. When the water is dropping and clearing after a rain, crane fly imitations tumbled along the bottom can be very effective.

Many species are predaceous. They crawl through the bottom sediments in search of midge larvae and other small insects. The majority, however, feed on the organic debris in which they are found.

Pupation takes place in damp soil along the margins. The pupal stage is of no account to fly fishermen.

Adult crane flies are usually quiescent, hiding in moist, shady, sheltered places. They favor the undersides of broad leaves, rotten logs or crevices in rocks. During a light summer rain shower they come out and dance clumsily above the water. Though they are not so available that fish become selective to them, they are usually so large that fish will not refuse them.

Eggs are usually laid along the water's margins or on logs and rocks at the water's surface. The adults are thus not available to fish when they oviposit.

Imitation

Cranefly imitations are useful only in the limited conditions already mentioned. The larvae are available after high water, the adults after light rains.

Larvae

Larval imitations should be simple and tube-like. Woolly Worms in sizes 6 through 14, tied on long shank hooks, are usually all that is needed to imitate crane fly larvae. They should be tied with cream, dirty-white, dirty-orange, tan or olive bodies.

> *MUSKRAT (Polly Rosborough)*
> *Hook: Mustad 38941 (3X long), Nos. 6-16.*
> *Thread: Black.*
> *Body: Muskrat fur.*
> *Legs: Speckled guinea fibers tied in at throat.*
> *Head: Black ostrich.*

This muskrat fur bodied pattern is tied by Polly Rosborough to represent grayish tipulid larvae. Variations in the colors listed above should also be effective.

> *WESTERN CRANE FLY LARVA (Ernest Schwiebert)*
> *Hook: Mustad 79580 (4X long), Nos. 10-12.*
> *Thread: Gray 6/0 nylon.*
> *Gills: Dark bluish-gray fibers tied short.*
> *Body: Dark bluish-gray muskrat dubbing.*
> *Ribbing: Fine oval tinsel.*
> *Thorax: Dark bluish-gray.*
> *Antennae: Dark bluish-gray fibers.*
> *Head: Gray nylon.*

This slightly more detailed pattern retains the simple tube shape of the tipulid while supplying a few short fibers at the tail to represent the gills of the natural, and a few more at the head to represent its antennae. It should be used as a model for color variations based on the larvae you collect in your own streams.

Presentation

Crane fly larvae have no swimming ability. Their imitations should be presented dead-drift and on the bottom. If they are fished after a spate, weight will be needed to get them down where they belong.

Adults

Crane fly adult dressings are usually impressionistic, designed to suggest the presence of an insect on the surface of the water, rather than offering the exact outline of the natural.

> **GINGER SPIDER**
> *Hook: Mustad 94838 (2X short), Nos. 10-16.*
> *Thread: Tan.*
> *Tail: Light ginger hackle fibers, long.*
> *Body: Dubbed cream fur.*
> *Hackle: Light ginger.*

This is one of the many spider patterns that can be tied to suggest crane fly adults. Others include Badger, Adams, Black, Blue Dun, Brown, Deer Hair, Furnace and Grizzly Spiders. The attraction of the spider flies lies in the pattern of the tail and hackle points as they rest on the water. The series of dimples in the surface film suggests the presence of an insect on the water, perfect for the long-legged, light-bodied crane flies.

> **GINGER VARIANT**
> *Hook: Mustad 94840 (1X fine), Nos. 10-16.*
> *Thread: Tan.*
> *Wings: Golden badger hackle tips tied upright and divided.*
> *Tail: Light ginger hackle fibers, long.*
> *Body: Cream fur.*
> *Hackle: Light ginger.*

Variant patterns are based on the same principle of over-sized hackle and tails as the spiders. A series of variant ties include Badger, Black, Blue, Brown, Furnace, Multi-Color and Red Variants.

Both spiders and variants represent insects hovering over the surface as well as those sitting on it. This traditional concept is perfect for the hovering and dancing crane flies.

> **DARBEE CRANE FLY (Harry Darbee)**
> *Hook: Mustad 9523 (5X short), Nos. 8-10.*
> *Thread: Yellow pre-waxed 6/0.*
> *Body and Wing: Mallard flank feather.*
> *Hackle: Medium blue dun, parachute.*

This exceptional tie incorporates the delicacy of light construction with an accurate silhouette of the natural crane fly adult. Detailed instructions for tying it are given in *Dressing Flies for Fresh and Salt Water* by Poul Jorgensen.

Presentation

Spiders and variants are well adapted to a skating presentation. When a drag-free float does not arouse the fish, a skating or skittering presentation will often stir them up. These patterns in large sizes are often used to get a splashy rise from lethargic trout. When the fish is located it is sometimes possible to switch to a smaller pattern and get a solid take.

You are most likely to see crane fly activity during and after a warm summer rain. On such days it is wise to consider the more exact Darbee Crane Fly. It, too, is of light construction and can be skated and skittered across the surface. The showy rises it often provokes are a delightful surprise, even if the fish misses the fly.

CONCLUSION

There is such a diversity of fishing conditions in our western states and provinces, and so many different insects, that there can be no substitute for local knowledge. A few major hatches have been catalogued on a few major waters; everywhere else the western angler is on his own.

We hope this book will be a help to those who seek that local knowledge; who want to approach any stream or lake and match its hatches; who want to understand the emergences on their own home waters. It is also our hope that those who are curious about the environment in which they fish will develop an increased awareness and appreciation of it from these pages.

How does an angler, in the face of such diversity, decide which stage of which insect to imitate at a given moment? Observation is the first step. Are there any insects on the water, or flying over it? Are there adults along the margins, or crawling over streamside vegetation? Are fish feeding actively, either at the surface or with flashing flanks under water? What are water and weather conditions—levels, temperature, and clarity— and how will these affect feeding fish? A few simple observations will often tell you all you need to know to stir up some action.

If no activity is obvious the next step is to make some simple collections from a variety of locations. Shake trees to find recently hatched adults. Pick up stones, branches, and leaf packs from shallow water. Sample riffles, runs and pools with a kick net. Sweep an aquarium net through weedbeds and along the shorelines of lakes. In all but the most sterile waters you will come up with a variety of insects from which to choose.

Selecting the insect to imitate should be based on the abundance, availability and maturity of the specimens collected. If one form dominates all others in your sample it probably is first in the eyes of feeding fish. If it is a form seldom available to fish, however, it might be a poor choice. For instance, a bottom sample might include a dominance of burrowing crane fly larvae, yet the fish will seldom see them. A few free-living caddis larvae in the net might be better candidates for imitation because they are active, and more likely to be available to the fish. Mature insects— nymphs with dark wingpads and pupae ready to leave their cocoons—are always good bets for imitation.

When you find one insect that is abundant, mature and available to the fish, and have selected a pattern that matches it, you are about to find yourself in the middle of some fine fishing.

Fish are unpredictable. Sometimes things that we don't know, and cannot observe, may please or displease them. Conditions change from hour to hour, day to day. This morning's success with an *Ephemerella* nymph may predict this afternoon's pleasure over a Green Drake hatch.

Fish drummed up sporadically yesterday may come easily today because the water is warmer and the March Brown hatch has started.

Observation is the first part of fishing success. Observation is also a never-ending pleasure as the angler becomes tuned to changes through the cycle of the seasons. Understanding the insects, their behavior and the response of fish as they feed on them, will not only increase the odds for success, but also the enjoyment of the places in which fish are found.

Glossary

Apex: the portion of a joint or segment opposite the base by which it is attached.

Caudal: pertaining to the anal end of the insect body.

Cercus: a slender, filamentous and segmented appendage (normally paired) on the tenth abdominal segment; usually called a tail.

Chitin: a hard secretion of the epidermis.

Costa: the thickened front margin of a wing.

Coxa: the basal, or first, segment of the leg.

Dorsal: the upper surface.

Eclosion: the process of hatching from the egg.

Elytra: the anterior (front) chitinous wings of beetles which cover the hind wings and abdomen.

Emargination: a notched place in an edge or margin.

Exoskeleton: the external skeleton of an insect.

Femur: the third and usually principal segment of the leg.

Gravid: pregnant; having fertilized eggs.

Halteres: in Diptera the moveable clubbed filaments in place of the hind wings.

Imago: the adult and sexually mature insect; mayfly spinner.

Instar: the period of growth between molts in immature insects.

Labial: referring to the labium.

Labium: the compound structure which forms the floor of the mouth in mandibulate insects; the lower lip.

Labrum: the structure which forms the roof of the mouth; the upper lip.

Mandibles: the first pair of jaws in insects.

Maxilla: the second pair of jaws of mandibulate insects.

Maxillary Palp: the segmented appendage attached to the insect maxilla.

Mesothorax: the second thoracic segment; bearing the middle legs and first pair of wings.

Metamorphosis: the series of changes an insect passes through during its development from egg to adult.

Metathorax: the third thoracic segment, bearing the hind legs and second pair of wings.

Molt: the process of casting off the outgrown skin during nymphal or larval development.

Ocelli: the simple eyes of insects.

Operculate: plate-like; a lid.

Periphyton: the algae attached to submerged objects.

Prolegs: the fleshy, unjointed legs of certain insect larvae; false legs.

Pronotum: the upper surface of the prothorax.

Prothorax: the first thoracic segment bearing the front legs, but no wings.

Puparium: the thickened and hardened larval skin in which the pupa is formed.

Sclerotized: definite hardened areas of the insect exoskeleton.

Spiracles: the openings of the insect body through which air enters the trachea.

Stemmata: the simple lateral eyes of insect larvae with complete metamorphosis.

Subimago: that stage of mayflies just after emergence from the nymph and before the final molt to the imago. Also called the dun.

Tarsal Claw: the claw at the end of the tarsus.

Tarsus: the part of the insect leg farthest from the body; consisting of from one to five segments.

Teneral: the adult insect shortly after emergence, before it is entirely hardened.

Tibia: the fourth division of the leg.

Trachea: an internal elastic air tube used for transporting oxygen.

Trochanter: the segment of the insect leg between the coxa and femur.

Ventral: the belly, or under surface.

Bibliography

Anderson, Norman H. *The Distribution and Biology of the Oregon Trichoptera.* Technical Bulletin 34, Agricultural Experiment Station, Corvallis, Oregon: Oregon State University, 1976.

- - - and Anderson, Margrett J. "Making a Case for the Caddis." *Insect World Digest:* Nov.-Dec. 1974, p. 1-6.

Atherton, John. *The Fly and the Fish.* New York: McMillan, 1951.

Bauman, Richard W., Gaufin, Arden R., and Surdick, Rebecca F. *The Stoneflies (Plecoptera) of the Rocky Mountains.* American Entomology Society, 1977.

Brooks, Charles E. *Nymph Fishing for Larger Trout.* New York: Crown, 1976.

- - - *The Trout and the Stream.* New York: Crown, 1974.

Caucci, Al and Nastasi, Bob. *Hatches.* Woodside, New York: Comparahatch, 1975.

Corbet, Philip S. *A Biology of Dragonflies.* H. F. & G. Witherby, Ltd., 1962.

Cummins, K. W. and Merritt, R. W., editors. *An Introduction to the Aquatic Insects of North America.* Kendall/Hunt, 1978.

Division of Entomology Commonwealth Scientific and Industrial Research Organization. *The Insects of Australia.* Melbourne: Melbourne University Press, 1970.

Edmunds, George F., Jr., Jensen, Steven L., and Berner, L. *The Mayflies of North and Central America.* Minnesota: University of Minnesota Press, 1976.

Hellekson, Terry. *Popular Fly Patterns.* Salt Lake City: Peregrine Smith, 1977.

Jennings, Preston J. *A Book of Trout Flies.* New York: Crown, 1970.

Jewett, Stanley, Jr. *Stoneflies (Plecoptera) of the Pacific Northwest.* Corvallis, Oregon: Oregon State University Press, 1959.

Jorgensen, Poul. *Dressing Flies for Fresh and Salt Water.* Rockville Center, New York: Freshet Press, 1973.

- - - *Modern Fly Dressings for the Practical Angler.* New York: Winchester Press, 1976.

Kaufmann, Randall. *American Nymph Fly Tying Manual.* Portland, Oregon: Salmon-Trout-Steelheader, 1975.

Koch, Ed. *Fishing the Midge.* Rockville Center, New York: Freshet Press, 1972.

Leisenring, James E. and Hidy, Vernon S. *The Art of Tying the Wet Fly and Fishing the Flymph.* New York: Crown, 1971.

Lehmkuhl, D. M. *How to Know the Aquatic Insects.* Dubuque, Iowa: W. C. Brown, 1979.

Meck, Charles R. *Meeting and Fishing the Hatches.* New York: Winchester Press, 1977.

Nemes, Sylvester. *The Soft-Hackled Fly.* Old Greenwich, Connecticut: Chatham Press, 1975.

Pennak, Robert W. *Fresh-Water Invertebrates of the United States.* John Wiley & Sons, 1978.

Richards, Carl and Swisher, Doug. *Selective Trout.* New York: Crown, 1971.

- - - *Fly Fishing Strategy.* New York: Crown, 1975.

- - - *Tying the Swisher/Richards Flies.* Eugene, Oregon: P. J. Dillan and Co., 1977.

Roberts, Donald V. *Fly Fishing Still Waters.* Portland, Oregon: Frank Amato Publications, 1978.

Rosborough, E. H. *Tying and Fishing the Fuzzy Nymphs.* Harrisburg, Pennsylvania: Stackpole, 1978.

Schwiebert, Ernest. *Matching the Hatch.* New York: McMillan, 1974.

- - - *Nymphs.* New York: Winchester Press, 1973.

- - - *Trout.* New York: E. P. Dutton, 1978.

Solomon, Larry and Leiser, Eric. *The Caddis and the Angler.* Harrisburg, Pennsylvania: Stackpole, 1977.

Wiggens, Glen B. *Larvae of the North American Caddisfly Genera (Trichoptera).* Toronto: University of Toronto Press, 1977.

Usinger, R. L., editor. *Aquatic Insects of California.* Berkeley, California: University of California Press, 1956.

Biological
Supply Houses

Carolina Biological Supply Company
2700 York Rd.
Burlington, North Carolina 27215
or
Box 7
Gladstone, Oregon 97027

VWR Scientific
P. O. Box 1004
Norwalk, California 90650
or
P. O. Box 3551, Terminal Annex
Seattle, Washington 98124
or
P. O. Box 1678
Salt Lake City, Utah 84110

Veniard Fly Tying Materials
John Veniard, Ltd.
4-6 High Street
Westerham, Kent, England
TN16 1RF

Index

PHOTOS

Chapter 1: Orders of Insects

Alderfly Adult, 26
Alderfly Larva, 26
Aquarium Net, 28
Backswimmer, 25
Beetle Adult, 26
Beetle Larva, 26
Caddis Adult, 16, 25
Caddis Larva, 15, 25
Caddis Pupa, 16, 25
Damselfly Adult, 24
Damselfly Nymph, 24
Diptera Adult, 27
Diptera Larva, 27
Diptera Pupae, 27
Dobsonfly, 26
Dragonfly Adult, 24
Dragonfly Nymph, 24
Hellgrammite, 26
Kick Net, 29
Mayfly Adult, 23
Mayfly Nymph, 23
Mesh-screen Net, 29
Stonefly Adult, 14, 23
Stonefly Nymph, 14, 23
Waterboatman, 25

Chapter 2: Mayflies

Ameletus Dun, 39
Ameletus Habitat, 39
Ameletus Nymphs, 39
Ameletus Spinner, 39
American March Brown, *90*
Baetis Compara-Spinner, *50*
Baetis Dun, 46
Baetis Emerger, *50*
Baetis Habitat, 47
Baetis No-Hackle, *49*
Baetis Nymph, 46
Baetis Nymph, *48*
Baetis Soft Hackle, *47*
Baetis Spinner, 46
Baetis Spinner, *50*
Big Yellow May, *95*

Big Yellow May Dun, *95*
Big Yellow May Spinner, *96*
Black Drake, *36*
Black Drake Spinner, *38*
Black Quill, *67*
Black Quill Spinner, *68*
Blue Quill Spinner, *51, 72*
Brown Drake, *99*
Brown Drake Nymph, *98, 99*
Brown Drake Spinner, *100*
Brown Wulff, *99*
Callibaetis Compara-Dun, *56*
Callibaetis Dun, 52
Callibaetis Habitat, 53
Callibaetis No-Hackle Dun, *56*
Callibaetis Nymph, 52
Callibaetis Spinner, 52
Clinger Nymph, *85*
Dark Blue Quill, *71*
Emerging Mayfly, 31
Epeorus Dun, 78
Epeorus Habitat, 79
Epeorus Nymph, 78, *80*
Epeorus Spinner, 78
Ephemerella doddsi underside, 59
Ephemerella Emerger Patterns, *61*
Ephemerella Habitat, 59
Ephemerella Spinner, 59
Female Red Quill Spinner, *72*
Flymph Body Block, 81
Flymph Under Water, 81
Ginger Quill Spinner, *51*
Gold Ribbed Hare's Ear, *54, 66*
Gordon Quill, *82*
Gray Drake, *36*
Gray Drake Dun, *37*
Gray Drake Spinner, *38*
Gray Wulff, *37*
Great Lead-Wing Olive Drake Nymph, *61*
Great Red Quill Spinner, *63*
Green Drake Compara-Dun, *62*
Green Drake Compara-Spinner, *64*
Green Drake Dun, 58
Green Drake Nymph, 58
Green Drake Spinner, *64*

Green Drake Wulff, *62*
Grizzly Wulff, *82*
Hare's Ear Flymph, *81*
Heptagenia Compara-Dun, *86*
Heptagenia Compara-Spinner, *86*
Heptagenia Dun, 84
Heptagenia Habitat, 84
Heptagenia Nymph, 83
Heptagenia Spinner, 84
Hexagenia limbata Dun, 93
Hexagenia limbata Habitat, 94
Hexagenia limbata Nymph, 93
Hexagenia limbata Spinner, 94
Ida May, *60*
Isonychia Bicolor, *41*
Isonychia Dun, 43
Isonychia Velma Nymph, *44*
Isonychia Velma Spinner, *45*
Leptophlebia Compara-Dun, *67*
Leptophlebia Habitat, 66
Leptophlebia Nymph, 65
Light Cahill, *55, 86*
Little Gray-Winged Dun Nymph, *85*
Little Olive, *49*
March Brown Compara-Dun, *90*
March Brown Flymph, *89*
March Brown Soft-Hackle, *89*
Mayfly Female With Eggs, 32
Medium Speckle-Wing Quill Nymph, *55*
Natant Nylon Nymph, *71*
Olive Midge, *76*
Pale Gray-Winged Olive Nymph, *48*
Pale Morning Compara-Dun, *63*
Pale Morning Dun, 58
Pale Morning Dun Nymph, 58, *61*
Pale Morning Dun Spinner, *64*
Paraleptophlebia Compara-Dun, *72*
Paraleptophlebia Dun, 69
Paraleptophlebia Habitat, 69, 70
Paraleptophlebia Nymphs, 69
Paraleptophlebia Spinner, 69
Partridge and Yellow Soft-Hackle, *80*
Red Quill, *71*
Red Quill Spinner, *82*
Rhithrogena Clinger Nymph, *89*
Rhithrogena Dun, 87
Rhithrogena Habitat, 88
Rhithrogena Nymphs, 87
Rhithrogena Spinner, 87
Siphlonurus Dun, 34
Siphlonurus Habitat, 34
Siphlonurus Nymph, 34
Siphlonurus Spinner, 34

Timberline, *54*
Tricorythodes Dun, 73
Tricorythodes Fallax Dun, *76*
Tricorythodes Fallax No-Hackle Spinner, *77*
Tricorythodes Fallax Nymph, *75*
Tricorythodes Fallax Spinner, *76*
Tricorythodes Habitat, 74
Tricorythodes Nymph, 73, 75
Tricorythodes Spinner, 74
Velma May, *44*
Western Black Quill Nymph, *67*
Western Blue Quill Nymph, *70*
Western Green Drake Nymph, *60*
Western Green Paradrake, *62*
Wet Blue Dun, *77*

Chapter 3: Stoneflies

Acroneuria californica Adult, 114
Acroneuria californica Nymph, 114
Acroneuria Habitat, 115
Alloperla Adult, 112
Alloperla Habitat, 112
Alloperla Nymph, 112
Bird's Stone Fly, *123*
Box Canyon Stone, *121*
Brown Bucktail Caddis, *107*
Bucktail Caddis, *110*
Capnia Adult, 104
Dark Stone Bi-Visible, *123*
Dark Stone, *122*
Dark Stone Wet, *124*
February Red Soft-Hackle, *106*
Golden Stone, *116, 118*
Golden Stone Wet Fly, *119*
Green Bucktail Caddis, *113*
Isogenus Adults, 109
Isogenus Nymph, 109
Isoperla Adult, 108
Isoperla Nymph, 108
Leuctra Adult, 104
Leuctra Nymph, 104
Little Brown Stone, *106, 107*
Little Brown Stone Habitat, 105
Little Yellow Stone, *110, 111*
Little Yellow Stone Female, *111*
Montana Stone, *122*
Nemoura Adult, 104
Nemoura Nymph, 103
Partridge and Green, *113*
Partridge and Orange, *106*
Partridge and Yellow and Fur Thorax, *110*

Perlodidae Habitat, 109
Pheasant Tail, *113*
Pteronarcys californica Adult, 120
Pteronarcys californica Nymph, 120
Pteronarcys Habitat, 120
Sofa Pillow, *118*
Stoneflies Mating, 102
Yellow Stone Nymph, *116*

Chapter 4: Dragonflies
    and Damselflies

Aeschnidae Adult, 129
Aeschnidae Habitat, 129
Aeschnidae Nymph, 129
Assom Dragon, *134*
Blue Damsel, *140*
Carey Special, *131*
Coenagrionidae Adult, 138
Coenagrionidae Habitat, 138
Coenagrionidae Nymph, 137
Damselfly Adult, 135
Damselfly Nymph, *139*
Dragon Fly, *132*
Dragonfly Emerging, 130
Dragonfly Nymph Shuck, 130
Ginger Damsel, *140*
Gomphidae Nymph, 134
Green Damsel, *139*
Heather Nymph, *139*
Lestidae Habitat, 136
Libellulidae Adult, 132
Libellulidae Nymph, 132, 133
Randall's Green Dragon, *131*
Woolly Worm, *131, 133*

Chapter 5: Waterboatmen
    and Backswimmers

Backswimmer, 142, *147*
Corixa Bug, *144*
Corixid, *144*
Corixidae, 144
Corixidae Habitat, 143
Notonectid, *146*

Chapter 6: Caddisflies

American Grannom, *171*

Blue Dun Hackle, *154*
Brachycentridae Adults, 169
Brachycentridae Larvae, 168
Brown Caddis Midge Nymph, *165*
Brown Microcaddis Pupa, *167*
Bucktail Caddis, *160, 176*
Caddisflies Mating, 149
Cased Caddis, *174, 175*
Cream Caddis Midge Nymph, *166*
Cream Soft-Hackle, *163*
Dark Bucktail Caddis, *155*
Dark Caddis, *177*
Dark Caddis Emergent, *175*
Dubbed Caddis Larva, *158*
Dun Microcaddis Pupa, *167*
Elk Hair Caddis, *160*
Glossosomatidae Adult, 162
Glossosomatidae Adult, 162
Glossomatidae Pupa, 162, 163
Gold Ribbed Hare's Ear, *159*
Gray Caddis Midge Nymph, *166*
Grayish Olive/Dun Caddis, *155*
Green Rock Worm, *152*
Hare's Ear, *161*
Hare's Ear Soft-Hackle, *163*
Herl Nymph, *170*
Hydropsyche Adult, 156
Hydropsyche Habitat, 157
Hydropsyche Larva, 156
Hydropsyche Larva and Net, 157
Hydropsyche Larva and Shelter, 157
Hydropsyche Pupae, 156, 159
Hydroptilidae Habitat, 164
Hydroptilidae Larva, 164
Latex Caddis Larva, *152, 158*
Lepidostomatidae Habitat, 169
Lepidostomatidae Pupa, 169
Limnephilidae Adult, 173
Limnephilidae Habitat, 173
Limnephilidae Larva, 172
Limnephilidae Pupa, 172, 173
Little Western Sedge Pupa, *159*
March Brown, *161*
March Brown Spider Soft-Hackle, *159*
Medium Cinnamon Sedge Pupa, *176*
Olive Caddis Midge Nymph, *166*
Olive Microcaddis Pupa, *166*
Orange Caddis, *177*
Orange Microcaddis Pupa, *167*
Pale Microcaddis Pupa, *166*
Partridge and Green, *153*
Quill-Wing Caddis, *161*
Rhyacophila Habitat, 150

Rhyacophila Larva, 150
Rhyacophila Life Stages, 150
Skittering Caddis, *155*
Solomon's Caddis Pupa, *153*
Strawman, *175*
Zug Bug, *152*

Chapter 7: Alderflies
   and Dobsonflies

Alder, *180*
Brown Woolly Worm, *180*
Corydalidae Adult, 181
Corydalidae Larva, 181
Hellgrammite, *182, 183*
Quill-Wing Alderfly, *180*
Sialidae Adult, 179
Sialidae Female With Eggs, 179
Sialidae Habitat, 179
Sialidae Larva, 178
Smoky Alder Larva, *180*

Chapter 8: Water Beetles

Brown Algae Larva, *189*
Brown Scavenger Beetle Larva, *189*
Dytiscidae Adult, 185
Dytiscidae Larva, 185
Hydrophilidae Larva, 187
Olive Diving Beetle Larva, *186*
Woolly Worm, *186*

Chapter 9: True Flies

Adams, *198*
Chironomidae Adult, 191
Chironomidae Habitat, 192
Chironomidae Larvae, 191
Chironomidae Pupae, 191
Culicidae Adult, 196
Culicidae Larva, 196
Darbee Crane Fly, *201*
Emerging Pupa, *194*
Emergent Mosquito, *198*
Ginger Spider, *201*
Ginger Variant, *201*
Griffith's Gnat, *194*
Henryville Special, *194*
Midge Larva, *193*
Mosquito, *198*
Mosquito Larva, *197*
Muskrat, *200*

Public Enemy No. 1, *197*
Rising Midge Pupa, *193*
Stillborn Midge, *194*
Traditional Midge Adult, *195*
Traditional Midge Larva, *195*
Traditional Midge Pupa, *195*
Tipulidae Adult, 199
Tipulidae Habitat, 199
Tipulidae Larva, 199
Western Crane Fly Larva, *200*

TEXT

A

Acroneuria, 114-119, 120
    A. californica, 102, 114-119
    A. pacifica, 114-119
Adams, 49, 67, 198
Aeschnidae, 129-132
Agria, 137
Alder, 180
Alderflies, 178-181
Alloperla, 111-114
Ameletus, 38-41, 42
American Grannom, 171
American March Brown, 90
Anderson, Margrett, 148
Anderson, Norman, 9, 148, 172
Anisoptera, 127, 128-135
Anisozygoptera, 127
Archilestes grandis, 136
Archynopteryx, 108
    A. compacta, 109
Assom Dragon, 134
Atherton, John, 48

B

Backswimmers, 142, 145-147
Baetis, 45-51, 90
    B. bicaudatus, 23, 46
Baetis Compara-Spinner, 50
Baetis No-Hackle, 49
Baetis Nymph, 48
Baetis Soft-Hackle, 47
Baetis Spinner, 50
Bailey, Dan, 132
Barker, Mims, 121, 122
Barnes, Pat, 118
Bauman, R. W., 102, 103, 125
Berosus, 188
Big Yellow May, 92, 95
Big Yellow May Spinner, 96
Big Yellow May Dun, 95
Big Yellow Mayfly, 118
Bird, Cal, 123
Bird's Stone Fly, 123
Black Diving Beetle Larva, 186
Black Drake, 33, 36
Black Drake Spinner, 38
Black Midge, 76
Black Quill, 67
Black Quill Spinner, 68

Black Scavenger Beetle Larva, 189
Black Woolly Worm, 182
Blackflies, 190
Blephariceridae, 190
Blue Damsel, 140
Blue Dun, 67, 68, 156, 167
Blue Dun Hackle, 154
Blue Quill, 68
Blue Quill Spinner, 51, 72
Blue-Winged Red Quill, 57, 91
Boaze, Raleigh, 152
Bodmer, George, 174
Box Canyon Stone, 121, 122
Brachycentridae, 168-171, 174
Brachycentrus, 168
Brachyptera, 102, 103, 104
Brooks, Charles, 9, 44, 60, 71, 116, 117, 122, 134, 154
Brown Algae Larva, 189
Brown Bi-Visible, 90
Brown Bucktail Caddis, 107
Brown Caddis Midge Nymph, 165
Brown Diving Beetle Larva, 186
Brown Drake, 96, 98, 99
Brown Drake Nymph, 98, 99
Brown Drake Spinner, 100
Brown Microcaddis Pupa, 167
Brown Scavenger Beetle Larva, 189
Brown Willow Fly, 114, 119
Brown Woolly Worm, 180
Brown Wulff, 99
Bucktail Caddis, 95, 107, 110, 111, 113, 118, 119, 155, 160, 161, 164,
    167, 171, 176, 177
Bunse, Richard, 10, 90

C

Calineuria californica, 102
Callibaetis, 51-57
    C. pacificus, 55
Callibaetis Compara-Dun, 56
Callibaetis No-Hackle Dun, 56
Canadian Sedge, 173
Capniidae, 102
Capnia, 102, 103, 104
Carey, Col. Thomas, 131
Carey Special, 131, 139
Cased Caddis, 174, 175
Caucci, Al, 9, 35, 41, 50, 56, 60, 62, 63, 64, 67, 72, 86
Ceratopogonidae, 190
Chironomidae, 191-195, 197
Chloroperlidae, 111-114
Christianson, Carl, 95
Cinnamon Sedge, 172

Cinygma, 77, 91-92
   C. ramaleyi, 91
Cinygmula, 77, 91-92
Clinger Nymph, 85
Clistoronia magnifica, 173
Coenagrionidae, 137-141
Coleoptera, 184-189
Corixa Bug, 144
Corixid, 144
Corixidae, 142, 143-145
Corydalidae, 178-183
Covert, Burt, 9
Crane Flies, 199-201
Cream Caddis Midge Nymph, 166
Cream Soft-Hackle, 163
Culicidae, 196-198
Cummins, K. W. , 149

D

Darbee Crane Fly, 201
Darbee, Harry, 201
Damselfly Nymph, 139
Dance Flies, 190
Dark Blue Quill, 71
Dark Bucktail Caddis, 155
Dark Caddis, 177
Dark Caddis Emergent, 175-177
Dark Sedge, 172
Dark Stone, 122
Dark Stone Bi-Visible, 123
Dark Stone Wet, 124
Dark Stonefly, 119
Davies, Russ, 10
Devil's Darning Needle, 129
Diving Water Beetles, 185
Dobsonflies, 178-183
Dragon Fly, 132
Dragon Fly Nymph, 139
Dubbed Caddis Larva, 158
Dun Microcaddis Pupa, 167
Dytiscidae, 185-187

E

Elk Hair Caddis, 160, 164, 167, 177
Emergent Mosquito, 198
Emerging Pupa, 194
Empididae, 190
Enallagma, 137
Epeorus, 23, 77, 78-83, 84, 90, 96
Epeorus Nymph, 80
Ephemera simulans, 92, 96-100

Ephemerella, 57-64, 66, 98, 202
   E. coloradensis, 57, 62, 63
   E. doddsi, 57, 58, 59, 62
   E. glacialis, 57, 58, 62
   E. grandis, 58, 61
   E. grandis grandis, 57, 58, 61, 62
   E. grandis ingens, 57, 58, 62
   E. hecuba, 57
   E. inermis, 57, 58, 63
   E. infrequens, 57, 58, 63
   E. subvaria, 57
Escola, Marshall, 139

F

Fall Caddis, 172, 174, 177
February Red Soft-Hackle, 106
Female Red Quill Spinner, 72
Fishfly, 92
Fly Fisherman Magazine, 75
Flyfishing the West Magazine, 95

G

Giant Salmon Flies, 108, 119-124, 182
Ginger Bi-Visible, 82, 86
Ginger Damsel, 140
Ginger Quill Spinner, 51
Ginger Spider, 201
Ginger Variant, 201
Glossosomatidae, 162
Glossosoma, 162-164
Gold Ribbed Hare's Ear, 54, 60, 66, 70, 80, 85, 89, 106, 113, 152, 158,
   159, 170, 174
Golden Stone, 102, 108, 109, 114-119, 122
Golden Stone Wet Fly, 119
Gomphidae, 134-135
Gordon Quill, 82
Gordon, Theodore, 82
Grannom, 168
Gray Caddis Midge Nymph, 166
Gray Drake, 33, 36
Gray Drake Dun, 37
Gray Drake Spinner, 38
Gray Nymph, 60
Gray Scavenger Beetle Larva, 189
Gray Wulff, 37
Grayish-Olive/Dun Caddis, 155
Great Lead-Wing Olive Drake Nymph, 61
Great Red Quill Spinner, 63
Great Western Lead-Wing, 42
Green Bucktail Caddis, 113
Green Damsel, 139

Green Darner, 129
Green Drake, 57-64, 202
Green Drake Compara-Dun, 62
Green Drake Compara-Spinner, 64
Green Drake Spinner, 64
Green Drake Wulff, 62
Green Rock Worm, 149, 152
Griffith, George, 194
Griffith's Gnat, 194
Grizzly Wulff, 82, 96

H

Halladay, Leonard, 198
Hare's Ear, 161, 167
Hare's Ear Flymph, 81
Hare's Ear Soft-Hackle, 163
Heather Nymph, 139
Hellekson, Terry, 140, 182
Hellgrammite, 178-183
Hendrickson, Harry, 140
Hendricksons, 57
Henryville Special, 194
Heptagenia, 77, 83-86, 91
    H. criddlei, 85
Heptagenia Compara-Dun, 86
Heptagenia Compara-Spinner, 86
Herl Nymph, 144-170
Herter, George L., 180
Hexagenia limbata, 35, 92-96, 98
Hidy, Vernon S. "Pete", 81, 154
Horse Stinger, 129
Hydrophilidae, 185, 187-189
Hydropsyche, 156-161, 173
Hydropsychidae, 156
Hydroptilidae, 164-167

I

Ida May, 60
Ischnura, 137
Isogenus, 108-110
Isoperla, 108-110
Isonychia, 40, 42-45
    I. bicolor, 40, 41
    I. sicca campestris, 42
    I. velma, 42
Isonychia Velma Nymph, 44
Isonychia Velma Spinner, 45

J

Jennings, Preston, 90, 123

Jewett, Stanley, Jr., 101, 125
Jorgensen, Poul, 80, 85, 89, 91, 158, 201

K

Kaufmann, Randall, 54, 131, 198
Klune, Frank, 72
Koch, Ed, 49, 165, 166

L

Lambuth, Letcher, 123
Latex Caddis Larva, 152, 158
Lead-Winged Olive, 57
Leadwing Coachman, 156
Leisenring, James, 9, 81, 154
Leisenring Lift, 155, 176
Leiser, Eric, 9, 154, 161
Lepidostomatidae, 168-171, 174
Lepidostoma, 168
Leptophlebia, 64-68
Leptophlebia Compara-Dun, 67
Lestidae, 135-137, 138
Leuctridae, 102
Leuctra, 102-104
Libellulidae, 132-134
Light Caddis Emergent, 176
Light Cahill, 49, 55, 56, 82, 86
Light Ginger Bi-Visible, 82, 86
Light Snipe and Yellow, 81
Limnephilidae, 172 -177
Limnephilus, 173
Little Brown Stone, 102, 103, 106, 107
Little Gray-Winged Dun Nymph, 85
Little Green Stone, 111-114
Little Olive, 49, 90
Little Red Stone, 102, 104
Little Western Red Quill, 71
Little Western Sedge Pupa, 159
Little Yellow May, 78
Little Yellow Stone, 114
Little Yellow Stone Female, 111
Little Yellow Stones, 108-111, 113

M

March Brown, 87, 161, 167, 203
March Brown Compara-Dun, 90
March Brown Flymph, 89
March Brown Soft-Hackle, 89
March Brown Spider, 54
March Brown Spider Soft-Hackle, 159
Mayfly, 92

McNeese, Dave, 10, 40, 155, 177
Meck, Charles R., 40
Medium Cinnamon Sedge Pupa, 176
Medium Speckle-Wing Quill Nymph, 55
Merritt, R. W., 149
Michigan Caddis, 92, 95
Microcaddis, 164-167
Midges, 191-195
Midge Larva, 193
Montana Stone, 122
Mooney, Paul, 10
Mosquito Larva, 197
Mosquitoes, 196-198
Muskrat, 200

N

Nastasi, Bob, 9, 35, 41, 50, 56, 60, 62, 63, 64, 67, 72, 86
Natant Nylon Nymph, 71
Near Enough, 36
Needle Fly, 102, 104
Nemes, Sylvester, 106, 110, 113, 153, 159, 167, 176
Nemouridae, 102, 103
Nemoura, 102, 103
Net-Winged Midges, 190
No-see-ums, 190
Notonectid, 146
Notonectidae, 142, 145-147

O

Octogomphus specularis, 134
Olive Caddis Midge Nymph, 166
Olive Diving Beetle Larva, 186
Olive Microcaddis Pupa, 166
Olive Midge, 76
Orange Caddis, 177
Orange Microcaddis Pupa, 167
Orange Sedge, 172

P

Pale Evening Dun, 83
Pale Gray-Winged Olive Nymph, 48
Pale Microcaddis Pupa, 166
Pale Morning Compara-Dun, 63
Pale Morning Dun, 57, 58, 60, 62, 63, 64
Pale Morning Dun Nymph, 61
Pale Morning Dun Spinner, 64
Pale Watery Dun Wingless, 81
Paraleptophlebia, 68-72
   P. gregalis, 68
   P. debilis, 68

P. bicornuta, 68
Paraleptophlebia Compara-Dun, 72
Parker, Barry, 36, 98
Partridge and Green, 153, 159
Partridge and Green and Fur Thorax, 113
Partridge and Orange, 106, 159
Partridge and Yellow and Fur Thorax, 110
Partridge and Yellow Soft-Hackle, 80
Periwinkle, 172
Perlidae, 114-119
Perlodidae, 108-111
Pheasant Tail, 54, 113
Philopotamidae, 165
Predaceous Water Beetles, 185
Progomphus borealis, 134
Pteronarcidae, 119-124
    Pteronarcella badia, 119
    Pteronarcella regularis, 119
    Pteronarcys californica, 119-124
    Pteronarcys princeps, 119
Public Enemy No. 1, 197

Q

Quill-Wing Alderfly, 180
Quill-Wing Caddis, 161, 167, 171, 177, 181

R

Randall's Green Dragon, 131
Red Quill, 68, 71, 72, 87, 90
Red Quill Spinner, 82
Rhagionidae, 190
Rhithrogena, 77, 87-90
    R. hageni, 87
    R. morrisoni, 87
Rhithrogena Clinger Nymph, 89
Rhyacophilidae, 149, 157, 173
Rhyacophila, 149-156
Richards, Carl, 9, 37, 38, 48, 49, 50, 56, 61, 62, 64, 75, 98, 99, 100
Rising Midge Pupa, 193
Roberts, Don, 10, 139, 140, 197
Rock Worm, 149
Rosborough, E. H. "Polly", 9, 36, 38, 40, 41, 44, 45, 94, 95, 96, 106, 107, 110, 111, 114, 116, 117, 118, 119, 122, 124, 139, 152, 175, 176, 177, 200
Roskelley, Fenton, 139

S

Salmon Flies, 109, 119-124
Sandfly, 92

Schwiebert, Ernest, 9, 12, 33, 48, 51, 55, 61, 63, 64, 66, 67, 68, 70, 71, 72, 75, 76, 85, 91, 106, 144, 159, 166, 167, 171, 176, 186, 189, 200
Sialidae, 178-181
Simuliidae, 190
Siphlonurus, 11, 33-38, 40, 41, 42
  S. occidentalis, 33, 36
  S. spectabilis, 36
Skittering Caddis, 155
Slate-Winged Olive, 57
Small Brown Stone Complex, 102-107
Smoky Alder Larva, 180
Snipe Flies, 190
Sofa Pillow, 118
Soldier Flies, 190
Solomon, Larry, 9, 153, 161
Solomon's Caddis Pupa, 153, 154
Speckle-Wing Quills, 51
Spotted Sedge, 156
Stillborn Midge, 194
Stratiomyidae, 190
Strawman, 174, 175
Swisher, Doug, 9, 37, 38, 48, 49, 50, 56, 61, 62, 64, 75, 98, 99, 100

T

Taeniopterybidae, 102
Taeniopteryx pacifica, 106
Teeny Nymph, 60, 106, 113, 144
Timberline, 54
Tipulidae, 199-201
Traditional Midge Adult, 195
Traditional Midge Larva, 195
Traditional Midge Pupa, 195
Tricorythodes, 73-77
  T. minutus, 73, 74
Tricorythodes Fallax Dun, 76
Tricorythodes Fallax No-Hackle Spinner, 76
Tricorythodes Fallax Nymph, 75
Tricorythodes Fallax Spinner, 76
Tricorythodes Nymph, 75
Troth, Al, 147, 160, 177
Trotter, Pat, 123
Tup's Nymph, 81
Turner, Hal, 9
Turtle-Case Makers, 162

V

Velma May, 44
Veniards, 90, 208

W

Water Beetles, 184-189
Water Scavenger Beetles, 187-189
Water Tigers, 185
Waterboatmen, 142-145
Watery Dun, 81
Western Black Quill, 64
Western Black Quill Nymph, 66, 67
Western Blue Quill Nymph, 70
Western Crane Fly Larva, 200
Western Green Drakes, 57, 60, 63, 98
Western Green Drake Nymph, 60
Western Green Paradrake, 62
Western March Brown, 87, 90
Wet Blue Dun, 77
Wetzel, Charles, 82
White-Winged Curse, 73
Whitlock, Dave, 193, 194
Winter Stone, 102, 104
Woolly Worm, 131, 133, 182, 186, 189, 200
Wright, Leonard, Jr., 155
Wulff, Lee, 37, 82, 99

Y

Yellow Drake, 33, 36
Yellow Stone, 122
Yellow Stone Nymph, 116
Young, Paul, 174

Z

Zug Bug, 60, 80, 144, 152, 153, 174
Zug, Cliff, 152
Zygoptera, 127-141